The theory and philosophy of organizations

SOCIAL ANALYSIS

A Series in the Social Sciences
Edited by Richard Scase, University of Kent

Beyond Class Images: Explorations in the Structure of Social Consciousness
Howard H. Davies

Fundamental Concepts and the Sociological Enterprise
C. C. Harris

Urban Planning in a Capitalist Society
Gwyneth Kirk

The State in Western Europe
Edited by Richard Scase

Autonomy and Control at the Workplace: Contexts for Job Redesign
Edited by John E. Kelly and Chris W. Clegg

The Entrepreneurial Middle Class
Richard Scase and Robert Goffee

Capitalism, the State and Industrial Relations: The Case of Britain
Dominic Strinati

Alcohol, Youth and the State
Nicholas Dorn

The Evolution of Industrial Systems
Timothy Leggatt

Sociological Interpretations of Education
David Blackledge and Barry Hunt

Sociological Approaches to Health and Medicine
Myfanwy Morgan, Michael Calnan and Nick Manning

School Organisation: A Sociological Perspective
William Tyler

Entrepreneurship in Europe
Edited by Robert Goffee and Richard Scase

Small Business and Society
David Goss

Deciphering the Enterprise Culture
Roger Burrows

Paths of Enterprise
James Curran and Robert A. Blackburn

The theory and philosophy of organizations

Critical issues and new perspectives

Edited by

John Hassard
University of Keele

and

Denis Pym
London Business School

London and New York

First published 1990
by Routledge
11 New Fetter Lane, London EC4P 4EE

Simultaneously published in the USA and Canada
by Routledge
29 West 35th Street, New York, NY 10001

Reprinted 1990, 1992, 1993, 1995

Typeset by LaserScript Ltd, Mitcham, Surrey
Printed and bound in Great Britain by
Biddles Ltd, Guildford and King's Lynn

British Library Cataloguing in Publication Data
A catalogue record for this book is available from the British Library

Library of Congress Cataloging in Publication Data
A catalog record for this book is available from the Library of Congress

ISBN 0–415–00428–4 (hbk) ISBN 0–415–06313–2 (pbk)

Contents

Acknowledgements

We would like to thank Andrew Lockett at Routledge, not only for acting as publishing co-ordinator but also for suggesting the title for the volume.

We are grateful, also, to Sally Jarratt for typing the manuscript and to Ian Atkin and Sudi Sharifi for assisting with the proofs.

Finally, we would like to thank the publishers of the journals cited below for their permission to produce revised/enlarged versions of: 'Overcoming hermeticism in organization theory' by John Hassard, originally published in *Human Relations* (1988), 41: 247–59; 'Opportunities arising from paradigm diversity' by Gareth Morgan, originally published in *Administration and Society* (1984), 16: 306–27; 'Organization/disorganization' by Robert Cooper, originally published in *Social Science Information* (1986), 25: 299–335; and 'Ethnomethodology and organization' by John Hassard, originally published in *Graduate Management Research* (1986), 3: 40–54.

Contributors

Peter Clark is Reader in Organizational Behaviour at the Business School, University of Aston.

Robert Cooper is a Lecturer in Organizational Behaviour in the Department of Behaviour in Organizations, University of Lancaster.

John Hassard is Director of the Centre for Graduate Management Studies, at the University of Keele.

Roger Holmes is a Senior Lecturer in Social Psychology in the Department of Social Psychology, London School of Economics.

Joanne Martin is a Professor of Organizational Behaviour in the Graduate School of Business, Stanford University, USA.

Gareth Morgan is Professor of Organizational Behaviour in the Faculty of Administrative Studies, York University, Ontario, Canada.

Michael Power is a Lecturer in Accountancy in the Department of Accounting and Finance, London School of Economics.

Denis Pym is Professor of Organizational Behaviour at the London Business School.

Michael Reed is a Lecturer in Organizational Behaviour in the Department of Behaviour in Organizations, University of Lancaster.

Burkard Sievers is a Professor of Organizational Development in the Department of Business Administration and Economics, Bergische University, Wuppertal, West Germany.

Barry Turner is Reader in Sociology in the Department of Sociology, University of Exeter.

Hugh Willmott is a Lecturer in Organizational Sociology in the School of Management, University of Manchester Institute of Science and Technology.

Introduction

This volume is a by-product of a running seminar on 'New perspectives on organizations' held at the London Business School between October 1986 and July 1987. This seminar provided a forum for exploring contemporary issues in organizational theory and analysis. The present volume contains not only papers from this seminar, but also others written in the same spirit of enquiry.[1]

The aim of the volume is to contribute to the debate on the status of organization theory as a discipline[2]. To accomplish this our authors draw, in the main, upon Kuhn's philosophy of science (Kuhn 1970) in order to identify new paradigms for organization analysis. This task is faced amidst what has been called the 'crisis' phase in organization theory (Benson 1983), a period in which the schismatic tendencies Gouldner predicted for Western sociology (Gouldner 1970) come to impinge upon theory development in organization studies.

In line with this aim, the volume seeks to accomplish two specific objectives: to illustrate some of the emerging perspectives available to organizational analysts; and to suggest how these perspectives (or paradigms) can be mediated for purposes of explanation. We take our lead from the study by Burrell and Morgan (1979) and argue that the field of organizational theory possesses a plurality of competing paradigms. However, we attempt to go further and to suggest that a number of new paradigms are emerging in the field, paradigms that we feel an adventurous organization theory should explore.

The volume explores these issues in three main sections under the headings theory, analysis, and philosophy. The contents are as follows.

Part one, 'Theory', addresses issues relevant to the contemporary debate on organizational paradigms. In Chapter one, 'Paradigm diversity in organizational research', Gareth Morgan suggests that paradigm diversity represents an 'opportunity' for organizational research rather than a 'threat'. He outlines four major paradigms for organizational analysis – functionalist, interpretive, radical, humanist, radical structuralist – and describes the contribution each one makes to our understanding of organizations. Morgan argues that we need to harness the research possibilities raised by different paradigms in order to yield the rich and varied explanations offered by multiple paradigm analysis. To realize this, however, he feels we must first overcome certain structural limitations present in the discipline. Specifically, we must modify the institutional constraints imposed by academic journals and university departments alike. Only by so doing will we facilitate the innovation and risk-taking necessary for exploring unconventional research perspectives.

The theme of theoretical heterodoxy is also at the heart of Chapter two by Joanne Martin, 'Breaking up the mono-method monopolies in organizational analysis', in which she too makes a case for harnessing multiple paradigms for research. Martin begins by distinguishing between two main positions in the paradigm plurality debate: first, that of writers who argue for the superiority of one paradigm over another; and second, that of writers who argue that one paradigm is better than another for the purpose of addressing a particular theoretical issue. Martin terms these positions the simple mono-method approach, and the complex mono-method approach respectively. She feels, however, that both positions are flawed; the first because it falls back on the 'my method is better than yours' mentality (one which is prevalent in discussions of qualitative and quantitative methods), and the second because it places strict limits on what can be accepted as paradigm methodology. In fact Martin suggests that these represent 'convergent' approaches, when we should be exploring 'divergent' ones. Martin proposes an alternative – for researchers to become 'methodological chameleons'. She argues that researchers should be more tolerant of paradigm diversity, and should come to prize and encourage the differing conclusions that emerge when we employ a range of paradigms. Like Morgan, she argues that we should encourage a more 'open-minded' approach to organizational research.

The final chapter of part one, Hugh Willmott's 'Beyond paradigmatic closure in organizational enquiry' (Chapter three) is also concerned with paradigm plurality. Willmott, like Morgan, examines the Burrell and Morgan (1979) scheme, although here to criticize one of its key premises – that of the 'dualism of subjective and objective paradigms' – which, according to Willmott, places 'undue limits upon the theorizing of organization'. Willmott explores the possibilities for reconciling what Burrell and Morgan regard as the irreconcilable ('incommensurable') features of their paradigms. He argues that the assumption of paradigmatic closure can be challenged by examining the attempts of Berger and Luckmann (1967), Giddens (1976, 1979, 1984), and Freire (1972), to integrate 'subjective' and 'objective' paradigms. Although Willmott feels that each of these approaches is found wanting, he argues nevertheless in support of their attempts to theorise the 'interpenetration of "subjective"/existential and "objective"/historical dimensions of social life'.

In part two, 'Analysis', we overlay the previous discussion of paradigm diversity with descriptions of some contemporary and emerging paradigm candidates. We examine the paradigm claims of labour process theory, organizational symbolism and ethnomethodology, before introducing new perspectives such as postmodernism, mortality, and time.

In Chapter four, Michael Reed offers a 'critique and reformulation' of 'The labour process perspective on management organization'. Reed provides an assessment of the contribution which labour process theory makes to the development of a 'systematic sociological understanding of management organization in advanced societies'. Starting with the seminal work of Braverman (1974), he documents the gradual disenchantment with the deterministic and mechanistic conceptions of management which underpin earlier contributions to the labour process debate. However, although noting the emergence of a perspective on management which is more voluntarist, Reed maintains that movement in this direction has been limited – to the extent that a continuing commitment to a rational and formal conception of management can be identified.

Reed suggests that voluntarist initiatives have not dealt adequately with the central problematic of the labour process debate on management, that is, with the 'complex interaction between operational control over the production process and allocative control over strategic, corporate decision-making'. Reed argues that the only way to correct this situation is to develop an action approach which can address the breaks and contradictions which occur, necessarily, between the forms of organizational control implemented by management within the production process. Subsequently, Reed attempts to outline such an approach. He argues that management should be regarded as a 'process' – as a 'related set of institutional mechanisms geared to the continual recoupling and regulation of diverse productive practices'. He feels that this approach facilitates analysis of the ways 'these integrative and regulative mechanisms are subjected to review and transformation as a result of the struggle to control them engaged in by various groups and classes'.

In Chapter five, Barry Turner considers 'The rise of organizational symbolism'. He suggests that a new set of concerns is invading organizational discussions through an awareness of symbolism and culture. He discusses developments in this field, starting with the symbolists' attack on the 'false rationality' of organizational life and draws upon the writings of interpretive analysts to illustrate the wealth of attacks on functional rationality. However, despite the 'luxurious embarrassment' of new writings on culture and symbolism, Turner feels we have not yet developed a new 'orthodoxy' for organizational analysis. On consulting numerous overviews of the field, he finds it difficult to summarize developments precisely, and thus to describe a 'paradigm'. Turner feels that part of the difficulty lies in defining the 'slippery notions' of culture and symbolism, especially as it is easy for discussions of culture to change, with little notice, from 'static, objectified notions' into analyses in 'processual terms'. Turner illustrates how for some writers it is social objects, such as values, rituals, myths or ceremonies, which constitute symbolism, while for others it is, or should be, 'the process which flows through the creation of these objects or occasions'. For these reasons it becomes difficult to pin down culture as a dependent or independent variable – because in so doing one loses the essence of culture as a metaphor.

In Chapter six, a discussion of ethnomethodology and organization, John Hassard suggests that ethnomethodology represents a truly ideographic approach for organizational research. First, by drawing upon the works of Garfinkel (1967) and Garfinkel and Sachs (1970), he outlines the basic principles of the approach, indexicality and reflexivity, together with its main research foci, linguistic and situational analysis. He explains how, in ethnomethodology, subjects make sense of verbal and non-verbal cues ('indexicals') whose meaning is dependent on the context of production; how interactions are regarded as ongoing accomplishments in which those involved take recourse to a range of assumptions, practices and conventions in order to define, sustain and reproduce everyday situations; and how the approach owes considerable debt to the phenomenological sociology of Alfred Schutz and to the symbolic interactionism of George Herbert Mead and Erving Goffman.

Hassard's second aim is to link this sociological analysis to the use of ethnomethodology in organizational research. He does this by explaining Bittner's thesis, 'The concept of organization' (Bittner 1974), before describing empirical contributions by Zimmerman (1971) and Silverman and Jones (1976). From Bittner, we find that the main fault of orthodox organizational research lies in its over-reliance on common-sense knowledge. Bittner suggests that Weber is particularly at fault here, notably in his development of ideal-type concepts for bureaucracy. Instead of coming to terms with the everyday presuppositions of his analysis, Weber offers a partial account which 'glosses' how competent participants make sense of, for example, notions of hierarchy and office. As empirical evidence from Zimmerman (1971) and Silverman and Jones (1976) shows, the ethnomethodological alternative is to analyse the *processes* through which competent participants use everyday knowledge of bureaucracy to account for specific activities in particular settings. In ethnomethodology, bureaucracy has no implicit meaning of its own – it exists only through 'the socially sanctioned occasions of its use'.

In Chapter seven, Michael Power discusses 'Modernism, postmodernism and organization'. In particular, Power wishes to 'speculate on the possible meaning of postmodernism for the concept of organization'. He concentrates upon the work of two thinkers, Jean François Lyotard and Jurgen Habermas, and attempts to sustain a dialectic between the former's 'postmodernist vision' (Lyotard 1984) and the latter's 'defence of a principle of modernity' (Habermas 1972, 1979). Power suggests that this contrast is important because the two share much common ground – including a critique of systems theory. In developing this analysis, Power describes the current postmodernist mood in order to set the stage for his comparison of Lyotard and Habermas. This latter comparison prepares the ground for Power's attempt to explicate the meaning of the modernist/postmodernist dialectic for the concept of organization, an analysis which expresses Power's views on the postmodernist motif of 'deconstruction'.

In Chapter eight, Burkard Sievers discusses the obsolescence of mortality in organization theory and practice. In a wide-ranging analysis, Sievers argues, *inter alia*, that mortality, although once regarded as a 'constituent part of human existence', has now been reduced to a 'critical episode at a certain point in time'. He suggests that in modern industrial societies death, like the dead body, has to be isolated and hygienically hidden. As long as we are not confronted by a catastrophic accident, such as a nuclear disaster, the 'societal displacement of death' is the strategy we deploy to let human mortality fall into oblivion. He suggests also that such processes are seen in work organizations - where we collectively repress death from experience in the search for success and survival; i.e. the organization's search for immortality. This process is expressed at many levels. Sievers develops analogies from Greek mythology to illustrate how senior managers become the immortal gods of corporate history, while workers, as expendable labour, become ephemeral mortals who, metaphorically speaking, end their days in Hades. For example, the senior manager wishes to make his mark on the history of the firm so that he can gain immortality; i.e. through becoming a hero of corporate legends. However, while senior managers seek immortality, this is often at the expense of treating workers as non-mortals. In difficult times the latter may have to be 'severed' because, if 'dead wood', they may threaten the immortality of the organization. Sievers argues that 'the splitting between life and death is enforced and concealed through the fundamental split in our employing organizations between those at the top and those at the bottom'.

The final chapter in the analysis section, Chapter nine, sees a discussion of organizational time or, more correctly, of 'Chronological codes and organizational analysis'. Here, Peter Clark argues that the organization sciences are at present a 'collection of research programmes and loosely bonded themata which are dominated by a theory and philosophy of time in the singular'. Clark suggests that organization theory must develop more sophisticated appreciations of time and temporality, and that researchers must recognize that 'corporations utilize and require a repertoire of chronological codes which blends homogeneous chronological codes (e.g. the calendar and the clock) with heterogeneous chronological codes (e.g. event time)'.

Clark argues that corporations differ in the 'robustness of their repertoires of chronological codes' and that 'robust, multilayered repertoires are essential to long-term survival, especially to efficient innovation'. He suggests that rigid chronological codes, like the timetable and its variants, are only relevant to the most basic forms of collective synchronization. Clark argues that increasingly we require 'complex individual forms of mutual timetabling which are exacting in their flexibilities and which operate on a multiplicity of layers'. He supports this argument by reference to organizational activity in the UK, USA, and Japan. He notes how these nations 'differ as societies in the clustering of the chronological codes which shape social choices'. Clark suggests that the domestic market structures of the UK, USA and Japan possess distinctive features 'reflecting the pace and saturation of collective consumer choices', and in particular that 'the temporal features of Britain and Japan tend to pose contrasting cases amongst the larger industrial nations'.

Part three, 'Philosophy', highlights some logical problems in our theorizing of organization. The section examines dialectical relationships between concepts central to debates in modern organization theory. The relationships and concepts examined are those of system and environment (open systems debate), person and role (alienation debate), and incommensurability and mediation (paradigms debate).

First, in Chapter ten, Robert Cooper considers the relationship between system and environment. Cooper's argument draws on structural linguistics and in particular on works by Derrida and Saussure to develop an analysis of 'systems of differences'. Cooper focuses on the concept of 'systemness', and examines how 'systemness relies singularly on a conception of unity' and how 'unity itself is a product of framing'. He argues for the centrality of the 'frame' in our understanding of the system/environment relation, and describes how the frame both includes and excludes, and that what it includes is 'subjected by the metalanguage to a process of logical ordering and organization'. From this position, Cooper attacks the functionalist view of systems where anything lying outside the system (or, more accurately, anything lying outside the frame that creates the system) is viewed as less ordered and less unitary than what is included. He notes how in functionalism, 'a privileging of unity and order is attributed to the inside of the system while the outside, presumed to be less organized, is by implication devalued'. This is problematic because it leads to a situation whereby the system (with its boundary) becomes conceptually detached from background or environment and thus takes on a life of its own. As Cooper notes, this has the effect of diverting attention from the all-important function of the frame, the paradox being that, 'while the social system is defined as a "pattern of relationships", the concept of relationship is its least systematically examined feature'. The result is that we end up with a 'nepotistic conception of social system'. Cooper argues that it is 'the frame which constitutes the relationship between system and environment and consequently it is the frame which provides the key to understanding the relationship between the two'.

In Chapter eleven, the analysis switches from system and structure to 'Person, role and organization'. Here Roger Holmes suggests that we must mediate the relationship between 'the personal and the social' in order to understand 'the organizational'. Holmes argues that person and role present logical and ontological difficulties in their simultaneous use. He suggests that these difficulties cannot be reconciled unless a very major step is taken; that is, to abandon empiricism, the theory of knowledge which has dominated scientific work for the last 350 years, and to replace it with a different approach to the knowable, constructivism (which is associated, particularly in psychology, with Piaget). Holmes outlines the constructivist position and explains how its definitions represent the 'result, not the ground, of the ordering of the world'. He suggests that by freeing the 'anchoring of the insistence of the senses', and thus the structural limitations of human perception, constructivism not only reconciles dialectical concerns of the personal and the social – the ideal subject-object – but also, and by extension, problems of human organization.

The dialectical approach common to the chapters by Cooper and Holmes is also central to Chapter twelve, by John Hassard. In this chapter Hassard returns to the problems of paradigm incommensurability raised in part one. However, rather than develop a sociological analysis, he develops a philosophical one to present 'An alternative to paradigm incommensurability in organization theory'. Hassard argues that 'a major logical problem in recent organizational analysis is the assumption that while paradigms are incommensurable, movement between them is nonproblematic'.

Citing works by Ritzer (1975), Burrell and Morgan (1979), and Pondy and Boje (1981), he notes how these writers all suggest that paradigms are exclusive yet advocate possibilities for inter-paradigm research. To make sense of this literature, and thus to establish an argument for paradigm mediation, Hassard returns to the origins of the debate in Kuhn's philosophy of science. However, in finding much equivocation in Kuhn, and especially in his debate with Popper, he draws upon the 'later' Wittgenstein in order to facilitate Giddens' concept of 'relativity without relativism' (Giddens 1976). Hassard's analysis rejects both Kuhn's 'strong' thesis of incommensurability and Popper's notion of liberal transitions in favour of a middle ground through Wittgenstein's 'language game of everyday life' (Wittgenstein 1953). For organizational analysis, Hassard argues for being 'trained into' new paradigms, given the premise that 'unorganized experience cannot order perception' (Phillips 1977).

On completion of the three main sections – theory, analysis and philosophy – the volume concludes with an epilogue by Denis Pym. This chapter acts as a coda to the foregoing analysis – it reflects upon the problems of traditional (especially 'scientific') organizational paradigms and makes a case for 'Post-paradigm enquiry'. The chapter begins with criticisms of the 'scientific method', Pym noting how the rejection of normal science and its methodologies has many supporters (e.g. Roszak 1972; Feyerabend 1975; Phillips 1977). Pym argues, however, that few of these critics focus on one of the most crucial problems facing scientific orthodoxy – the place of literacy in maintaining the institutions of science and the authority of the scientific estate. Pym explores this problem by developing personal 'post-paradigm' strategies for organizational analysis – strategies which account for his own divergence from the traditional posture. In particular, Pym uses post-paradigm enquiry to explicate the meaning and politics of literacy – 'the basis of the authority exercised by our major institutions'. For research, Pym advocates that we use post-paradigm enquiry to record information which doesn't fit with our presuppositions. This, he feels, will help us reclaim a more traditional view of information – as 'surprise' – and reject its current confirmational basis. Pym suggests that the only limitations to proceeding in this fashion are the 'enquirer's own personal confidence and self-awareness'.

In sum, this volume examines contemporary issues in the theory, analysis and philosophy of organizations. It contributes to recent debates about the status of organization theory as a discipline and introduces several new paradigms. In particular, it offers a sourcebook for readers who wish to explore the concept of organization by way of alternative perspectives to those found in standard methodology texts.

John Hassard
Denis Pym

Part one

Theory

Chapter one

Paradigm diversity in organizational research

Gareth Morgan

Introduction

In recent years, increasing attention has been devoted to understanding how the assumptions which scientists bring to their subject of investigation guide and influence what is seen and studied. In the field of organization studies, the problems involved have been most systematically explored through the notion of 'paradigm', and many rival modes of analysis identified and offered as alternative frameworks for the study of organization (Burrell and Morgan 1979; Morgan 1980; Evered and Louis 1981; Morgan 1986). The demonstrated existence of diversity, and more importantly the possibility of increased diversity in the future, poses organizational scientists with a situation that can be interpreted either as threat, opportunity, or some combination thereof.

Paradigm diversity is most often interpreted as threat by those organizational scientists committed to well-established models and methods for understanding organizations, and who wish to understand the generation of knowledge as a gradual, cumulative, well-ordered process. Paradigm diversity from their point of view is often seen as challenging the legitimacy of what they feel they already know about organization, and as opening a 'Pandora's box' of new problems and issues that must be addressed. For example, new paradigms entail new modes of theoretical conceptualization, the use of different research tools and techniques, and an appeal to new criteria for determining the legitimacy and quality of the knowledge which they generate. In essence, the perception of paradigm diversity as threat hinges on a celebration of past achievement and a fear and concern that a free and open pursuit of new directions will challenge and undermine this achievement.

The interpretation of diversity as opportunity, on the other hand, celebrates the possibility of obtaining new insights and understanding. Established paradigms for theorizing and research are recognized as providing at best partial modes of understanding which may be supplemented or even replaced by those of new paradigms. The constructive, perhaps cautious, opportunist seeks to emphasize the possibilities and advantages of exploring the new. The more dogmatic opportunist seeks to replace one orthodoxy with another, emphasizing the supremacy of one or more competing paradigms over the others. Either way, the challenge of diversity is seen as resting in the potential it offers for developing new modes of understanding the phenomenon of organization.

In this chapter I will adopt the role of constructive opportunist, and focus on the possibilities, prospects and challenges which paradigm diversity poses for the development of organization studies. To do so, I develop the analysis of paradigms offered by Burrell and Morgan, which analyses social theory (and hence the possibilities in organization theory and research) in terms of four broad world views, characterized as functionalist, interpretive, radical humanist and radical structuralist (Burrell and Morgan 1979). Each of these paradigms identifies a basic structure of social thought, based on a cohesive set of underlying reality assumptions.

The paradigms discussed by Burrell and Morgan are not merely typologies, and the primary purpose of conceiving social theory and organizational analysis in these terms is not simply to classify theory and research in terms of different dimensions and to determine the location of one social or organizational theorist *vis-à-vis* another. The paradigms and the dimensions through which they are characterized present the interested social scientist with an invitation to discern and explore the deep structure of assumptions which underlie different modes of theorizing. Theorizing characteristic of the different paradigms constructs the social world in very different ways, and leads us to see and understand the nature of organization in different ways. The fundamental challenge posed by a recognition of this paradigm diversity is to see and understand how we can research organization (and any other aspect of social life) in ways that tell us something new about the phenomenon in which we are interested. This challenge also leads to others, explored elsewhere (Morgan 1983, 1986), such as the need to reconcile the form, legitimacy and claims of one mode of knowledge against another, by reflecting on the way organizational researchers attempt to understand their subject of investigation.

We can begin to see the prospects and possibilities which the different paradigms offer organizational analysis by posing the question, 'What does each paradigm contribute to our understanding of organization?' In the following four sections of this chapter, I attempt to answer this question by adopting the different perspectives which characterize each paradigm, identifying just four or five of the major contributions which each has to offer. In the final section of the chapter, I identify some of the issues that need to be addressed if the rich possibilities of the different paradigms are to be realized in practice.

The functionalist contribution

The functionalist paradigm has provided the foundation for most modern theory and research on the subject of organization. For those committed to its underlying assumptions, which in effect treat organization as an aspect of a wider societal system that serves the interests of its members, the paradigm has been spectacularly successful. It is seen as providing the basis for an organization and management theory that contributes to the progress and development of formal organization, and to the progress and development of the wider society. Organization theorists and researchers are seen from this point of view as making substantive and helpful contributions to the development of our organizational society.

While it is recognized that this mode of organizational research may in practice serve to enhance one set of individual or societal values as opposed to another, or one set of interests as opposed to another, this is seen as involving a problem of its use rather than of its fundamental nature. Functionalist theory is seen in principle as being able to serve management, workers, government, interorganizational networks or any client's perspective, according to the orientation of its user. The perspective generates theories, techniques, and detailed research findings that claim to contribute to our knowledge about the empirical nature of organization, and encourage us to see the role of values as a separate variable in the research process.

Specifically, it is possible to identify a number of major contributions to which functionalist organization theory can lay claim. Though functionalist theorists do not often list them in the way shown below, the listing does in fact capture the essential contribution which they make.

Functionalist organization theory creates and elaborates a 'language' for the management and control of organizations

Functionalist theory has typically viewed organization as a problematic phenomenon, and has seen the problem of organization as synonymous with the problem of 'efficiency' and, more recently, of 'effectiveness'. Theory and research has sought to generate useful perspectives, models, metaphors, concepts and detailed research findings which help to structure and control organized activity in pursuit of system states deemed efficient and effective. Taylorism, Human Relations, Theory X, Y, Z, concepts of structure, technology, environment, etc., all share this common property. They attempt to create and systemize a language of organizational life that helps to structure organizational reality in a way that makes controlled performance possible. Modern organization and management theory constitutes a language of control which has evolved in nature and sophistication to cope with changing requirements of organizational control. New theories – networks of concepts and relationships – are offered as new languages for structuring organizational life, and in many cases have been adopted in the actual management of organization with spectacular success. Functionalist organization theory can lay claim to great practical success, for it provides a direct means of structuring organization as a practical activity.

Functionalist organization theory provides its clientele with a 'mirror' through which it can see and assess itself

In addition to creating new languages for organization, functionalist theory has borrowed heavily from existing organizational language as a means of structuring and understanding organizational reality. To this extent, organization theorists engage in an act of unwitting collusion with the ideas and actions of those they attempt to study, articulating and refining theories in use (Bittner 1965). Much of classical management theory is of this kind, codifying practices in terms of general principles. Such codification performs a 'mirroring' function against which clients, for example managers, can reflect on and assess their current practice.

The codified theories in use provide clients with an opportunity to affirm or negate and change their practice. It allows them to see and assess more clearly exactly what they are doing. Much discussion on management courses involves the use of theory as a mirror, and of course, is about the appropriateness of new as against existing languages of organization. In the mirroring function, as in the creation of new language, much modern organization theory can claim spectacular success, as witnessed by the marketability of its ideas to client groups, particularly organizational managers.

Functionalist organization theory generates problem-solving ideas and practices designed to enhance the adaptive capacity of organization as a continuing process

The 'problems' which a functionalist theorist sees in an organizational context usually hinge upon the perception of some form of breakdown in the control of ordered activity. An inefficiency in management procedure, a conflict between superior and subordinate, or some form of withdrawal from work as in the case of an employee strike, may be defined and recognized as problems. In each case the functionalist theorist seeks to find ways in which these problems can be overcome, and ordered operation restored. Much of the theory and practice of organizational development (OD), for example, is devoted to this activity.

Somewhat paradoxically, the change orientation which characterizes OD is in point of fact geared towards the creation of a continuity of process. The tensions which underlie the 'problem', if left to themselves, may lead to disruptive changes in the system, perhaps of a qualitative kind (e.g. in those dramatic cases where management control is replaced by workers control). The 'problem-solving' solutions of the OD change consultants will usually contribute to the emergence of new forms of order based on a new-found or newly developed adaptive capacity. In this sense, organizational change agents often work to preserve the status quo, not in the sense of creating stability, but in the sense of fostering homeostasis. The same is true of organization theorists concerned with the adaption of an organization to its environment through the development of strategy-structure relationships that preserve the organization as a successful, evolved member of an existing species. The functional study of power and politics often serves the same ends, yielding insights which help to make political activity manageable, often by making managers better politicians.

The status quo orientation of functionalist theory (frequently seen and regarded as a criticism) must in point of fact be regarded as its *raison d'être*, and one of its major strengths. Functionalist organization theory in essence actively strives to create adaptability and organized change to minimize and counteract the possibility of more extreme forms of disruptive disjunctural change.

Functionalist organization theory attempts to generate generalizable knowledge that can be regarded as valid and reliable

Drawing inspiration from achievements in the natural sciences, functionalist research seeks to discern the regularities and relationships that characterize the world of organization, in a way that renders them subject to prediction and control. The knowledge generated by the functionalist researcher thus serves the general regulative orientation of the underlying paradigm or world view which it expresses. Realistically, the knowledge thus generated provides a set of generalizable ideologies which can be used with some certainty for the management and control of organizations. Thus 'generalizable knowledge' on the relationships between job design and employee satisfaction, organization – environment – effectiveness, etc., serves to provide guidelines for organizational action in different situations. The knowledge generated in effect creates or reinforces a system of belief for guiding action.

The equation here of knowledge and ideology is not intended as a specific criticism of the functionalist viewpoint. The knowledge generated by all paradigms must be regarded as ideological to the extent that there appear to be no independent reference points for determining validity. The particular strengths which the functionalist can claim for the knowledge he or she strives to obtain is that it is *internally* valid and reliable, generalizable to some degree, and hence useful as a basis for action. Usefulness is celebrated as a major criterion for judging the worth and legitimacy of knowledge.

Functionalist organization theory in effect attempts to create a world characterized by certainty

This contribution is in many respects a corollary of the four listed above. The whole thrust and direction of functionalist theory is towards the development of a cohesive system of thought, where everything has a place within a web of ordered relationships that are intelligible, predictable and controlled. Its quest is for a bedrock of knowledge and an armoury of technique through which human beings can manage and regulate their world in relatively clear-cut, systematic ways. It could be said that it is intellectual response to the experience of the uncertainty and ambiguity of the world, and provides much solace and comfort to those desiring such structure.

Interestingly, the way functionalist theory hinges on and responds to the problem of uncertainty is clearly reflected in many conceptions of the nature of organization. For example, classic works in organization theory such as March and Simon (1958) and Thompson (1967) characterize organization as a process of reducing uncertainty, and external environments are often characterized in terms of the uncertainty dimension. The functionalism logic of organization is based on the idea that it is possible for humans to master and control context and destiny. Functionalist organization theory draws on and fosters this belief and contributes operative ideologies and technologies of organized action which can claim major short-run success in the creation of a world believed to be certain, real in nature and effect, and amenable to control.

The history of functionalism is of course, very short, and whether it will be able to claim success in the long run remains to be seen.

The interpretive contribution

The interpretive paradigm directly challenges the preoccupation with certainty that characterizes the functionalist perspective, showing that order in the social world, however real in surface appearance, rests on a precarious, socially-constructed web of symbolic relationships that are continuously negotiated, renegotiated, affirmed or changed. The interpretive theorist's problematic is to understand the meaning and significance of this web of relationships, and how it exists as such. The perspective, though often expressed in ways that seem opaque and geared to providing no more than an intellectual and purely destructive critique of all that is 'useful' in functionalist theory, does have many direct and important implications for understanding and managing organization.

An interpretive approach to organization theory suggests that we must understand 'certainty' and the quest for certainty as a socially constructed phenomenon, and that organization theorists and practitioners (lay theorists) should confront this and the other myths and ideologies which underwrite their practice

For the interpretive theorist and researcher all human beings are in various degrees makers and believers of practical myths, through which they make sense of action and acquire coherence in their lives. The world of organization is seen and understood as a realm of activity characterized by particular forms of myth-making that express significant networks of rules or models of action and give form to contextually based systems of meaning. The realization that we construct organization symbolically generates a healthy respect for the tentativeness of its fundamental nature, and cautions the organization theorist, lay and academic, against excessive commitment to favoured conceptions of organizational reality.

The interpretive perspective suggests that we treat our conception of organizational reality as a useful fiction which we use to guide our understanding of activities and events in this milieu. The perspective suggests that we should see and understand every person as his or her own personal theorist, living life in accordance with the dictates of the theories and explanations thus constructed. This view of organizational reality provides an injunction to organizational members to remember and own the role they play in the construction of their reality, and appreciate the power and control they have over their own situations. The perspective deconcretizes our view of organizational reality and suggests that we should not be held in awe by the practices and structures in which we find ourselves. This general insight has a number of specific implications for the understanding and conduct of organizational practice, as discussed below.

An interpretive view of organizational reality provides an impetus for innovation

When organizational members specifically realize that they guide their lives through means of fictions, the way is open for innovation through the creation of new fictions. Thus organizational members may specifically begin to see the same situation in different ways, juxtaposing insights to create new modes of organizational theory and practice. Through the sytematic use of new metaphors of organization, new languages of organization can be developed in a coherent and systematic way and, equally important, the limitations and implications of existing languages more clearly appreciated.

An interpretive view of organizational reality sensitizes organizational members to the importance of understanding organization as a cultural phenomenon rich in contextually based systems of meaning

An appreciation of organizational life from this perspective hinges on an appreciation of the shared meanings that permit organized activity to emerge and assume coherence as an ongoing social form (Van Maanen 1981; Smircich 1984; Pondy *et al.* 1983). The management of organized activity in this view hinges on the successful management of meaning, and points to the importance of managers being fully aware and skilled in the use of various symbolic modes of discourse through which situationally significant patterns of meaning and attention can be created and changed. An understanding of the symbolic nature of organization also provides the basis for an epistemology of management based on an appreciative wisdom that recognizes organization as resting not simply on the manipulation of cause and effect relationships, so much as on the patterning of symbolic discourse. Symbols and their relationships, i.e. patterns of contextually based meaning, become a principal focus of attention.

Organizational practice is understood as a continuous process of enactment

Implicit in the points made above, the idea that organizational members enact their own reality (Weick 1979) deserves special mention as one of the clearest and most important implications of the interpretive perspective. For it stresses that although organizational reality may at times appear 'all too real', the realness is of a socially constructed kind. What is real in organizations ultimately depends on the human beings that sustain the realness. Even the brute force of assembly line technology, for example, depends ultimately on the decisions of human beings to work within such a system or, from a managerial or trade union point of view, to adhere to the technology on which such a system depends. Some situations may appear more real than others, but the realness is always the product of human agency. Reality as a consensually valid system of meaning is at best an intersubjective phenomenon, with different individuals enacting reality in a similar way. Interpretive theory points to the unwitting collusion that underwrites the realness of organizational structure, rules, roles, and virtually every feature of organizational life.

Organizational contexts are enacted domains

This particular kind of enactment deserves special emphasis, for among all organizational concepts, that of the environment is often seen as being most independent and real in its consequences for any given organization. Yet it is clear that environments are enacted social processes. The independence and robustness of an environment stems from the actions of significant actors that comprise and shape 'the environment'. The environment which an organization encounters is also a product of the past enactments of that organization, and in this sense, it is a dimension of its own action and behaviour, and to this extent is under a measure of direct control. Present and future are defined and inhabited by past decisions which often come to haunt organizations like ghosts from the past. By way of example, I take a vivid illustration relating to the US motor industry, which I owe to Bill Starbuck. The US motor industry views itself as occupying a stagnating environment which, apart from its failure to offset foreign competition through an earlier move to the production of smaller cars, is seen as independent of their own decisions, and certainly not of their own choosing. One wonders, however, what the motor industry would be like if it had evolved technologically as fast as the computer and information processing industry. On this score we might expect some change in the whole concept of transportation or, with some exaggeration, cars that travel somewhere close to the speed of light. The motor industry has not evolved technologically in this way, and the non-actions in this regard in part account for its current predicament. The whole thrust of the interpretive paradigm is to suggest that the world which we inhabit is much more of our own making than we are usually prepared to recognize.

The radical humanist contribution

The radical humanist paradigm is specifically concerned with studying the self-laid traps which interpretive theory shows us that human beings are so adept at constructing. In essence, it is concerned with understanding the way humans construct a world which they often experience as confining, and most importantly, with finding ways in which humans can exercise control over their own constructions that allow them to express and develop their nature as human beings. The critical edge which characterizes radical humanist thought derives from the view that social life should express rather than constrain our humanness. The perspective offers a number of potentially important contributions to an understanding of organizations.

The radical humanist perspective searches for the ideological traps and blinders that lead human beings to feel powerless in dealing with the contingencies of their everyday world

For many in organizations, the enacted world appears 'all too real'. Workers and managers alike often function as alienated automatons, claiming no influence or power over the actions in which they engage (see, for example, Jermier 1981). The nature of organization and environment confronts the individual as imperatives, guided by impersonal forces or even blind necessity. The individual stands apart from a world experienced as an objective reality. Much of this seeming objectivity stems from those processes through which humans have learned to attribute a false correctness to their milieux.

Workers and managers alike often experience the concepts through which they structure their world as real forces; they believe their reality to be real, rather than merely an extension of themselves, i.e. an objectification of *their* experience of the world. This feeling of false concreteness is, from the radical humanist standpoint, one of the great barriers to the development of a reflexive awareness of the interactive relationships between subject and object, i.e. of the process of enactment. Radical humanist critique of the alienation and false concreteness embedded in our use of language, ideology, etc., provides an important means of developing in individuals a power and responsibility for guiding their own actions. The perspective provides a means of regaining power over our social constructions, so that individuals can consciously attempt to make their organizational and everyday life, rather than experiencing that they are merely being made by it.

The radical humanist perspective draws attention to the power dimension underlying enactment processes

Some people's processes of enactment are more important than others, for by virtue of position or charismatic qualities, they may assume great influence over the sensemaking processes of others. Leadership roles, for example, are characterized by a process of power-based reality construction in which certain individuals may perceive or are perceived to hold a right and obligation to define the reality of others. Such situations enact a pattern of dependency relations in which leaders feel obliged to define situations, and others to engage in a kind of 'trained inaction', waiting upon the definition of others, i.e. 'to follow' and 'be led'. Radical humanism offers a critical understanding of such phenomena showing, for example, that the 'all too realness' of leadership is predicated in a power that derives as much from the enactment of followership, as on the initiatives of the leader. Throughout the organization of social life, it is possible to discern institutionalized power relationships which sustain social forms constraining human development. Radical humanism serves, through critique of these forms, the democratic ideal of restoring power to people.

The radical humanist perspective reveals the ethical dimension embedded in systems of meaningful action

John Van Maanen notes in a consideration of the way radical humanist thought can enrich interpretive theory, that meanings are ultimately practical, and in essence provide solutions to the problems of existence (Van Maanen 1981). Different systems of meaning offer different kinds of solutions, and have different consequences. Viewed in this way, it becomes clear that configurations of meaning have an ethical or moral dimension amenable to both discussion and critique. Radical humanist thought presents an approach for understanding and confronting the moral codes which underwrite modes of organizational life, posing organizational choice as as much a problem of moral principle as it is of technique.

Radical humanism highlights the unconscious significance of organization

One of the most important but often neglected aspects of radical humanist thought focuses on the role of the unconscious mind in shaping the world of everyday activity. Organizations from this point of view are rich in symbolic significance, and many organizational events and activities are to be understood as manifestations of deep psychic processes that are at best poorly understood (Pondy *et al.* 1983; White and McSwain 1983). An appreciation of the deep psychological significance of various aspects of organizational practices generates important insights on the paradoxes and double-binds underlying the enactment of organizational realities that make effective action difficult, if not impossible.

Radical humanism advocates an ideology which places people first

Organization is seen as being ultimately for people rather than the other way around. Whereas most theories of organizations view human beings as either tools or resources to be used for the purpose of organization, radical humanism stresses that organization should express our humanness and its potentialities. In this way, radical humanism sets the foundations of a truly humanistic vision for the practice of organized activity.

The radical structuralist contribution

Of all the paradigms, the radical structuralist is perhaps among the most misunderstood, particularly because of its roots in Marxist theory and the popular but misguided view that Marxism constitutes no more than a set of beliefs as to what society should be like. In point of fact, Marxist theory presents a rigorous mode of social analysis which generates insights of a distinctive kind. In judging the merits of this mode of analysis, it is largely irrelevant as to whether one believes in capitalism, socialism, communism or whether any other mode of organization constitutes an ideal kind. The important point is that its mode of analysis leads us to see social phenomena in ways that elude the perspectives characteristic of other paradigms, and which have major relevance for understanding modern organization.

The radical structuralist perspective provides us with a theory of organization which emphasizes the importance of self-generated change

Most traditional explanations of social change draw in one way or another upon causal models which look to external factors as a means of understanding how change as a phenomenon is shaped. The radical structuralist view, on the other hand, is premised on the dialectical notion that everything changes itself as a result of the tensions which its very existence creates. All organized forms, for example, are negated by what they are not. Any act of management, for example, immediately sets up a dialectical tension between itself and the managed situation which it has created. The managed situation stands in opposition to the act of management. Although this force for change may appear to be externally generated, in point of fact it emerges as a direct consequence of the original action. All organized forms can be seen as embodying this characteristic, which sets the basis for their own transformation. The implications of understanding change from this point of view are enormous, and provide the basis for a dialectical theory of management which recognizes the negational consequences of its own action.

Radical structuralist theory focuses attention on the generative mechanisms that characterize the deep structure of a mode of organization, to reveal its fundamental logics of action

The dialectical processes referred to above produce a world amenable to empirical observation which is of awesome complexity. The radical structuralist maintains that beneath the clutter of facts and observations which characterize this empirical world (and with which, incidentally, most conventional social science is almost exclusively preoccupied) it is possible to discern generative mechanisms that provide important structural explanations of the whole (Bhaskar 1975; Burrell 1981; Benson 1983). In other words, radical structuralist analysis discerns logics of action within social systems that provide unique insights on and explanations of the nature of the surface phenomena that characterize the empirical world. This perspective offers a mode of organizational analysis that allows us to identify the major dialectical oppositions that shape our culture. It can be argued that this has direct consequences for the entropic system tendencies which underlie the turbulence of our organizational society, and has direct implications for the formulation of governmental and corporate strategy.

The radical structuralist perspective encourages an understanding of the role organizations play in the total social formation in which they are set

Organizations, from this point of view, are empirical facets of an underlying mode of organization, and their nature and significance can only be understood in terms of the role they play within the whole. Radical structuralist analysis encourages a perspective on organization which has considerable relevance for understanding the role of the state, and the distinctions between various kinds of public and private institutions. For example, it offers a specific view on the nature of regulative agencies, suggesting that we understand their role in terms of the under- lying contradictions in the mode of social organization which has produced them. This mode of analysis has direct relevance for the formation of public policy, particularly in the late twentieth century, an era when policies on regulation and deregulation swing like a political pendulum, in ignorance of the role and function of regulation in the mediation of contradictions.

The radical structuralist perspective offers a distinctive understanding of organizations in crisis

Crisis is of special interest to the radical structuralist, because in such situations it is often possible to discern the workings of a social system much more clearly than in those periods of surface stability when potentially contradictory elements are 'overdetermined' and in a state of temporary balance. The approach of the radical structuralist is to understand crises in terms of the logic of the whole social system, and to draw distinctions between the crises that are functional for maintenance of the whole against those which herald major transformations of the whole. Here again these insights have direct implications for the way we respond to and handle organizational crises.

The radical structuralist perspective offers a conception of organization as a form of praxis concerned with the self-transformation of collective action

Organizational praxis is not so much concerned with instrumental, practical problem-solving of a social engineering kind, such as that associated with usual discussions on the nature of innovation, as with the development of a capacity for self-organization which allows transcendence of existing constraints embedded in subject and object worlds (Heydebrand 1983). Praxis constitutes a form of action which seeks to transform itself through its interaction with the object world. As an example, we can point to the collective self-transformation which appears to be taking place in late twentieth century Poland, where trade unions are attempting to transform their situation, not in a piecemeal fashion, but through action designed to create a new social form. An understanding of this process, whereby new social forms emerge from contradictions in the old, provides the basis for a new way of conceptualizing and facilitating the process of social innovation in the widest sense.

Harnessing new opportunities for organizational research

Throughout the above discussion, emphasis has been placed on identifying the contributions which different paradigms can make to our understanding of organization. This approach has been adopted to move debate about paradigms beyond recognition that different perspectives exist, to a stage at which we can begin to harness the possibilities which they offer. If the chapter has made its case effectively, there can be no doubt at all that the paradigms are worthy of investigation for organizational analysis. Each paradigm offers important insight which eludes other perspectives, and while the implications of the contradictory nature of many of the assumptions on which they are based must ultimately be addressed (Morgan 1983 deals with this problem) much can be done to advance organizational analysis immediately by attempting to realize the rich possibilities they offer.

Organizational analysis, interpreted in the widest sense to incorporate the usual distinctions between organizational behaviour, theory, development, policy, etc., should grasp the opportunity and challenge which paradigm diversity presents, and explore the new perspectives which are available.

In order for this to be achieved in practice, attention needs to be given to the barriers posed by a number of institutional constraints associated with the way scientific enquiry is presently organized. There are a number of factors which serve to encourage organization researchers, particularly those who are just embarking on their academic careers, to engage in research which is 'safe' to the extent that it builds on past achievements in different subject areas and presents little challenge to the status quo. In line with the constructive nature and intent of this chapter as a whole, it will be useful to discuss the constraints in terms of the challenges which they present. I will confine attention to just three.

There is a need to develop a greater sensitivity for the practice and requirements of intellectual craftsmanship

Much conduct of organizational research, and the training of researchers on contemporary graduate programmes, is dominated by the requirements of methodology or technique. It is perhaps an exaggeration to suggest that organizational research is driven by methods searching for problems and situations to be researched, but it makes the fundamental point. In comparison with the attention given to methodology, the need for researchers to become familiar with and understand the multifaceted nature of the phenomenon being studied is given relatively little attention. It is in this sense that there is a need for a greater sense of intellectual craftsmanship.

A craftsperson, whether engaged in creative or relatively functional work, cannot perform effectively simply by knowing his or her tools. Craftsmanship also depends on an understanding of the material being worked. For organizational researchers, this material is found in the phenomenon of organization, and an understanding of this material depends on careful examination and experience of the phenomenon. An understanding of the way we can constitute the phenomenon in different ways on the basis of different paradigms provides one means through which we can make sense of our experience of the phenomenon. An understanding of the intellectual traditions which define these paradigms provides us with access to the thoughts and insights of the great theorists who have recorded their experience of social organization from these different standpoints.

The notion of paradigm can thus be used as a tool for exploring the nature of the phenomenon that we are concerned to investigate. Even

though a researcher may eventually decide to conduct research from the perspective of one given paradigm, an exploration of the nature of other paradigms provides an invaluable basis for understanding what one is doing, and why other alternatives are to be rejected. An understanding of the different paradigms also opens up the possibility of engaging in dialectical modes of research which attempt to counterpose the insights generated from competing perspectives.

There is a need to develop and refine the strategies and tools of research appropriate to different paradigms, and to develop appropriate criteria for determining the quality of the research conducted

There is a need for methodological innovation, and in particular for consideration of the logics of research practice characteristic of different paradigms. There is a special need to develop understanding of the vital link between theory and method in social research, and to appreciate the way sound research practice must be true to the logic of the assumptions which underwrite that practice.

Steps in this direction were taken in a research methodology project which counterposed the logics of twenty different kinds of research practice, and assessed the nature of their competing insights (Morgan 1983). This approach offered the possibility of replacing debates about the merits of competing methodologies with a consideration of the merits of rival logics of research. It offered the possibility of opening a new frontier of debate; one which assesses the significance of research strategies from the perspectives of different paradigms rather than from the traditional standpoint of a simple correspondence theory of truth.

There is a need to justify the institutional constraints imposed by academic journals and university departments on research practice, to facilitate the innovation and risk-taking necessary to explore unconventional research perspectives

One of the most frequent responses to the suggestion that there is a need for exploration of different paradigms in organizational research is that those who do so will fail to 'get published', and fail to 'get tenure'. At a recent *Academy of Management* doctoral consortium, numerous doctoral students responded to a debate on paradigms for organizational research with the view that they felt there was little room for innovation in their doctoral work, since only conventional research activities were appreciated and rewarded. In other words, there are signs of a well-spread feeling in many academic departments that there are few practical alternatives to orthodoxy, even among those newcomers to organizational research who might be expected to relish the challenge of a new opportunity. The control systems developed by journals and university departments alike exert a confining if well-meaning hold on the jugular of scholarship, which threatens to strangle the development of new possibilities. The existence of paradigm diversity thus presents a special challenge to those who control sources of publication, and to those who administer research opportunities through control of funding and careers. At a minimum, it is a challenge to become proactive in encouraging the pursuit of new endeavour, and to be tolerant, helpful and understanding toward those who are sufficiently inquisitive and courageous to explore the new research frontiers which are in such obvious need of attention.

Chapter two

Breaking up the mono-method monopolies in organizational analysis[1]

Joanne Martin

During the last ten years, efforts have been made to improve the breadth and quality of empirical approaches to the study of organizations (e.g. Burrell and Morgan 1979; Van Maanen 1979; Mitroff and Mason 1981; Hackman 1982; Morgan 1986). Partially in response to such efforts as these, organizational researchers are discussing methods and methodology more openly than before.[2] Often, one of two positions is argued. The first, a simple mono-method argument, proposes that one type of method is generally better than another. The second, a complex mono-method approach, argues that one type of method is better than another for the purpose of addressing a particular theoretical issue. Because these two positions have been advocated frequently, this chapter explores both seriously.

After some introductory definitions, this paper presents versions of the simple and complex mono-method approaches. Each of these one-sided positions is then rebutted. In conclusion, a more complex alternative is proposed – the methodological chameleon.

Qualitative vs. quantitative: a false dichotomy

In order to discuss these issues, labels are needed to describe the different types of methods available. In order to facilitate discussion of previous work, this paper uses the terms quantitative and qualitative.

The label quantitative is used here to refer to methods that primarily seek to express information numerically – in terms of amounts or counts. To use Daft's terminology, quantitative methods rely on low variety research languages, such as analytic mathematics (e.g. calculus, dynamic equilibrium models), linear statistics (e.g. correlations, regressions), and categorization (e.g. frequencies, percentages, cross-tabulations) (Daft 1980: 623–4). Although associating the label 'quantitative' with specific techniques can sometimes be misleading, statistical analyses of experimental, survey, and archival data are generally considered quantitative.

Qualitative methods, according to Van Maanen, are best defined in terms of axiom-like beliefs of the researcher (e.g. the importance of detailed observation; first-hand witness; studying normal, ordinary behaviour; sensitivity to meanings and contexts) (Van Maanen, Dabbs and Faulkner 1982: 16). Qualitative methods rely on high-variety research languages, such as verbal expression (e.g. open-ended interviews, reports of observations) and non-verbal modes of communication (e.g. photographs, videotapes, illustrations). A broad variety of specific techniques are used in a qualitative way, including participant observation, videotaping, formal and informational interviewing, ethnomethodology, historical and conversational analysis.[3]

Two caveats should be noted in order to avoid the confusion often associated with these labels. First, some methods are difficult to classify. For example, some kinds of qualitative data can be counted and texts can be systematically content-analysed (e.g. Webb, Campbell, Schwartz, and Sechrest 1972; Downey and Ireland 1979). Thus it is essential to conceptualize the qualitative *vs.* quantitative distinction not as a dichotomy, but as a continuum, with mixed methods at the midpoint of the scale. Secondly, these definitions are not meant to imply that quantitative research is objective, while qualitative research is subjective. Any research – whether qualitative or quantitative – must include subjective elements.[4]

Arguments about the relative merits of method choices are often phrased in terms of the inherent superiority of qualitative – or quantitative – types of methods. The next section of this paper describes two common forms of these arguments: the simple mono-method approach and the complex mono-method approach. Quantitative and qualitative versions of each of these arguments are described. Although these arguments have been elaborated and enacted by the practising researchers in more moderate and complex terms, this chapter uses extreme examples in order to clarify and highlight the essences of these positions.

The simple mono-method approach

This position is mono-method in that it considers well-executed quantitative methods to be inherently superior to well-executed qualitative methods or vice versa. It is simple because that superiority is said to hold across a broad spectrum of organizational research questions. There are currently quantitative and qualitative versions of the simple mono-method approach.

The quantitative version

According to this point of view, well-executed quantitative methods are seen as superior to well-executed qualitative approaches, irrespective of the topic being studied. An example is Blau's influential critique of the case-study approach to organizations (Blau 1965). In order for knowledge of organizational phenomena to expand, Blau argued that researchers should collect quantitative data from large numbers of organizations, rather than focus qualitatively on a single setting. The prevalence of this point of view is demonstrated by the steady increase in the proportion of quantitative papers accepted by the Administrative Science Quarterly between 1959 and 1979 (Daft 1980: 629).

Because this position dominates the field, it is usually not necessary to state it explicitly. Instead, the quantitative version of the simple mono-method approach usually remains a tacit assumption, the truth of which need not be explicated to those who are already true believers. It surfaces primarily when newcomers are being indoctrinated (as in some methodology textbooks) and when someone has the temerity to use qualitative methods.

The qualitative version

Because the organizational field is dominated by quantitative methods, qualitative researchers are often asked to, or feel it helpful to, defend their unorthodox method choices. Understandably, some of these discussions are one-sided arguments for the superiority of qualitative over quantitative methods, as if the point were, 'My method is better than your method.'

These defences often begin by extolling the advantages of qualitative approaches, citing for example the richness of the data, the strengths of a holistic approach that eschews decompositions, and the ease with which contradictions and paradoxes can be explored. A classic example of the qualitative version of the simple mono-method approach begins, 'Although questionnaires and interviews have their value, systematic observation has a number of advantages for organizational analysis. . . ' (Light 1979: 552).

Some proponents of qualitative research take their argument one step further by denigrating quantitative research. Those who take the stance that reality is a socially constructed phenomenon are particularly likely to express discontent with all forms of quantitative methods: 'The large-scale empirical surveys and detailed laboratory experiments that dominate much social research. . . . become increasingly unsatisfactory and, indeed, inappropriate' (Morgan and Smircich 1980: 498).

As these examples illustrate, some proponents of the simple mono-method position sound like lawyers presenting one side of a case. They catalogue the merits of their preferred method and the demerits of the unchosen alternatives, as if it would be unintelligent to give the opposition (such as a critical editor, reviewer, or reader) ammunition by admitting the strengths of the opposite point of view. This contentious approach to methodological discussions reinforces the simple mono-method position and makes it less likely that adherents of this approach will appreciate research findings obtained using non-preferred methodologies. Thus, the simple mono-method approach impedes the sharing of knowledge about organizational phenomena.

The complex mono-method approach

Many theoretical problems are characteristically addressed with either quantitative or qualitative methods. For example, a review of articles published in key organizational journals during the last decade yielded a list of sixteen frequently studied topics (Campbell, Daft, and Hulin 1982). Most of these topics were addressed predominantly with one or more quantitative methods. Studies of macro-level issues, such as organizational structure, technology, and size, generally relied on archival data. Goal-setting and expectancy theory were usually studied using experimental laboratory methods. Surveys were the preferred mode of assessing job attitudes. In contrast, organizational culture is usually studied using qualitative methods (e.g. Jelinek, Smircich, and Hirsch 1983).

The complex mono-method position justifies these observed affinities between substantive areas and method choices by arguing that quantitative or qualitative methods are better for addressing particular kinds of theoretical problems. The tone and content of these arguments can be more clearly understood if a substantive example is presented. The discussion below examines the complex mono-method justification for using qualitative methods to study culture. This substantive example was chosen because methodological disagreements are surfacing in this domain. Similar disputes, however, have focused on other substantive issues, such as decision-making, organizational symbolism, and cognitive approaches to the study of organizations.

The complex mono-method justification for qualitative culture research

Some organizational culture researchers argue that research on culture should depend predominantly on qualitative methods. For example, Daft categorizes the study of organizational culture as a research topic of the highest order of complexity. He states that 'low variety' research languages, such as quantitative methods, are not suited to the study of such a complex topic, due to the danger of oversimplification (Daft 1980: 632).

Smircich has made a similar argument. Defining culture as a network of shared meaning, she states, 'Networks of shared meaning do not lend themselves to study by methods of detachment and objectivity' (Smircich 1980: 9), so that qualitative methods such as 'participant observation for significant time periods with interviews conducted after some time in the setting is the favoured strategy for data gathering (on this topic)' (Smircich 1980: 19). Although others may not express the complex mono-method position as explicitly as these two researchers, qualitative methods have dominated culture research to date (e.g. Jelinek, Smircich, and Hirsch 1983; Pondy, Frost, Morgan, and Dandridge 1983; Frost, Moore, Louis, Lundberg, and Martin 1985).

Two justifications for this methodological preference are frequently given. First, qualitative research methods are said to be particularly appropriate for topics about which little is known. Perhaps the best-known presentation of this view is Mosteller and Tukey's contention that qualitative methods are best suited for exploratory research, while quantitative methods such as experimentation are more appropriate when knowledge has advanced to the point that hypotheses can be articulated (Mosteller and Tukey 1968). Research on culture is clearly in an embryonic stage. Accordingly, quantitative methods are said to be inappropriate for addressing the unformed questions that will arise in this relatively uncharted research domain.

A second reason for preferring qualitative approaches to the study of this topic stems from the advantages of 'thick descriptions' of cultures (Geertz 1973). According to this point of view, the researcher must attempt to study cultural phenomena in context. The nuances of socially constructed meanings should be recorded in rich detail. Presumably, qualitative approaches are better suited than quantitative methods to capture the complexity of cultural phenomena. The next section of this paper challenges both these arguments for the complex mono-method approach.

Critique of the complex mono-method approach to studying culture

There is nothing inherent in quantitative methods that restricts their use to empirically familiar territory. Even novel or empirically unfounded questions can be explored using quantitative methods. For example, little is known about the process of cultural change. Periodic collection of questionnaire data could provide a dynamic model of this process. Similarly, it is unnecessary to limit the usefulness of qualitative methods by restricting their use to exploratory studies. For instance, qualitative methods could be used to see if humanitarian cultural values have a beneficial effect on satisfaction or productivity. Thus, both qualitative and quantitative methods can be used for both exploratory and confirmatory research.

However, even if a researcher believes that qualitative methods are best suited to exploratory studies, some aspects of culture research are relatively well established and could be further explored using quantitative methods. For example, a number of researchers argue that organizational cultures generate employee commitment by such means as passing on stories that illustrate the institution's values or philosophy of management (Selznick 1957; Clark 1970; Wilkins 1979; Ouchi 1981; Pascale and Athos 1981; Deal and Kennedy 1982; Peters and Waterman 1982). Because most of the evidence supporting this culture-commitment proposition is qualitative, the accuracy of the proposition is questionable on a number of grounds.

First, this proposition posits a causal relationship between cultural activities, such as the sharing of stories, and commitment. Many qualitative researchers are not committed to establishing causal relationships (cf. Bateson 1979), in part because it is extremely difficult to demonstrate the existence and direction of causality using qualitative data. In this case, it is possible that employees in the organizations studied were already highly committed to the values in question, independently of any story-sharing activities.

Qualitative data makes it difficult to disentangle the effects of potentially confounding variables. For example, the relationship between cultural activities and value commitment may simply be due to length of employment. Employees who have worked longer for a particular organization may be more committed to its values and, simply because they have been around for a long time, may also know more about that organization's shared stories.

A third difficulty stems from the fact that qualitative research seldom includes adequate control or comparison groups. Thus, for example, the available data does not demonstrate that cultural phenomena, such as the sharing of organizational stories, cause more commitment than other means of communicating information, such as the presentation of statistics.

Finally, there is the question of generalizability. The time and effort involved in qualitative research makes the in-depth study of large numbers of organizations difficult. The qualitative evidence that supports the culture-commitment proposition comes either from large numbers of organizations, not studied in systematic depth, or from more detailed investigations of a relatively small number of settings. As a result, the generalizability of this proposition is questionable.

Of course, not all culture researchers are concerned about developing abstract, generalizable theories. Some prefer to present a detailed, thick description of a single setting. However, the culture-commitment proposition claims to be a generalizable statement. Therefore, it is necessary to provide appropriate comparisons and controls, disentangle potential confounds, and explore the existence and direction of causal relationships. Quantitative methods perform these tasks. For example, laboratory experiments have examined the relationship between one cultural activity, sharing stories, and commitment (e.g. Martin 1981).

A brief description of one of these experiments illustrates the types of information this quantitative method can, and cannot, provide. In one study, MBA subjects read about an organization's humanitarian values and then were randomly assigned to read one of three types of information indicating that these values had been translated into practice: a story about a single employee, statistics about many employees, and the story and the statistics combined. These humanitarian values, the story, and the statistics were drawn from a qualitative case study of an actual organization (Wilkins 1979). After reading the materials, the subjects were asked questions about their commitment to this kind of value and their reactions to this particular company.

The results of this study demonstrated that this cultural activity, the sharing of organizational stories, caused higher levels of commitment than other means (such as statistics) of transmitting the same sort of information. The experimental evidence, unlike the qualitative evidence on this issue, demonstrated a causal relationship unconfounded by the effects of long-term employment. To find these results in an experimental laboratory study, as well as in a series of qualitative field studies, is powerful evidence of generalizability.

In summary, quantitative approaches to the study of culture provide information that is difficult to obtain using qualitative methods. However, on a more abstract level, this discussion so far has simply replaced a qualitative justification for a mono-method approach to culture with a quantitative one. This is unfortunate, because quantitative approaches also have their limitations. Morgan has suggested that one way to transcend methodological parochialism is for researchers to engage in conversations about their methodological preferences (Morgan 1983). Below, one such conversation, among 'true believers', is imagined.

Arguing the merits of complex mono-method rationales

Imagine that two culture researchers are comparing the relative merits of their versions of the complex mono-method argument introduced above. One researcher is a psychologist who favours quantitative methods, and the other is an anthropologist who prefers qualitative techniques.

Anthropologist: 'Quantitative methods have difficulty providing "thick descriptions" of cultural phenomena. There are two aspects to this problem: cultural phenomena are taken out of context and their complexity is reduced. The implications of the first of these issues can be illustrated with the experiment described above. A cultural manifestation, in this case a story, was taken out of its natural context and studied in a laboratory. The experimental subjects knew nothing about the organization from which the story came. The subjects had no histories of interaction with organizational members to serve as a source of relevant interpretative information. Thus, the story inevitably lost some of its symbolic meanings. In contrast to actual employees at the organization where the story was told, the experimental subjects undoubtedly had a different, probably more simplified, interpretation of the story.'

Psychologist: 'There is another side to this issue. If culture is such a rich and complex phenomenon, then any analysis which captures this complexity will have difficulty separating the interwoven strands of organizational history and personal relationships. For example, when an employee hears an organizational story from a superior, the employee's reaction will be influenced by the history of interaction between those two people. If the relationship has been troubled, the employee may dismiss the story as corporate propaganda, particularly if some story element serves as a symbolic reminder of past disagreements. Quantitative methods can focus on the impact of the story, independent of the complicating effects of personal and organizational history. For example, in an experimental setting, subjects can be strangers and organizational history can, in effect, be erased. The effects of other potentially confounding variables can be statistically controlled or dispersed through random assignment of subjects to experimental conditions.'

Anthropologist: 'Who cares about the outcomes of that kind of research? Stories never exist independent of personal and organizational histories. Why research something that is so controlled and simple that it never would exist? No matter how many potentially confounding variables a quantitative researcher studies, this type of method inevitably restricts attention to a subset of variables, in effect reducing the complexity of cultural phenomena. This problem is particularly acute for experimental methods. Most experimenters hesitate to manipulate more than three independent variables in a single study. Thus, quantitative studies lack the conceptual breadth necessary for encompassing a phenomena as complex as culture.'

Psychologist: 'Yes, but there are good reasons for narrowing one's attention to a few variables at a time. It is important for the development of theory, irrespective of the percentage of variance accounted for in a complex field setting, to understand the relationships that would occur in the absence of confounding factors. There are also practical reasons why only a few independent variables are examined in a single study, including the difficulties of interpreting n-way interactions and obtaining adequate cell sizes. Furthermore, a sequence of experiments can build a carefully expanded theory, incorporating a larger range of variables than can be examined within a single study.'

Anthropologist: 'With such a narrow approach you risk discovering relationships that may be insignificant, may not even exist, in complex natural settings.'

Psychologist: 'But the richness of your qualitative data is an invitation to conceptual chaos.'

This debate, like many simple and complex mono-method arguments, ends in a stand-off. The same points, however, could be made in the context of a discussion of inevitable trade-offs. Qualitative approaches to the study of culture have unavoidable weaknesses and irreplaceable strengths. Quantitative methods also have unique advantages and inescapable disadvantages for the study of culture. The next section of this paper develops a more systematic analysis of trade-offs among inherently imperfect method choices and argues that the relevance of this trade-off analysis is not restricted to the topic of culture research.

The research dilemma: inevitable trade-offs

McGrath presents a systematic analysis of the inevitable trade-offs that underlie the choice of any one method (McGrath 1982). He examines eight 'pure' or idealized techniques: laboratory experiments, experimental simulations, field experiments, field studies, computer simulations, formal theoretical exercises, sample surveys, and judgement tasks. While some of these techniques fall on the 'mixed' or 'variable' midpoint of the qualitative–quantitative continuum, others are defined by McGrath in terms that are clearly quantitative (such as laboratory experiments) or qualitative (non-experimental field studies). Each of the eight techniques is classified according to the extent to which three criteria are maximized: controlled and precise measurement of behaviour, generalizability across subjects and detailed knowledge of contexts.[5]

McGrath argues that method choices which maximize any one of these criteria will necessarily minimize the other two; and that the choices that would 'optimize' on any two will minimize on the third. For example, non-experimental field studies, as defined by McGrath, are as unobtrusive as possible. They take place in settings that are existentially real for participants. Thus, realism of context is maximized, at the cost of precision and generalizability. In contrast, laboratory experiments involve deliberately contrived settings. Realism of context and generalizability are sacrificed in order to maximize precision of measurement. Although space limitations make it impossible to summarize the rest of McGrath's analysis of the trade-offs involved in method choices, these two examples illustrate his fundamental conclusions – any method has inherent weaknesses; no method is perfect. Moreover, one method's strengths are another method's weaknesses.

If method choices do have complementary strengths and weaknesses, the simple and complex mono-method positions are misguided. The simple version ignores the weaknesses of the preferred method and does not allow the accumulation of knowledge to benefit from the strengths of the non-preferred methods. The complex mono-method position suffers from similar problems. If research on any one topic, such as culture, relies on any one method, such as ethnography, the inherent weaknesses of the method will cause blindspots in knowledge about that topic. Thus, both the simple and the complex mono-method positions inhibit the development of knowledge.

These conclusions have implications for the behaviour of researchers. First, the simple mono-method approach should be discarded. One-sided 'my method is better than your method' discussions are oversimplified and, to the extent that they are persuasive, are dangerously misleading. The complex mono-method approach is equally misleading, although within the narrower constraints of a single topic area. It too should be abandoned. Instead, multiple methods should be used to address topic areas, so that the weaknesses of one method would be compensated for, over time, by the strengths of other methods. Multi-method approaches have been frequently advocated and, less frequently, practised. If the argument above is correct, it is important to understand why such eminently sensible practices are avoided.

Triangulation and hybrid methods

Perhaps the most familiar of the multi-method techniques is triangulation. According to classic definitions, a successful triangulation study uses different methods to come up with the same answer to a single theoretical question (cf. Fiske and Campbell 1959). McGrath's analysis suggests a different, perhaps equally desirable, outcome. Because different methods must address somewhat different aspects of a problem, they will yield divergent answers. Rather than invalidating each other, such conflicting results may offer insight into different aspects of the problem.[6]

Even if researchers see the risk of divergent results as a desirable outcome, there are a number of practical reasons why they may avoid triangulation. It is conceptually and technically difficult, time consuming, and costly (cf. Jick 1979). Even when these problems are resolved, it is often impossible to publish the results in a single journal article, so that discrepant findings can be discussed in the context of detailed information about the methods used. Journals have stringent space limitations and, in a few cases, have well-developed preferences for either quantitative or qualitative methods. Thus, the hard-earned insights gained from triangulation are often buried in a footnote which begins, 'A survey concerning these issues was also administered. . .'.

Advocates of triangulation often stress the advantages of selecting 'pure' methods which are as different as possible (e.g. Runkel and McGrath 1972). A second multi-method approach uses a quite different strategy. Rather than using several different methods, the researcher develops a hybrid method which has a blend of strengths and weaknesses uniquely suited for addressing a specific topic.

Because organizational researchers must be able to relate the results of their work to what goes on in organizations, they have developed a variety of hybrid techniques. For example, laboratory experiments have used full-time employees as subjects, adapted stimulus materials from organizational archives, and structured the experimental context to approximate subjects' normal working environments (e.g. Fox and Staw 1979; Salancik 1978; Staw and Ross 1980; Zucker 1977). Materials from a qualitative observational study of culture have been used to create a standardized survey, designed to assess systematically knowledge of, and commitment to, some aspects of an organization's culture throughout all levels of the institution (Siehl and Martin 1984). Unobtrusive measures and systematic sampling procedures have been used to integrate quantitative techniques into the traditionally qualitative case-study approach (Campbell and Stanley 1963; Webb, Campbell, Schwartz, and Sechrest 1972; McClintock, Brannon, and Maynard-Moody 1979; Van Maanen, Dabbs, and Faulkner 1982).

Hybrid methods such as these involve trade-offs, because some advantages of the 'pure' forms of these methods are sacrificed. It is often difficult to make these choices, particularly if the trade-offs are to be uniquely suited for addressing a specific problem. Even if the choices can be made appropriately, to the researcher's satisfaction, others must also be convinced. In addition to these difficulties, there are broader reasons why multi-method approaches are often avoided. These are discussed below.

Garbage cans and the scarcity of multi-method competence

Researchers who choose triangulation or who develop hybrid methods are making method choices in a well-reasoned, self-conscious manner. In accord with the procedure described in research textbooks, these researchers are defining a theoretical problem and then letting the nature of that problem dictate their careful choice of an appropriate method. However, the sequence of research decisions described in the textbooks may not be an accurate description of how researchers actually make method choices.

Instead, the research decision-making process may resemble the garbage can model of managerial decision making (Cohen, March, and Olsen 1972), so that the sequential assumptions of the research textbook model are suspended (Martin 1982). Instead of theoretical problems always dictating the choice of a method, method choices may be determined by the availability of resources, the preferences or limited skills of a researcher, or even the likelihood that particular results may be found. Indeed, the textbook sequence may be reversed, so that methodological preferences dictate what theoretical problem is studied. For example, some of the projects of Michigan's Institute for Survey Research, such as the Detroit Area Study, can be characterized as a method (survey) in search of a theoretical problem to address.

There is considerable evidence that the garbage can model is more accurate than the textbook model in its portrayal of how method choices actually are made (e.g. Webb and Ellsworth 1975; Ellsworth 1977; Campbell and Cook 1979; Knorr 1979; McGrath, Martin, and Kulka 1982). If this is so, it may be very difficult to convince researchers to make method choices in the complex, well-reasoned, self-conscious manner that is a prerequisite for the multi-method approaches advocated above.

A second difficulty is that triangulation and, to a lesser extent, hybrid methods require that a researcher becomes a jack-of-all-trades, adept in several different methods. Most researchers are adequately trained in one, or at best a few, methods. Multi-method approaches may require changes in skills and attitudes that are unlikely, perhaps impossible.

Methodological chameleons

There is another alternative. Researchers could become more appreciative of, and more able to judge the merit of, studies in their field of interest that use unfamiliar or non-preferred methods, so that the results of these studies could be integrated into their own work. Researchers could learn to be tolerant of different methods, coming to prize and encourage divergent conclusions that emerge from divergent method choices. This open-minded stance is rare. Even in an openly interdisciplinary, multi-method field such as organizational behaviour, theoretical integration of results obtained using different methods is proceeding in a slow, crude and inefficient fashion (Roberts, Hulin, and Rousseau 1981).

Methodological open-mindedness may be rare because some people feel that a complex or simple mono-method position is the only intellectually honest alternative – that one method is, in fact, superior. This tendency may be particularly strong among those who believe in a single epistemological point of view and feel that point of view justifies a simple or complex mono-method approach to research (Burrell and Morgan 1979).[7] All too often, methodologies are discussed as if they were scientific religions – each one labelling itself the one true faith.[8]

Methodological – and perhaps even epistemological – conflicts could be overcome by drawing from existentialism. As atheists, the existentialists disavowed belief in all ideologies except that which asserted that no ideology was valid. Regarding the void left by the absence of any kind of faith, existentialists felt themselves faced with a brutal choice: to commit suicide or to act as if they believed in something. Those that chose the latter alternative often aspired to act in accordance with some of the ethical principles of religious ideologies, even though they had discarded some of the basic premises of religion, such as a faith in God (cf. Camus 1948; Hartt 1962).

It is possible to take an 'existential' approach to method choices by admitting that no alternative is free of flaws or inherently superior to the others. The researcher who believes this is faced with a choice. He or she could stop doing research, or he or she could continue to do research within the constraints of a quantitative or qualitative preference, but with full awareness that those constraints have no monopoly on truth; alternative types of methods may well be equally valid (and equally invalid).

A researcher who adopts this position would be a methodological chameleon. While conducting a study, the researcher would act like – perhaps even temporarily become – an advocate of one of the mono-method positions. When reading completed studies, even his or her own, the researcher would evaluate the results with the scepticism of a methodological atheist, with no belief in the supremacy of any mono-method position. In this state of mind, the existential methodologist could draw on research results using any well-executed method.

The image of a chameleon may not capture the quality and intensity of commitment required by this existentialist stance. It is exceedingly difficult to adopt an existential approach to research. We seem to need to believe in the superiority of the method we use, perhaps because otherwise we might have to question the worth of doing research at all. Like religious faiths, mono-method justifications are comforting, making multi-method-appreciators, if not -practitioners, an all-too-rare phenomenon.

Breaking up the monopolies

In our efforts to improve the breadth and quality of empirical studies or organizations, researchers have begun to invest more time and energy in discussing methodology. This is good. Unfortunately, the tone of that discussion has, all too often, taken the form of a one-sided justification of a given method choice: either a simple or a complex version of a mono-method argument.

This chapter argues that we should refrain from this type of argument and, instead, actively work to break up mono-method monopolies. The difficulties inherent in this task should not be minimized. Methodological existentialists are rare, in part for the understandable reasons outlined above. These problems are exacerbated by the difficulties of designing and publishing triangulated studies, inventing effective hybrid methods, and overcoming the lack of self-consciousness that is often inherent in the garbage can approach to making method choices.

Nevertheless, if we could overcome these difficulties, the benefits of breaking up the mono-method monopolies would be considerable. As individual researchers, we would have a better understanding of the phenomena we study. If we could – in our own research or in our reading – draw on the insight of a variety of quantitative and qualitative studies, our theories might be less riddled with blindspots caused by mono-method monopolies. Expanding and deepening our knowledge of organizations is, after all, the business we are in, and there are those who would argue that breaking up monopolies is good for business.

Chapter three

Beyond paradigmatic closure in organizational enquiry[1]

Hugh Willmott

Introduction

In the 1960s, reflection upon the metatheoretical assumptions underpinning organization studies was virtually absent. So, too, were alternatives to orthodox, functionalist organization theory. Today, following the publication of Burrell and Morgan's *Sociological Paradigms and Organizational Analysis* (1979), an appreciation of the relationship between accounts of organization and the framing of these accounts within paradigmatic frameworks has become a commonplace within the discipline. The intellectual imperialism of the functionalist orthodoxy has been challenged by perspectives that are attentive to the significance of organizational actors' definitions of the situation and the class-invested basis of organizational structures.

This chapter has two objectives. One is to reflect critically upon a fundamental premise of Burrell and Morgan's *Sociological Paradigms and Organizational Analysis* – namely, the dualism of subjective versus objective paradigms that sets limits upon the possibilities of theorizing organization. More positively, it involves an exploration of attempts to theorize the social world in a way that denies the mutual exclusivity of the distinguishing attributes of these paradigms. The second objective is to examine the basis upon which these denials are made. A contrast is drawn between those attempts which seek to overcome the dualism of subjectivity and objectivity in theory (e.g. Berger and Luckmann 1967; and Giddens 1976, 1979, 1984), and those which are primarily concerned with overcoming this dualism in practice (e.g. Freire 1972). Despite its theoretical deficiencies, which are discussed, Freire's approach is sensitive (however imperfectly) to the dialectic of theory and practice. That is to say, his work is informed by the understanding that theory is conditioned by the practical experience of dualism and, in this sense, he grasps more adequately than Giddens the connectedness of theory and practice.

The chapter is organized as follows. First, recent developments in organizational theory are reviewed. It is suggested that three theoretically distinctive approaches – forms of contingency theory, ethnomethodology and Marxism – have emerged out of the earlier juxtaposition of 'systems' and 'action' perspectives. Second, it is noted how, in recent years, differences in these approaches have been theorized in terms of incommensurable paradigmatic assumptions about the nature of science and society. Third, the writings of Berger and Luckmann, Giddens and Freire are examined, each of which, it is argued, pose a challenge to the assumption of paradigmatic closure. Finally, through a review of the assumptions underpinning their work, an alternative foundation for critical organizational analysis is briefly sketched.

The career of organization theory

Orthodox approaches to the analysis of organizations have assumed that their reality is objectively given, functionally necessary and/or politically neutral (Donaldson 1985). Enquiry is informed by a technocratic concern to improve the design of corporate structures and processes, the assumption being that such modifications will be broadly beneficial for all groups. In both open systems theory and contingency analysis, for example, the existence of the 'outside' world is conceptualized as an environment comprising a variety of factors that must be registered and controlled if strategic adjustments are to be successfully achieved. There is minimal consideration of the relevance of social theory – of theories of society and theories of knowledge – for the study of organizations.[2]

Initially, an alternative to 'systems' analyses of organization developed within studies that were attentive to fundamental similarities between formal organizations and other social institutions (e.g. Selznick 1949; Gouldner 1954; see also Perrow 1972). Employing neo-Weberian methods of enquiry, an important outcome of these studies was their discovery of a variety of often conflicting purposes and perceptions held by individuals and groups within organizations. In turn, this revelation pointed towards the phenomenon of power, rather than functional imperatives or complex contingencies, in privileging particular definitions of, and strategies for securing, 'organizational goals' (Krupp 1961).

However, it was not until the publication of David Silverman's *The Theory of Organizations* (1970) that orthodox, 'systems' accounts of organization were subjected to a comprehensive critique. Drawing heavily upon Berger and Luckmann's *Social Construction of Reality* (1967), Silverman advocated a method of enquiry designed to provide a dialectical analysis of '*social relations* within organizations' (Silverman

1970: 147, emphasis added) wherein 'society defines man, [and] man in turn defines society' (p. 127). This methodology, the action frame of reference (AFR), provided an alternative framework for the study of organizations. But its more lasting effect has been to expose and deepen the rift between, on the one hand, those who have been impervious to the critique of 'systems' analyses of organizations (i.e. contingency theorists who are preoccupied with the construction of 'objective' models and the measurement of variables, as exemplified in the Aston studies); and, on the other, those who have radicalized Silverman's critique of orthodox organization theory in divergent directions. Uncomfortable with the commonsensical attribution of meaning to actors within the AFR, ethnomethodology has explored how actors practically accomplish a common sense of their reality. And, moving in an opposite direction, the absence of historical specificity within the AFR has prompted radical organization theorists to return to classical social theory and, in particular, to the writings of Marx.

By the beginning of the 1980s three main metatheoretical directions in organization analysis had become established: contingency theory, ethnomethodology and Marxism.[3] Building upon the legacy of the 'systems' tradition, contingency theory continues to exert the most pervasive and influential effect upon organization analysis. Ranging from population ecology to strategic choice analysis (Aldrich 1979), the broad church of contingency harbours a studied disinterest in the relevance of social theory for the study of organizations (Donaldson 1985). Even in strategic choice analysis, Silverman's critique of systems theory is accommodated within a contingency framework in which its insights are employed to reveal the influence of managerial values in the selection of organizational structures best fitted to respond to environmental contingencies. Attending to this design as the outcome of 'a political process in which constraints and opportunities are functions of the power exercised by decision makers in the light of ideological values' (Child 1972: 16), executive action is theorized as a neglected variable which must be identified and measured if 'greater predictive certainty' about the contingent relationship between contextual and structural variables is to be achieved (Child 1972: 16). In effect, the metatheoretical assumptions of contingency theory ensure that little can be learned about the commonsense reasoning of organizational members or about the institutional structures that empower their actions.

A second, much less influential, metatheoretical direction has been taken by ethnomethodology. Here the process of objectification (i.e. the ascription of meaning) is itself treated as a problematic, indexically constituted topic of investigation. In contrast to the AFR, ethnomethodology is attentive to the mundane reasoning that makes these actions accountable to organizational members.[4] In its radicalization of the

AFR's attention to meaning, ethnomethodology adopts an attitude of 'ethnomethodological indifference' to the ontology of the organizational and institutional structures that are the medium and outcome of this mundane reasoning (Garfinkel 1967; Zimmerman 1971; Silverman 1975).

Although informed by very different theoretical positions, both orthodox analyses and ethnomethodological studies exclude from their perspectives any appreciation of history and social structure as conditions of possibility for the construction and transformation of organizational realities. This is because they each 'subscribe to a conception of organizational analysis which severely fractured, if not totally sundered, the historical link between organization theory and social theory' (Reed 1985: 61). In part, it is the concern to restore the broken link between organizational theory and social theory that has stimulated the emergence and growing influence of neo-Marxist (e.g. Benson 1977) and neo-Weberian (e.g. McNeill 1978) forms of analysis.

This third approach to organizational analysis has sought to reveal how the structure and dynamics of capitalism is reflected in both the organization of work and the theories that inform and legitimate its design. As the capitalist organization of work extends and strengthens its grip upon society, the organization of the labour process (including the processes of distribution) becomes more complex and requires more sophisticated forms of control (and ownership). Braverman, for example, has described the widespread adoption of Taylorian principles in the design of work as 'the verbalization of the capitalist mode of production' (Braverman 1974: 86).[5] In this light, orthodox theories of organization are seen to assume and secure processes of rationalization and innovation necessary to satisfy the process of accumulation (cf. Clegg and Dunkerley 1980: 538–9). In contrast, neo-Marxist analysis addresses questions of which class is the primary beneficiary of current organizational structures and practice; who is empowered to maintain or to change these structures; and what is the source of the institutional power that enables or constrains the actions of different individuals and groups, etc.

To summarize, the recent history of organization analysis has been one of growing theoretical pluralism. A critical rupture followed the publication of *The Theory of Organizations* in which Silverman provided a penetrating examination of the functionalist premises underpinning mainstream analyses of organization. Coinciding with the rapid growth in the teaching of organizational behaviour in higher education, its most significant effect was to facilitate the opening up of the area to approaches that marked a radical departure from the systems orthodoxy. It was the mapping of these departures that provided the inspiration for the book that has probably had the greatest impact on theorizing within the discipline in the 1980s – Burrell and Morgan's *Sociological Paradigms and Organizational Analysis* (1979). It is to a consideration of this book that the chapter now turns.

Paradigms of organization analysis

In *Sociological Paradigms and Organizational Analysis*, contingency theory, ethnomethodology and radical forms of analysis are located in hermetically sealed paradigms, paradigms that are differentiated by their espousal of contrasting philosophies of science and theories of society. Burrell and Morgan write:

> The four paradigms are founded upon *mutually exclusive* views of the social world. Each stands in its own right and generates its own distinctive analyses of social life. With regard to the study of organizations, for example, each paradigm generates theories and perspectives which are *in fundamental opposition* to those generated in other paradigms.
>
> (Burrell and Morgan 1979: x, emphasis added)

The thesis that analyses of organization are unavoidably informed by some (usually undisclosed) conceptions of science and society is uncontentious. More problematical, however, is the assertion that conceptions of science and society can, in each case, be boiled down to a binary opposition between 'subjectivist' and 'objectivist' philosophies of social science on the one hand, and 'regulation' and 'radical change' theories of society on the other; and that these can then be arranged in a 2 x 2 matrix to provide a comprehensive and reliable map of the terrain in which specific forms of organization analysis may be located.

Burrell and Morgan recommend that analyses of organization should be guided principally by the assumptions of the paradigm in which the favoured approach is positioned. Referring to work being undertaken outside of the functionalist paradigm, they advise:

> There is a real need. . .to ground their perspective in the philosophical traditions from which it derives; to start from first principles; *to have the philosophical and sociological concerns by which the paradigm is defined at the forefront of their analysis*; to develop a systematic and coherent perspective *within the guidelines which each paradigm offers*. . . . Each paradigm needs to be developed in its own terms.
>
> (Burrell and Morgan 1979: 397, emphasis added)

In part, this advice arises from the desire to explicate the ontological, epistemological and methodological assumptions underlying different forms of analysis and to defend the legitimate concerns of 'interpretive' and 'radical' forms of analysis from colonization by the dominant functionalist orthodoxy. A danger, which Burrell and Morgan strongly scent, is that other approaches will be used to strengthen this dominance – either by appropriating elements to bolster the functionalist regime, or by reasserting the authority of functionalism through a derisory dismissal of their radical thrust. However, though well intentioned, the effect of this advice, where followed, is to constrain analysis within one of the four paradigms, and thus to exclude the possibility of forms of analysis that deviate from, or transcend the limitations of, the paradigmatic guidelines. Paradoxically, the recommended replacement for the functionalist orthodoxy is a world-view that acknowledges a wider field of vision but is no less myopic in respect of its own constraints.

The fundamental flaw in Burrell and Morgan's thesis arises from the assumption that theories and perspectives are actually determined, in structuralist fashion, by the pre-existence of four 'mutually exclusive' paradigms (p.25). Certainly, the outer boundaries of the 2 x 2 matrix suggest plausible limits for social theorizing. More questionable is the sense of dividing this intellectual territory into four paradigmatic enclaves. A more defensible approach would be to recognize both the diversity of assumptions guiding analysis *and* the ways in which they may be combined. Instead, the tendency in organization analysis (following the intellectual lead of social theory) to construct, solidify and defend such dualisms is presented as a metaphysical principle. Similarly, in differentiating between the political leanings of analysis towards 'regulation' or 'radical change', Burrell and Morgan specify a dualism in which there is no room for any ambiguity about the political impulse and impacts of particular forms of organization analysis.

In sum, *Sociological Paradigms and Organizational Analysis* provides a valuable heuristic device, in the form of the 2 x 2 matrix of paradigms, for appreciating how different approaches to the study of organizations are implicitly informed by philosophical and political assumptions about the nature of science and society. Its appearance has heightened awareness of the foundations of organization analysis; it has also identified the existence of vast expanses of intellectual terrain that have been ignored or prematurely written off by organization analysts. However, by denying the presence (and the possibility!) of approaches that are neither exclusively 'subjective' nor 'objective', and which are not governed solely by the principles of 'regulation' nor by those of 'radical change', *Sociological Paradigms* exerts an inadvertently repressive force as it denies the very possibility of analysis that is much more sensitive to the ambiguous and contradictory nature of social reality than is allowed by its own one-dimensional vision of the mutual exclusivity of paradigms (Dawe 1979).

Beyond paradigmatic closure

This section examines a number of attempts to overcome the limitations associated with a belief in paradigmatic closure – a belief that denies the possibility of transcending the dualistic foundations and identity of Burrell and Morgan's four paradigms. Three such efforts will be reviewed: those of Berger and Luckmann (1967), Giddens (1976, 1979, 1984) and Freire (1972). When examining these attempts, it will be argued that they are themselves underpinned by contrasting assumptions about the nature of the social world. Berger and Luckmann found their analysis upon the understanding that social reality is the product of a process involving a continuous series of subjective and objective moments.[6] Rejecting this rather mechanistic account of social reproduction, Giddens advances a theory in which there is only one moment – the moment of reproduction – which is analyzed from two analytically distinct perspectives. In each case, the effort to overcome the dualism of subject and object is informed by a concern to overcome dualisms in social theory rather than dualisms in practice or dualisms between theory and practice. In contrast Freire is concerned to develop a theory capable of penetrating and transforming the practical manifestations of dualism – in the experience of oppression and the fear of freedom.

Berger and Luckmann

In *The Social Construction of Reality* (1967), Berger and Luckmann set out to integrate 'objectivist' and 'subjectivist' accounts of social life. As they put it, 'Since society exists in both objective and subjective reality, any adequate theoretical understanding of it must comprehend both these aspects.' (p. 149)

Based upon the understanding that society is both an objective facticity *and* built up by activity that expresses subjective meaning, Berger and Luckmann have sought to develop a conceptual framework capable of explicating how and why subjective meanings (externalization) become objective facticities (objectivation) which then 'act back' as they socialize present and future generations (internalization). Referring to these as three dialectically related moments in the construction of social reality, they observe, 'Society is a human product. Society is an objective reality. Man is a social product. . . .an analysis that leaves out any one of these three moments will be distortive'. (p. 79, emphasis omitted)

Berger and Luckmann's thesis is of particular interest here because it provides the theoretical basis for Silverman's action frame of reference (AFR). In mounting his challenge to orthodox organization theory, Silverman pays greatest attention to the understanding that the apparent objectivity of the social world (i.e. the everyday world which is routinely taken for granted) 'does not acquire an ontological status apart from the human activity that produced it' (Berger and Luckmann 1967: 78). Though it may be experienced as a reality *sui generis*, it is a construction whose appearance of objectivity depends wholly on the (inter) subjectivity of the actors who are continuously (re) constructing it. In order to understand organization, Silverman argues, it is essential to appreciate the subjective meanings that support this process. Silverman's reading of Berger and Luckmann is summarized in 'seven propositions', of which numbers 4 to 6 are central:

4 While society defines man, man in turn defines society. Particular constellations of meaning are only sustained by continual reaffirmation in everyday actions.
5 Through their interaction men also modify, change and transform social meanings.
6 It follows that explanations of human actions must take account of the meanings which those concerned assign to their acts; the manner in which the everyday world is socially constructed yet perceived as real and routine becomes a crucial concern of sociological analysis.

(Silverman 1970: 126–7)

Despite Silverman's emphasis upon the role of meaningful interaction in the reproduction of the world-taken-for-granted, Burrell and Morgan site the AFR in an 'objectivist' paradigm. How can this be? The answer is that they give more weight to proposition 3 which states that 'meanings are given to men by their society' and that 'shared orientations are experienced by later generations as social facts'. Although Burrell and Morgan acknowledge that this '"realist" ontology' is immediately 'qualified' by the '"nominalist" ontology' of subsequent propositions, they none the less assert that proposition 3 leaves the reader in 'no doubt that the actors occupy a "realist" social world which is external to the individual and has a reality which is independent of any individual's social construction of it' (pp. 198–9). Not surprisingly, they conclude that the AFR 'is based upon an ontology which is essentially realist in orientation' (pp. 198–200), a reading which allows Burrell and Morgan to place the AFR unambiguously in an 'objectivist' paradigm, and thereby to reaffirm their faith in the mutual exclusivity of the four paradigms.

Burrell and Morgan's denial of the sense of critical reflection upon the assumption of paradigmatic closure blinds them to the possibility of exploring any further what they characterize as equivocality and confusion in Silverman's position (p. 199). All approaches have to fall decisively on one side or the other of the 'subjective'–'objective' divide. Elements in the AFR that might otherwise expose limitations of the 2 x 2 matrix are swept aside by arbitrarily privileging the contents of proposition 3 over those that follow. Accordingly, 'the overall position' of the AFR is characterized as follows:

> . . .whilst recognising that there is an external world which is ontologically prior to man, its crucial significance as far as the study of social affairs is concerned lies in the way in which its 'meaning' resulted from the interpretations placed on it by individual actors.
>
> (Burrell and Morgan 1979: 199)

This interpretation of the AFR reflects the assumption that forms of analysis that assume the existence of a 'real', external world that pre-exists actors' reproduction (or transformation) of it are essentially 'objectivist'. The recognition in proposition 3 that in order to make sense of their experience, actors draw upon 'shared orientations', experienced by them as 'social facts', is interpreted by Burrell and Morgan as an expression of 'objectivism'. Conveniently overlooked is the AFR's equal, and arguably greater, emphasis upon the idea that the reality of these 'shared orientations' and 'social facts' is entirely sustained through a continuous process of social construction. That this insight into the dialectics of social existence is then applied in a mechanistic manner is not in question. The point is that Burrell and Morgan's faith in the mutual exclusivity of paradigms leads them to deny the very possibility of developing a social theory wherein this dialectical process may be more adequately conveyed. It is precisely this project to which Giddens' theory of structuration is dedicated.

Giddens

In seeking to develop a theory in which the 'subjective' and 'objective' of social reality are integrated, Giddens (1976, 1979, 1984) has stressed the central role of agency in the reproduction of social institutions.[7] In this respect at least, Gidden's theory of structuration can be directly compared and contrasted with that of Berger and Luckmann.[8] The most significant difference, perhaps, is that Giddens' framework is designed to reveal how 'agency' and 'structure' are simultaneously present in the accomplishment of social practices. Or, as he puts it, 'the constitution of agents and structures are not two independently given sets of phenomena, a dualism, but represent a duality' (Giddens 1984: 25). Echoing Burrell and Morgan's distinction between 'subjectivist' and 'objectivist' approaches to social science before urging the possibility of transcending their mutually reinforcing imperialism, Giddens observes:

> What is at issue is how the concepts of action, meaning and subjectivity should be specified and how they might relate to notions of structure and constraint. If interpretive sociologies are founded, as it were, upon an imperialism of the subject, functionalism and structuralism propose an imperialism of the social object. One of my principal ambitions in the formulation of structuration theory is to put an end to each of these empire-building endeavours. The basic domain of study of the social sciences, according to the theory of structuration, is neither the experiment of the individual actor, not the existence of any form of societal totality, but social practices ordered across space and time.
>
> (Giddens 1984: 2)

In the theory of structuration, attention is focused upon the way in which actors accomplish their practices by drawing upon a knowledge of rules (e.g. procedures and techniques) and a command of resources (e.g. valued material and symbolic goods), and thereby to reconstitute the considerations that provide for the very possibility of such accomplishments. In this formulation, 'structure' or 'objective facticity' does not exist independently of the actor. Rather, what other analysts routinely conceptualize as a determining constraint upon human action is theorized as sets of rules and resources drawn upon by actors in the reproduction and transformation of social worlds. These rules and resources enable as well as constrain their practices and, in doing so, 'bind' time–space into routines, institutions and social systems.

> The knowledge of social conventions, of oneself and other human beings, presumed in being able to 'go on' in the diversity of contexts of social life is detailed and dazzling. . . . Structure has no existence independent of the knowledge that agents have about what they do in their day-to-day activity.
>
> (Giddens 1984: 26)

In this light, the reproduction of practices in the form of routines, etc., depends upon actors continuing to mobilize the particular sets of rules and resources that are supportive of such practices – a capacity which is itself dependent upon their positioning within routines, institutions and social systems. It is in this sense that the rules and resources are at once 'a medium and outcome of the practices they recursively organise' (p.25).

In order to analyse the process of social reproduction, Giddens argues, it is necessary to adopt two complementary standpoints, each of which is separated out by means of a methodological epoch. On the one hand, it is possible to examine how actors mobilize these properties as they accomplish and reproduce their social practices. In which case the analytical focus is upon actors' use of rules and resources to 'bring off' the interaction in which they are engaged. On the other hand, when an epoch is placed upon strategic conduct, these rules and resources may be studied as institutional features of systems of social interaction. The analytical focus is then upon the location of particular rules and resources within the totality of social relations (Giddens 1979: 80; 1984: 28–30). Thus, whereas Berger and Luckmann tend to theorize 'action'/subjectivity and 'structure'/objectivity as two separable moments in the construction of social reality, Giddens presents them as a medium and outcome of each other. In doing so, he stresses that his twin foci of analysis are based upon a self-conscious methodological bracketing. That is to say, they do not refer to separate moments in the reproduction of reality, or even to substantively different aspects of reality. Or, as he puts it, 'they are not two sides of dualism, they express a duality, the duality of structure' (Giddens 1979: 80).

A number of organization analysts have been attracted by Giddens' theory of structuration (e.g. Riley 1983; Smith 1983; Pettigrew 1985). Like Giddens, they have been concerned to move away from approaches based upon a dualism between action and structure. For example, drawing a contrast between a 'structural perspective' which specifies abstract dimensions and abstract constraints and an 'interactionist perspective' which attends to symbolic mediation and negotiated processes, Ranson *et al.* (1980: 1) seek to apply the work of Giddens to argue that 'these procedures and perspectives which, until now, have tended to be regarded as incompatible, must be incorporated in a more unified methodological and theoretical framework'. However, in doing so, they have tended to interpret the theory of structuration from within a position that supports the very dualism of 'structure' and 'action' that Giddens seeks to transcend (Willmott 1981; 1987).

To summarize, in marked contrast to Berger and Luckmann, Giddens' concern has been to go beyond the mechanistic combination of 'subjective' and 'objective' perspectives to develop a radically different approach in which dualistic formulations of the relationship between structure and action are superceded. Space has not permitted an evaluation of its success in achieving its objective, though assessments are available elsewhere (Knights and Willmott 1985; Willmott 1986). Instead, it has been argued that Giddens' theory of structuration is sufficiently robust to cast doubt upon Burrell and Morgan's faith in paradigmatic closure and outlines a means of progressing beyond it. Not only does it assert the need to comprehend both 'subjective' and 'objective' aspects of reality but it advances an understanding in which traditional, dualistic approaches to the study of social life are, in part, transcended.

Freire

Freire's *Pedagogy of the Oppressed* (1972) provides a third example of an approach that eschews the dualism of subject and object. Where it differs from the formulation of Berger and Luckmann and Giddens is in its attention to dualism in practice. Freire writes:

> One cannot conceive of objectivity without subjectivity. Neither can exist without the other, nor can they be dichotomised. The separation of objectivity from subjectivity, the denial of the latter when analysing reality or acting on it, is objectivism. On the other hand, the denial of objectivity in analysis or action. . .denies action itself by denying objective reality.
>
> (Freire 1972: 27)

Freire shares with Berger and Luckmann and Giddens the view that 'one cannot conceive of objectivity without subjectivity' (p. 27). However, in contrast to the analyses of Berger and Luckmann and Giddens, which are overtly motivated by a concern to displace inadequate or confused understandings of the social world, Freire's critique of dualistic conceptions of social life is grounded in a prior, *practical* concern to replace injustice, exploitation and oppression with freedom and justice (p. 20). His concern to overcome the dualism between subjectivity and objectivity encompasses a commitment to acting upon reality as well as providing analytical accounts of it.

In Freire's assessment, the distinguishing feature of the reality of oppression is the division of subjectivity from objectivity within social relations that are structured by a division between oppressors and oppressed. On the one hand, the subjectivity of the oppressed is unnecessarily confined by their restricted access to valued material and symbolic goods. As Freire (p. 24) observes, their experience has led many of them to adapt and become resigned to 'the structure of domination in which they are immersed', and to be unwilling to run the risks associated with a struggle for freedom.

On the other hand, the oppressors, who occupy a comparatively privileged position within the social structure, are inclined to view themselves as the benefactors of what is enjoyed by the oppressed, an interpretation which ensnares their own subjectivity within the confines of the exploitative relations that they are so anxious to protect and maintain. The disadvantaged position of the oppressed is justified by interpreting it individualistically, as a product of the latter's failings (incompetence, laziness, etc.). In so far as the oppressors may be prepared to provide minimal protection for the weak, they are inclined to engage in a paternalistic charade of false generosity, whose principal effect is to secure their privileged position through its reinforcement of relations of dependence.

> The oppressors do not perceive their monopoly of *having more* as a privilege which dehumanises others and themselves. They cannot see that, in the egotistic pursuit of *having* as a possessing class, they suffocate in their own possessions. . . .If others do not have more, it is because they are incompetent and lazy, and worst of all is their unjustifiable ingratitude towards the 'generous gestures' of the dominant class. Precisely because they are 'ungrateful' and 'envious', the oppressed are regarded as potential enemies who must be watched.
>
> (Freire 1972: 35)

Central to Freire's thesis is the understanding that the dualism between subjectivity and objectivity is a problem in, and of, theory. Defined in terms of the separation of subjectivity and objectivity, this problem is expressed in the existence of an oppressive reality comprising oppressors and oppressed. The contradiction of oppression, wherein the dependence of the oppressors upon the oppressed provides for the possibility of emancipation from this relationship, is established in concrete situations. In other words, liberation involves a practical fusion of subjectivity and objectivity. Because oppression is a concrete, practical problem of social relations, it is one which can be resolved only by engaging in emancipatory forms of action (praxis) (cf. Jackson and Willmott 1987). The nature of this problem is such that it can be verified only through its solution in practice. Critical analysis of the sources of oppression is a necessary condition for the reconciliation of subjectivity and objectivity. But without the application of theory through the transformation of subjectivity, it degenerates into mere verbalism.

Since the oppressed are least insulated from the violent and degrading effects of oppressive social relations, it is the oppressed who Freire identifies as the principal agents of liberation. But, at the same time, he examines how this mission is continuously undermined and deflected by the domesticating effects of oppression. The very constitution of their subjectivity within relations of oppression tends to deny them the possibility of assertiveness, of confidence in their right to challenge their oppressors – it is not their place, they have no right. To become an oppressor or a 'sub-oppressor' appears to offer the only realistic possibility of escape from oppression. Any alternative, which involves a struggle to emancipate their subjectivity of oppression, arouses a fear of freedom – a fear generated by the demands of autonomous and collective action. Moreover, the realization of oppression compounds its oppressiveness. It is this which stimulates resistance. But it can also inhibit the praxis of emancipation.

> When they discover within themselves the yearning to be free, they perceive that this yearning can be transformed into reality only when the same yearning is aroused in their comrades. But while dominated by the fear of freedom they refuse to appeal to, or listen to, the appeals of, others, or even to the appeals of their own conscience. They prefer gregariousness to authentic comradeship; they prefer the security of conformity with their state of unfreedom to the creative communion produced by freedom and even the very pursuit of freedom.
>
> (Freire 1972: 24)

Not that the unnecessary limiting of subjectivity is restricted to the oppressed. Some of the oppressors, too, may recognize the presence of oppression and actively work to transform an unjust order. However, in so far as their criticisms of oppression are based upon pity for the oppressed and guilt about their own privileges, there is a tendency to act as 'proprietors of revolutionary wisdom' (p. 37) who dispense prescriptions for change that marginalize the participation of the oppressed in the processes of transformation. This problem is compounded when the latter's identification with bourgeois or reactionary values and ideas is interpreted as a sign of their innate ignorance, stupidity or gullibility rather than as a manifestation of the constitution of their subjectivity within an oppressive reality.

In the sum, the most important contribution of *Pedagogy of the Oppressed* is its exploration of how relations of oppression tend to constitute the subjectivity of both oppressors and oppressed in ways that lead them to impede or pervert emancipatory action. Instead of direct engagement in transforming the objective experience of oppression, subjectivist responses substitute analysis of paternalism for action that might result in a real change in the situation. Similarly, objectivist responses sustain the status quo by assuming that emancipatory action must wait upon changes in the objective situation. However, support for Freire's concern for the practical reconciliation of dualism does not require an uncritical acceptance of his theorizing of subjectivity and social relations. Specifically, it is necessary to reject both the reductionism in his theory of oppression and the essentialism in his theory of emancipation.

The major flaw in Freire's theory of oppression concerns his reduction of the complex, systematic *practices* of oppression to the identification of a *class* of oppressors that is juxtaposed with a *class* that is oppressed. Indeed, as Freire himself argues, the *experiential* reality of oppression involves a division of subjectivity and objectivity, a division that is not the exclusive preserve of any one class. This flaw in Freire's analysis is directly related to his essentialist conception of human nature. Freire assumes autonomy and responsibility to be the most fundamental characteristics of human nature. Driven by this condition, the process of humanization is perceived to be 'man's vocation'. Or, as he puts it, oppression involves:

> a distortion of the vocation of becoming more fully human. . . . Because it is a distortion of being more fully human, sooner or later being less human leads the oppressed to struggle against those who made them so.
>
> (Freire 1972: 20–1, emphasis omitted)

This theory of emancipation assumes an essential quality in human nature that leads us to struggle against the reality of oppression. Founded upon a blind faith in the innate goodness of human beings, this superficially attractive and reassuring assumption is no more or less plausible and defensible than the opposing view that man is irrecoverably flawed or fallen. Its shortcomings are compounded when, instead of being theorized as a pervasive, institutionalized endowment of social relations, the experience of being oppressed is attributed to the members of *one* class. Not only does this interpretation neglect the interpenetrating oppressions of 'gender', 'ethnicity', 'age', and so forth, it also fails to theorize the ways in which, at different moments, most of us are both victims and perpetrators of oppressive social relations.

Discussion

Assessments of where, and how far, efforts to move beyond paradigmatic closure take us inevitably reflect the position from which these movements are surveyed. If paradigmatic closure is assumed, then they will be dismissed as wish-fulfilling figments of a deluded imagination. From positions that accommodate the possibility of moving beyond the dualism of paradigmatic closure, a variety of assessments may be made. If Giddens' theory of structuration is adopted, Berger and Luckmann's framework appears both mechanistic and politically conservative. Mechanistic because it fails to theorize structure (objective reality), conservative because it does not centralize relations of power and domination in its account of the social construction of reality.

If, on the other hand, Freire's formulation is favoured, Giddens' theory is criticized for its failure to go beyond a form of intellectual life in which 'critical analysis' is equated with the development of theoretical frameworks that offer a more sophisticated, intellectually satisfying account of social reproduction but make rather marginal contribution to our ability to understand and accomplish a practical, embodied reconciliation of the dualism between subject and object. For, in contrast to the writings of Giddens, and Berger and Luckmann, which are more likely to alter how we interpret our world without prompting a struggle to change our relations with others, *Pedagogy of the Oppressed* has a greater capacity to penetrate our lived experience and, thus, to have a deeper impact on the way in which we lead our lives.[9] This position is exemplified in the observation that:

> The oppressor shows solidarity with the oppressed only when he stops regarding the oppressed as an abstract category. . .when he stops making pious, sentimental, and individualistic gestures and risks acts of love, in its existentiality, in its praxis. It is a farce to affirm that men are people and thus should be free, yet to do nothing tangible to make this affirmation a reality.
>
> (Freire 1972: 26)

However, in criticism of Freire, it has been argued that emancipation does not wait upon the essential humanity of subjects to surface from an oppressive reality. Nor, it has been suggested, is it plausible to assume that the humanity of 'the oppressed' is invariably more distorted than that of 'the oppressors', and therefore that the oppressed are necessarily the more promising agents of emancipatory change. Instead, critical analysis must take very seriously Freire's observation that 'the oppressed' are submerged in the reality of oppression so that, despite their immediate experience of greater relative deprivation, they are constituted within practices that render them more resistant to the transformation of their subjectivity than those who are less disadvantaged.

Conclusion

This chapter has critiqued the assumption of paradigmatic closure underpinning Burrell and Morgan's *Sociological Paradigms and Organizational Analysis*. It has reviewed the development of different theoretical approaches to the analysis of organizations and their alleged locations within mutually exclusive paradigms. Through an exploration of the work of Berger and Luckmann, Giddens, and Freire, it was suggested that moves to overcome the dualism of 'subjectivist' and 'objectivist' analysis of social life are both possible and desirable. Possible because there are approaches to social analysis that deny this dualism. And desirable because a theoretical appreciation of the interpenetration of 'subjective' and 'objective' dimensions of social reality is a condition of their practical reconciliation.

However, in addition to exposing the incoherence of analysis that conceives of objectivity without subjectivity (or vice-versa), this chapter has argued for the importance of connecting dualisms in theory to dualism in practice. If critical analyses of organization are to address practical expressions of dualism then its development must be guided by its capacity to expose the experience of oppression and the possibilities of liberation. To this end, it is necessary to move away from a theory in which oppression is formulated as an objective reality comprising those who are oppressors and those who are oppressed. For, instead of promoting reflection upon the possibilities within our 'own' practices for reducing socially unnecessary suffering, this dualistic understanding of oppression tends to be restricted to identifying an external 'oppressor' and engaging in the struggle to change 'their' practices.

A rational critique of oppressive theories (of organizations) and practices (in organizations) can only proceed on the basis of a rejection of the assumption of paradigmatic closure. This cannot be based upon an appeal to an essence of man that is being denied. Nor can it be the identification of an oppressive class, since this obscures the extent to which everyone is engaged in the reproduction of oppressive social practices. Instead, by focusing upon organizational practices which reflect and sustain the contradictory separation of subjectivity and objectivity, the task of critical organizational analysis is to penetrate its practical production in order to reveal how this dualism simultaneously promotes and impedes the possibilities for emancipatory change.

Part two

Analysis

Chapter four

The labour process perspective on management organization: a critique and reformulation

Michael Reed

Introduction

The publication of Harry Braverman's *Labour and Monopoly Capital* in 1974 seemed to herald a 'paradigm shift' in the sociology of work organizations. This was so to the extent that the book set a new agenda for the latter, and provided radically different theoretical tools through which the agenda could be pursued to that found within 'traditional' industrial sociology (Thompson 1983). In particular, Braverman's analysis called for renewed efforts to explicate the intimate relationship between managerial control of social relations at the point of production and the broader structures of class power and domination in which it was located. For Braverman, the causal connection between the imperative of capitalist accumulation and the structure of managerial control in the workplace was axiomatic for the analysis of historical developments in organizational forms.

However, the research tradition spawned by this pioneering work almost immediately began to display all the qualities of 'chronic disputation' normally associated with schools of social scientific analysis. Disputes over matters of historical interpretation and appropriate theoretical equipment were soon overtaken by intense disagreement over the philosophical foundations on which the labour process approach was constructed and the strategy of political intervention – if any were advocated – which they legitimated. More recently, considerable scepticism had been expressed over the capacity of the labour process perspective to provide an analysis of work relations and behaviour which is sufficiently sensitive to the historical and empirical complexities of actual organizational practice (Wood 1985; Edwards 1986; Salaman 1986a; Hyman 1987). A distinct theoretical predilection for structural determinism has been superceded by a voluntaristic stress on 'strategic choice' in forms of organizational control (Reed 1985).

Yet, this has produced a situation in which the intellectual certainties of an earlier period have given way to self-doubt and re-evaluation.

The purpose of this chapter is to provide an assessment of the contribution which labour process theory had made to the development of a systematic sociological understanding of management organization in the 'advanced societies' (Giddens 1973). This assessment will provide the basis for a set of recommendations concerning the way in which labour process theory needs to be reformulated in order to make a more substantial contribution to the achievement of the latter task than has been the case to date.

The first section of the chapter will provide a critical review and evaluation of the underlying conceptions of management organization which have informed labour process analysis, beginning with the seminal contribution of Braverman (1974). It will identify a growing disenchantment with the more deterministic and mechanistic conceptions of management that underlay earlier contributions to the labour process debate and the gradual emergence of a perspective on management which is much more voluntaristic and pluralistic in its approach (e.g. Salaman 1982). However, it will also maintain that movement in this direction has been limited, to the extent that a continuing analytical commitment to a rational and formal conception of management can be identified.

The second section will maintain that these analytical developments have not dealt adequately with the central 'problematic' which lies at the core of the labour process debate over management organization; that is, the complex interaction between 'operational control' over the production process and 'allocative control' over strategic corporate decision-making (Pahl and Winkler 1974) within the structural constraints embedded in a continuous process of capital accumulation (Storey 1985).

It will also be argued that the only way of correcting this theoretical lacuna is to develop an analytical framework which can cope with the breaks and contradictions which necessarily occur between the forms of organizational control implemented by management within the production process and the broader structures of corporate control in which they are located (Salaman 1982; Tomlinson 1982; Burawoy 1985; Child 1985; Fox 1985). As Salaman contends, we need to:

> Move beyond the abstract statement of the differentiated functions and requirements of capital, to a consideration of how these are actually achieved, in the context of concrete mechanisms mediating between economy and work designs. And such a consideration must bring to light the complexity, and contradictoriness, of a process which occurs constantly within the

> context of changing frontiers of control between classes, and fractions of classes.
>
> (Salaman 1982: 62)

The third section outlines an analytical framework through which this task may be realized. Salaman's analysis suggests two areas of theoretical concern which should provide the foundations for this framework: first, the 'concrete mechanisms mediating between economy and work designs'; second, 'the complexity, and contradictoriness, of a process which occurs constantly within the context of changing frontiers of control between classes'. Both of these themes – mediating mechanisms and contradictions generated by the struggle for control – can be pursued within a conceptual framework which focuses on management organization as a loosely coupled network of social practices geared to the assembly and regulation of those basic activities necessary for the production of goods and the provision of services. In this way, management organization is conceptualized as a process and a related set of institutional mechanisms geared to the continual recoupling and regulation of diverse productive practices inherently prone to disengagement and fragmentation. This approach facilitates an analysis of the manner in which these integrative and regulative mechanisms are subjected to review and transformation as a result of the struggle to control them engaged in by various groups and classes located in a dynamic socio-economic context always likely to subvert established patterns and routines (Reed 1985).

A brief concluding section reviews the arguments developed in the chapter and considers their broader implications for the sociology of management as one substantive contribution towards a sociology of human agency (Dawe 1979).

Managing the labour process

A growing disenchantment with the intellectual capital that the labour process tradition has inherited from Braverman has been evident in recent years. This relates to both the underlying methodological position which Braverman adopts and its implications for the treatment that he gives to various substantive themes such as developments in job design, managerial control strategies, forms of worker resistance, gender relations at work, and their impact on class struggle within the production process (Giddens 1982; Littler 1982; Salaman 1982; Thompson 1983; Burawoy 1985; Storey 1985; Wood 1986). Thus Giddens argues that the 'objectivist' methodology which Braverman advocates produces a form of analysis that:

> drastically underestimates the knowledgeability and capability of workers faced with a range of management imperatives. Braverman is mistaken to say that his work is unconcerned with 'subjective will': the 'subjective will' of *management*, as expressed in Taylorist strategies of control, is more than adequately represented in the book. What is lacking is an adequate discussion of the reactions of the workers, as themselves knowledgeable and capable agents, to the technical division of labour and Taylorism.
>
> (Giddens 1982: 40)

Giddens' warning about the deterministic predilections evident in Braverman's analysis, and the severe limitations which they impose on the study of industrial conflict as a social process, finds clear echoes in the contributions of other commentators (Zimbalist 1979; Salaman 1986 b). However, his qualified support for the conceptualization of management control strategies offered by Braverman has not been reflected to anything like the same extent in the work of labour process theorists attempting to provide a better understanding of the historical development of different forms of management organization and their impact on the dynamics of class struggle.

Indeed, mounting dissatisfaction with Braverman's analysis of management has resulted in a number of theoretical reformulations and empirical case studies that have considerably enriched our understanding of the complex processes whereby managers attempt to exert effective control over productive activity and their consequences for the crystallization of class relations through industrial conflict (Mackenzie 1982; Littler 1982; Salaman 1982; Knights *et al.* 1985).

Two recent contributions to this continuing process of critique and reformulation are to be found in Storey (1983, 1984, 1985) and Burawoy (1985). Their work will be discussed in some depth as a prelude to a more detailed consideration of the problems which still remain in developing a more subtle understanding of the management practices through which control strategies are generated.

Storey offers three major criticisms of post-Braverman labour process analysis of management control strategies and structures as discovered in the work of Freidman (1977), Edwards (1979), Clawson (1982), and Gordon *et al.* (1982). First, that the functionalist analytical framework in which these studies have been conducted leads to a serious underestimation of the diversity and complexity of managerial control processes. Second, that the former also encourages neglect of the inherent contradictions of different managerial control strategies and structures which 'undermine any ultimate or absolute logic in the means of control' (Storey 1985: 197). Third, that these analytical and methodological inadequacies culminate in the failure to develop a 'dialectical' analysis of managerial control strategies and structures which is equipped to deal with the coexistence of a variety of means of control within work organizations and resist the monistic tendencies of orthodox labour process accounts of developments in control systems (see also Edwards 1986).

Burawoy criticizes Braverman for attempting to develop an understanding of management control strategies without due attention to the 'subjective' components of work and the economic determinism which tends to flow from this neglect (Burawoy 1985: 21–84). As a result:

> he makes all sorts of assumptions about the interests of capitalists and managers, about their consciousness, and their capacity to impose their interests on subordinate classes. . . .Braverman's restricted attention to the 'objective elements' of work does not allow us to understand the nature of control – for, by definition, control involves what Braverman would refer to as 'subjective' aspects of work and what I will refer to as political and ideological processes.
>
> (Burawoy 1985: 25–35)

In an attempt to fill this conceptual gap, Burawoy develops the notion of 'factory regime' as a way of integrating a concern with the control implications of different forms of work organization within the labour process, and the distinctive political and ideological apparatuses through which surplus value is secured and obscured. With this concept of factory regime, he reworks the idea of 'work games' which co-ordinate the interests of workers and managers, and legitimate the conditions under which they are played and the substantive outcomes that they generate (Burawoy 1985: 38–40). Both of these concepts (factory regimes and work games) are subsequently deployed to explain the historical development of different forms of management control systems in advanced capitalist and socialist states, and in developing countries. This analysis highlights the crucial role of the state in creating and maintaining the material and ideational preconditions for the political and ideological structures of domination through which economic power is exercised in particular work organizations. In this context, management provides that crucial mediating mechanism through which the strategic interests of the dominant class groupings located within the state system are translated into practical control objectives within the labour process. Both Storey and Burawoy are clearly aware of the danger of the 'panacea fallacy' highlighted by Littler and Salaman, and the 'search for the Holy Grail' of the 'magic strategy that successfully stabilized capital/labour relations' which tends to go with it (Littler and Salaman 1984: 264). Yet the theoretical alternatives which they offer seem to fall back into the very conceptual and methodological confinements from which they wished to escape.

Littler and Salaman warn that descriptive classifications and evolutionary schemes of management control strategies constructed and applied by labour process theorists such as Friedman (1977) and Edwards (1979) tend to:

> fail to grasp the variety of aspects of organizational control; that they focus on the 'formal' and official, and ignore the informal aspects of control; and that they compare forms of control which are incomplete and therefore incomparable.
>
> (Littler and Salaman 1984: 264)

These failures are compounded by an even more serious failure to appreciate the significance of the fact that 'conflicting principles of labour management may be woven into the structure of the firm' (Jones 1978: 13) and to ignore 'the obvious fact that all control strategies are developing strategies which involve combinations of management practices and which may involve perpetual contradictions' (Littler and Salaman 1984: 264).

If Storey and Burawoy had taken these admonitions and their implications seriously, then they would have been forced to reject the functionalist and determinist residues present within their own theoretical reformulations. Storey's dialectical approach calls for a more 'emphatic focus' to be accorded to the practical activity of managers in the development of various control strategies and structures within the labour process of capitalist systems. Yet this does not allow him to support a voluntaristic model of managerial action; neither does it prevent him from advocating a conception of a global model of competitive production which exercises hegemonic domination over the contingent managerial control strategies through which work is organized (Storey 1985: 197). Burawoy quickly retreats into a functionalist analysis of the role of the state in activating various institutional mechanisms which stabilize the material and ideological preconditions necessary for the exercise of managerial control over the labour process (Burawoy 1985: 62). Thus he maintains that British workers, 'the acme of shopfloor control, find themselves helpless before job loss through rationalization, technological change, and, particularly, the intensification of work' (Burawoy 1985: 150 – compare this, for instance, with the level of active resistance found in Batstone 1984 or, more appropriately in this context, Thompson and Bannon 1985).

In this way, both Storey and Burawoy are unable to detach

themselves completely from a logic of analysis which assumes that the interlocking structural components of the wider 'social totality' in which work organizations are located attain explanatory primacy over the long-term. Consequently, the starting point for their analyses is the structural requirements of class domination within a capitalist mode of production and the variety of managerial control systems which are implemented within the labour process in response to these requirements. While this retreat into functionalist logic is much more strongly expressed in Burawoy (and even the latter admits to the 'precariousness' of capitalist domination as a theoretical possibility but not, it is relevant to note, as an integral social condition and structural characteristic), Storey's critique of the deterministic streak in labour process thinking and the rationalistic explanations of managerial conduct that flow from it would seem to require a deeper attachment to voluntarism than he is prepared to accept.

Indeed, the failure to overcome the agency/structure analytical duality within labour process thinking, and the tendency to fall back on a functionalist explanatory logic of one form or another (or at one level of analysis or another – such as the 'social totality'), would seem to indicate that Littler's plea that the 'relative autonomy' of employers' control strategies be taken as a starting point for analysis (Littler 1982: 34) has fallen on deaf ears. This would seem to be even more the case in relation to his argument that the link between the process of capital accumulation and historical transformations of the labour process needs to be re-thought in terms of an indirect and variable relationship mediated through human action rather than as a functional relationship determined through structural necessity (Littler 1982: 34).

The implications of this argument for the manner in which the interaction between 'allocative' management and 'operational' management is dealt with is reviewed in the next section.

Allocative controllers and operational managers

The relationship between corporate management and operational management has become a central theme for those working within a labour process framework. As Willmott (1984) has argued, the need to reveal the manner in which routine organizational arrangements reflect and advance the interests of a dominant ruling class or economic elite lies at the core of labour process analysis to the extent that managers are regarded as the principal 'bearers' of the inner logic which is at work within capitalism:

> when examined from this perspective, the question of whether individual managers act with the intention of securing or advancing

> the interests of capital, or accept this account of their work, is irrelevant. . . managerial work is seen to be primarily governed by the structure of relations of production that it 'bears'. . . . As agents of capital, managers are seen to develop and/or implement strategies and structures that ensure productive subordination of labour to the demands of capital. Fundamentally, managerial work is thus understood to involve creating and maintaining a structure of relationships in which those who are 'in control' act in the interests of capital.
>
> (Willmott 1984: 362)

If this characterization is accepted, then the process whereby strategic controllers transmit the control imperatives required to attain a commercially acceptable surplus to lower-level administrative management is clearly central to an understanding of the structural transformations which the labour process may undergo as a result of those imperatives being altered in any way.

Recently, Scott has provided an elegant analysis of this relationship through a highly sophisticated synthesis of the 'business policy' and 'labour process' traditions which draws heavily on a neo-Marxist interpretation of long-term capitalist economic development (Scott 1985). Within this framework, Scott argues that corporate strategy is the outcome of a struggle for control, sometimes latent, between members of the dominant coalition within the corporation boardroom whose actions 'are shaped by the network of intercorporate relations in which the enterprise is embedded and, beyond this, by the actions of the state and other political agencies' (Scott 1985: 180). The control strategies and structures implemented and administered by lower level managers are tightly conditioned by the longer term imperatives imposed by senior managers and directors as constituent members of the structures of intercorporate networks which dominate capitalist economies (Scott 1985: 193).

However, this model of a hierarchical control system in which multiple levels of management are closely conditioned by a centrally-determined and co-ordinated strategy of accumulation has not a great deal of support from the analyses which have been carried out on the relationship – or lack of it – between corporate management and labour management (Winkler 1975; Gospel 1983a and 1983b; Purcell and Sissons 1983; Thurley and Wood 1983; Pettigrew 1985; and Rose and Jones 1985). Indeed, these studies suggest that a striving for 'logical incrementalism' in the design and implementation of corporate strategy (Storey 1985) is the very most which one can hope for; the process whereby the broad guidelines produced by the latter are translated into relevant and workable labour control strategies and practices to be implemented and administered by managers at lower levels of the organizational hierarchy remains something of a mystery, although the broad outlines of an explanation are beginning to emerge. Purcell has expressed the nagging doubts, not to say downright scepticism, over the empirical veracity and theoretical adequacy of the formalistic and rationalistic model with some force:

> Constant reference is made to managerial strategy in the labour process debate but it is difficult to find a clear exposition of how ideas come to be transmitted, interpreted and acted upon, or more specifically on the trade union role in opposing or encouraging the use of these managerial techniques. As these techniques are important in structuring the wage-work bargain and are designed to control or channel individual and collective worker behaviour, the need is to study what could be best described as the sociology of management knowledge.
>
> (Purcell 1983: 9–10)

It seems unlikely that we will be able to achieve this objective if we accept many of the central assumptions of the labour process perspective concerning managerial control strategies and systems within work organizations, and their relationship to higher levels of management decision-making and corporate structure. As Rose and Jones suggest, the underlying problem with the labour process approach to management is that 'the various forms of levels of control are not explained on their own terms. Instead, various features of British enterprise organization, work group autonomy and bargaining relationships are mistaken for subsidiary elements of the overriding strategy of control' (Jones and Rose 1985: 90). This approach, they continue, leads to a reductionist account of the complex link between corporate and operational management in two respects: first, it ignores the problematical character of the vertical integration between different levels of managerial activity; second, it seriously underestimates the 'muddying effect' of the simultaneous intervention of a broad range of horizontal functional management specialisms 'that may seriously handicap the feasibility of any 'strategic' pursuit of co-ordinating control objectives through the various departments and dimensions of management activity which might be concerned' (Rose and Jones 1985: 90–1).

These points have been borne out by recent research on changes to labour management's strategy in Britain which occurred during the 1970s. Such research suggests a somewhat hesitant and fragile move away from the strategy of indirect or delegated control (relying on lower-level line management and/or employers associations) highlighted by Gospel (1983a and b) towards a more direct engagement with labour representatives through corporate level bargaining structures and centralized personnel management functions. This is best interpreted as an unplanned consequence of piecemeal reform rather than the outcome of deliberate long-term planning (Brown 1981; Daniel and Millward 1983; Batstone 1984).

Thus the analysis of the complex interaction between 'allocative control' processes and 'operational control' processes, as Pahl and Winkler (1974) have labelled them, would seem to call for a much less deterministic and rationalistic theoretical framework than most labour process researchers seem prepared to provide. While the reality of unavoidable contradictions and breaks within and between different forms and levels of control is obviously recognized, the theoretical framework retained by labour process writers is based on a logic of explanation that minimizes both the significance of these complexities and their implications for the kind of conceptual equipment which we need in order to construct more sensitive accounts of managers' efforts to organize and control productive activity.

The concept of 'logical incrementalism' (Quinn 1980) would seem to resonate more closely with the form of analysis provided by Pahl and Winkler to the extent that they both rest on an 'action definition' of the social processes through which control is attempted and the unintended consequences that they inevitably set in motion. Pahl and Winkler indicate that the conceptual distinction between 'allocative' and 'operational' control can be identified in two interrelated ways. First, to differentiate first order decisions concerning the implementation of the former; second, to distinguish between control over the distribution of economic resources (particularly labour power) within work organizations (Pahl and Winkler 1974: 239 and 114). The also maintain that:

> there will be overlap between the two forms, in the sense that some individuals will have both. There will be a reciprocal relationship between them, in the sense that a man starting with one form may acquire the other. There will be gradations in both forms of control, in the sense that for any company or group they may be divided among several people who will have more or less control. . . . In sum, the locus of control governing the allocation of capital for a given economic organization may lie inside or outside the organization or shared between internal and external controllers.
>
> (Pahl and Winkler 1974: 114–15)

This focus on the protean quality of managerial control processes within and between work organizations neatly dovetails with Pettigrew's development of the concept of logical incrementalism in his study on strategic change in ICI (Pettigrew 1985). Logical incrementalism, Pettigrew argues, interprets strategic change as a cautious, step-by-step evolutionary process in which there is a continuous effort in constructing and maintaining a workable political consensus within management, although this may be punctuated by relatively brief and dramatic spurts of political activity during which there may be total upheaval in accepted ideas, perceptions and ideologies (Pettigrew 1985: 442). It is crucial, Pettigrew contends, to reject single-factor theories of organizational change. Indeed, he cautions against such approaches in the strongest terms:

> Beware of the singular theory of process, or indeed of social and organizational change. Look for continuity and change, patterns and idiosyncracies, the actions of individuals and groups at various organizational levels, and processes of structuring. Give history and social processes the chance to reveal their untidiness. To understand strategic change, examine the juxtaposition of the rational/analytical and the political, the quest for efficiency, growth, power and business survival, the role of exceptional men and of extreme circumstances, the vicariousness of chance, the enabling and constraining forces of the environment, the way organizational culture shapes people's interpretations of environmental forces, and explore some of the conditions in which mixtures of these occur.
>
> (Pettigrew 1985: 444)

If we are to explore the conditions under which these 'mixtures' occur and to reveal the 'untidiness' of the social process through which managerial control strategies and structures (at whatever level or whatever form they emerge) are transformed (Hickson *et al.* 1985), then many of the key assumptions which have informed labour process analysis are in need of substantial revision. This is so in a number of respects. First, in relation to an excessive reliance on a rational model of managerial behaviour and the over concentration on formal strategies and structures of labour management control which this encourages (Littler 1982: 40). Second, the tendency to assume a relatively tight functional fit between different decision-making levels secured through processes or mechanisms that are not clearly specified or explained (Pettigrew 1985: 33). Third, a penchant for a restrained structural determinism in which the breaks and contradictions which inevitably occur between the 'malleable constrained domination' (Hickson *et al.* 1985) enjoyed by allocative controllers, and the 'organized anarchy' experienced by operational managers, tend to be subsumed within a development logic that eventually asserts itself against the temporary diversions resulting from human recalcitrance.

The following section attempts to outline an alternative conception of management which is more sensitive to these problems.

Management as a social practice

As we have already seen, labour process analysis focuses on managerial control strategies and structures which both enable and constrain the formulation and implementation of certain labour management practices rather than others. The conceptual framework outlined in this section refocuses attention on the managerial *practices* through which control strategies and structures are generated and takes seriously Littler and Salaman's earlier reminder of 'the obvious fact that all control strategies are developing strategies which involve combinations of management practices and which may involve perpetual contradictions' (Littler and Salaman 1984: 264). While some commentators may be fearful that this approach will degenerate into a facile pragmatism 'in which each management and workplace is analysed separately as if there were no common features and external pressures' (Thompson and Bannon 1985: 3), it will be argued that a conception of management as a social practice can provide the analytical means necessary to cope with the complexity of those general processes through which managers attempt to exert control over social relations within work organizations.

The preceding discussion of labour process analysis of managerial control strategies and structures indicates the need for a reconsideration of the conceptual equipment through which we approach the theoretical, methodological, empirical and ideological issues that coalesce within the sociology of management. It seems to suggest that we require an approach that is sensitive to the empirical diversity and the social ambiguity of those managerial practices through which collective social action becomes sufficiently structured to take on a coherent and reasonable stable institutional shape in the form of 'work organizations'.

To date, the clearest expression of an approach to the study of management which displays the required degree of theoretical and methodological sensitivity to empirical diversity and social ambiguity is to be found in the work of Burns (1977, 1982; Burns and Stalker 1961). Over a period of thirty years, his work has exhibited a keen theoretical sensitivity to the political and ethical dilemmas that managers necessarily face in their struggle to come to terms with the inherent complexity and 'messiness' of organizational life. His more recent research has also served to emphasize the importance of understanding the intricate social processes whereby these dilemmas are institutionally reflected in the makeshift, and often internally contradictory, assemblies of practices that constitute contemporary work organizations as 'bricolages' of partially articulated and half-digested sets of principles or rationalities (Burns 1982).

Tomlinson has also provided a similar theoretical characterization of management as consisting of:

> the containment of separate and other contradictory practices – a matter of keeping the show on the road. Management is then seen as facing such problems as 'How can the practices of sub-agency A be made compatible with those of B?' and 'How can the decisions of C be summarized in their negative impact on D' rather than how the practices of A, B, C and D can be subordinated to the goals of the enterprise.
>
> (Tomlinson 1982: 128)

In this way, 'management' is treated as a process or activity aimed at the continual recoupling or 'smoothing over' of diverse practices always prone to disengagement and fragmentation. It is based on the often contested capacity to control the institutional mechanisms through which some degree of overall co-ordination and integration can be secured. This implies a contrasting view of work organizations to that conveyed in the approach reviewed in preceding sections of this chapter; that is, as the point of intersection for a wide range of social practices which are subject to various strategies of institutional combination and recombination rather than as hierarchically structured social units subordinated to the performance of an essential function within the economic, technical, administrative or political imperatives imposed by a particular socio-economic sector or system.

It may be appropriate at this point to offer a rather more formalized specification on the 'practice perspective' which builds on recent development of the concept of 'social practice' within social and political analysis, before moving on to its broader implications for the sociology of management. This can be achieved in three stages: first, by providing a general theoretical characterization of the concept of social practice; second, by elaborating upon this basic conception in the form of a crucial distinction between 'primary' and 'secondary' social practices; and third, by developing this distinction in regard of management as a particular type of secondary social practice. (For further elaboration see Reed 1984, 1985.)

The concept of social practice has figured prominently in the recent contributions of a number of writers and researchers in the fields of philosophy, anthropology, sociology, organizational studies and economics (Bordieu 1977; Giddens 1979; Macintyre 1981; Anthony 1985). Harris (1982) provides a useful definition of the concept which can form the starting point for further elaboration. To engage in a social practices involves:

> engaging in a class of actions which are intelligible in and through the concepts which inform them, which have to be understood as directed towards ends which all members of the community of practitioners share, and is defined through the means adopted to the achievement of those ends which are to be understood as determined by the conditions under which the practice is undertaken.
>
> (Harris 1982: 29)

From this basic definition, it is possible to identify five interrelated conceptual components which together form the analytical framework for organizing our thinking about management which is on offer within this paper. Conceptualizing management as an identifiable social practice requires that five distinct, but interrelated, factors are specified:

1. The concepts through which certain shared aims or problems are identified in a meaningful way by practitioners.
2. The shared aims or problems to which the practice is directed as communicated in the practitioners' conceptual vocabulary.
3. The means or resources through which achievement of these meaningful objectives is pursued.
4. The activities through which these resources are organized in pursuit of common objectives.
5. The situational conditions under which these activities, and the relationships they engender, are collectively undertaken.

Given this broad outline of the concept of social practice, it is necessary to move on to Harris's distinction between 'primary' and 'secondary' social practices which will have a crucial bearing on the way in which we treat management. Primary social practices are aimed at transforming the environmental circumstances in which human life is carried on through the production of goods and services and the ideas which inform our conceptions of them (Harris 1982: 64–5). Secondary social practices are directed at achieving overall integration and co-ordination of primary social practices through the design, implementation and monitoring of various judicial, political and administrative mechanisms. They 'assemble' the diverse and complex array of primary practices in which human populations are necessarily involved into institutional structures which exhibit a minimum degree of normative coherence, social cohesion and temporal continuity.

Considered in these terms, 'management' can be broadly defined as that secondary social practice through which administrative regulation and control is established and maintained over those activities and relationships in which non-managerial practitioners are engaged by virtue of their membership of communities of primary productive practice. It is directed at assembling diverse and complex primary practices into institutional structures which exhibit an acceptable degree of conceptual and material communality through the application of a range of physical and symbolic resources and the implementation of various co-ordinating mechanisms through which incipient fragmentation and decay can be temporarily resisted. Consequently, management constitutes both a mechanism through which conflict over the possession and control of resources necessary for primary productive activity can be regulated at least temporarily, and a means which provides a focus for struggle over the institutional arrangements through which this regulation is achieved.

This approach offers three main theoretical advantages over that discussed in previous sections of this chapter. First, it provides a conceptual synthesis of three key aspects of management which have previously been isolated from each other – that is, 'technique', 'process' and 'structure'. Second, it rejects the more orthodox treatment of management as a unitary control device which ensures the single-minded pursuit of an unambiguous technical, political or ideological imperative to which all aspects of social action, including managerial action, must be rigidly subordinated. In its place, the practice framework suggests that the task of management is to ensure a minimum degree of overall co-ordination and control of diverse primary productive practices which contain very powerful centrifugal forces pushing in the direction of even greater complexity and fragmentation. It also indicates that, in pursuing this institutional containment and regulation, managerial practitioners will have to rely on a wide range of specialized mechanisms and supporting rationales to achieve their aims, which may come into conflict with one another.

The interests of those who possess and/or control the basic material resources and instruments necessary for primary productive activity are likely to be the most influential consideration informing management's design and implementation of the various integrative mechanisms through which overall co-ordination and assembly may be attempted. However, managerial practitioners will also be exposed to alternative sources of pressure and demands, which will shape the particular mechanisms and rationales they follow in attempting to recouple diverse primary productive practices which have become, or are in danger of becoming, disengaged. As such, they will be required to develop an acceptable, and necessarily shifting, *modus vivendi* between competing rationales, each with their own internal logics and supporting justifications (Batstone 1987).

The third theoretical advantage offered by the approach outlined in this section is that it provides an integrated conceptual framework which can interrelate behavioral, organizational, and institutional levels of analysis without falling prey to the deterministic functionalist analysis which alternative perspectives tend to retreat into when faced with the diversity and complexity of managerial existence. This is achieved by focusing upon the array of regulative and co-ordinating mechanisms which managers must rely upon to organize productive practices and the problems which their usage presents to the continued integrity and viability of the institutional structures in which they are loosely grounded. Consequently, individual managers are forced to cope with the tension that necessarily arises between maintaining the long-term integrity and viability of the bureaucratic control systems on which they rely to achieve overall integration, and the operational requirement for the application of specific devices and understandings which undermine the coherence and stability of the former. The contradiction between a bureaucratic logic which requires strict adherence to the rule of imperative co-ordination and an operational practice that demands managerial reliance on devices, techniques and agreements which have no place within the former provides the focal point for the conceptual framework which has been developed in this section.

As such, it is the allocative controllers located at the corporate level who are primarily concerned with designing and imposing the bureaucratized monitoring systems through which operational controllers are managed. Yet the latter exercise a considerable degree of 'constrained autonomy' in deciding how the broad parameters established at corporate level will be interpreted in their establishments (Edwards 1987). At the same time, they provide much of the basic information on which allocative controllers are forced to rely in framing their decision-making rationales (Whitley 1987). These rationales will inform decision-making processes and outcomes relating to the acquisition, divestment and transformation of the productive resources on which the corporation depends. Their analysis needs:

> to incorporate an understanding of how management teams co-ordinate and direct resource allocation, rather than simply presume they do by virtue of their position. The social processes by which management teams secure adherence to and maintain control of human and material resources have to be specified, if we are to understand fully how and why firms act as they do.
>
> (Whitley 1987: 143)

This suggests that the managerial practices through which putative structural imperatives are transformed into operational rationales and mechanisms cannot be explicated in terms of a strict hierarchy of control levels. Rather, they must be understood in relation to the complexities of intra- and inter-organizational politics. Pahl and Winkler suggest that a subtle form of manipulative collusion between directors, senior managers and middle-level experts takes place, that shapes the allocative parameters within which operational decisions and mechanisms are formulated and implemented. They conclude that information manipulation and control was the key process for analyzing this collusive relationship:

> Successful manipulation in this way depends on the skilful structuring of the information which the board has available for assessing proposals. The power which the managers exercise over boards is power based on information control. Essential to such power is the sealing off of any sources of contradictory information. . . .The answers to the questions 'Who initiated?' 'Who is ultimately responsible for a given decision?' 'Who has power?' 'Who controls?' will be buried by the normal priorities of organizational politics. . . .Once we recognise the processes of manipulation, screening and pre-emption, then any serious consideration of decision-making must allow that decisions may be thrust up from below.
>
> (Pahl and Winkler 1973: 109–11)

Acceptance of this view of the relationship between allocative and operational control indicates the need for a firm rejection of the determinist – not to say reductionist – logic implicit in much labour process analysis. A conception of management as a loosely integrated configuration of social practices geared to the assembly of and control over the diverse resources and activities required for large-scale production facilitates realistic understanding of the actual processes through which 'structural imperatives' and 'operational mechanisms' interact to generate organizational outcomes.

Management practices, and the mechanisms through which they are enacted, will necessarily reflect the competing priorities of diverse groups struggling to impose their 'rationales' on the decision-making process. The assumption of a structural logic which leads directly from class domination to organizational control is replaced by a socio-political process in which the interaction between economic imperatives and social action is mediated by practices which cannot – and will not – guarantee the domination of one set of decision-making rationales to the exclusion of all others.

Managerial practice and the problematic of human agency

The analytical perspective outlined in this paper rests on the fundamental proposition that the sociology of management is most fruitfully considered as one element of a much larger intellectual enterprise, carried on by social and political theorists through many centuries, which has striven to provide a more sophisticated and insightful understanding of what Dawe has called the problematic of human agency (Dawe 1979). Dawe argues that:

> the idea of social action has been central to sociological thought less as a theory or set of theories in any formal sense, than as a fundamental moral and analytical preoccupation. What it does have is a vast body of theorizing about social action: its nature, its sources, its consequences. And this theorizing around a single idea, has. . . been decisive for and definitive of the entire history and nature of sociological analysis from its very inception.
>
> (Dawes 1979: 363)

He further maintains that the history of sociological analysis is a history of repeated failures to come to terms with the ambiguous and paradoxical nature of human agency to the extent that it has been intellectually dominated by a scientistic methodology which transforms ambiguity and contradiction into certainty and consistency.

In his attempt to recover the 'problematic of human agency' as the leitmotiv for the history of sociology and for the development of an historical sociology, Abrams suggests that:

> The problem of agency is the problem of finding a way of accounting for human experience which recognizes simultaneously and in equal measure that history and society are made by constant and more or less purposeful individual action and that individual action, however purposeful, is made by history and society. How do we, as active subjects make a world of objects which then, as it were, become subjects making us their objects? It is the problem of individual and society, consciousness and being, action and structure; a problem to which the voices of everyday life speak as loudly as those of scholars.
>
> (Abrams 1982: xiii–xiv)

He also contends that the dilemma of human agency needs to be approached in historical terms so that the relationship between action and structure is conceptualized as a 'matter of process in time' (Abrams 1982: xv). This shifts the focus of attention to those social practices through which social structures are created, maintained and transformed over time rather than treating the latter as entities or objects that evolve according to a hidden developmental logic in which human agency is conspicuous by its absence.

Thus the sociology of management needs to be regarded as one manifestation of a broader intellectual endeavour to explore the process of structuring in which 'human agency becomes human bondage because of the very nature of human agency' (Dawe 1979: 398).

In this way, the analysis which has been developed within this chapter is undertaken with a view to improving our understanding of the inevitable dilemmas and paradoxes which are encountered in the attempt to assemble and maintain workable institutional structures that reflect the uncertainties and ambiguities of the practices through which they are constructed. Managers cannot avoid these uncertainties and ambiguities; indeed, the very nature of the social practice in which they are involved expresses the contingent and paradoxical quality of human agency to the extent that it simultaneously denies and attempts to cope with the seemingly intractable problems which stand in the way of creating and sustaining some sort of order in the face of chaos. The public rhetoric of technocratic ideology conveys a 'Platonic' image of the manager as a rational planner and controller of an organizational machine which is infinitely adaptable to rapidly changing conditions. The private language suggests a very different picture of somebody struggling to come to terms with a reality which stubbornly refuses to conform to this organizational blueprint or to fit the universal categories and laws which it specifies. It is time that the credibility gap between public image and private reality was bridged by a theoretical perspective which is focused on the unavoidable dilemmas which managers have to contend with in their struggle to construct a workable *modus vivendi* between structural constraints and human recalcitrance. This will be unable to fall back on a deterministic mode of analysis in which inherent ambiguity and contradiction are transformed into certainty and consistency by recourse to structural imperatives and functional requirements.

This exploration of the contribution which management makes to the process of structuring can be pursued in relation to a number of crucial themes which recur in the sociology of management. First, there is a need to achieve a better understanding of the historical development of the multifarious forms of organizational control which managers have tried to implement in different institutional settings as a means of securing 'effective' structuring of work performance. Second, the impact of these forms of control on the nature and quality of managerial work must be examined with a view to realizing a more rounded and sensitive appreciation of its inherent dilemmas and the manner in which they are contained. Third, the responses which this 'organizational work' has elicited from those subjected to the mechanisms of control which it produces need to be reviewed with particular reference to the generation and regulation of industrial conflict. Fourth, the implications of the previous themes for the location and role of managerial groups within the class structure of the 'advanced societies' should be outlined. Finally, the insights derived from the exploration of managerial structuring conducted above will provide the basis for a more general assessment of the alternative futures faced by managers in a social world which is unlikely to become completely amenable to their attempts to eradicate its inherent uncertainties and perversities. This is certainly true at a time when they have as much cause as any to be fearful of what the future holds for them, as creators and protectors of organizational communities which are increasingly under threat from rationalizational processes which they themselves may have to implement but cannot hope to control (Anthony 1977, 1985; Reed 1988).

Conclusion

A continued analytical commitment on the part of labour process theorists to a rationalistic and formalistic model of managerial control strategies and structures has been identified in this chapter. This commitment produces explanations of managerial behaviour and organization which retain strong residues of a functionalist logic that specifies a deterministic relationship between the imperatives of capital accumulation and a hierarchial structure of control systems within management.

The arguments advanced in this paper suggest that the study of management should focus on the range of social practices through which managers attempt to retain a semblance of control over productive activity within the shifting pattern of material and ideational constraints contained within the social situations in which they operate. These practices are deemed to be inherently unstable and contradictory to the extent that they are geared to the assembly of productive activity through the implementation of control mechanisms at different levels of the organization, based on divergent rationales and logics. This divergence is seen to create severe problems of managerial co-ordination and control which produce organizational solutions that generate novel instabilities and conflicts calling for alternative 'coping strategies' on the part of management.

It is in terms such as those outlined above that the sociology of management can make a major contribution to a better understanding of the 'problematic of human agency' as it has emerged through successive waves of theorizing on social action within western socio-political thought.

Chapter five

The rise of organizational symbolism

Barry Turner

> Of the operations of the spirit, the least frequent is reason.
>
> Fenelon

A manifesto associated with the recent growth of interest in organizational symbolism would declare that many of the most important phenomena occurring within the human groupings known as organizations lie outside the precincts of classical rational-technical organization theory and systems analysis. Drawing attention to deeply held values and emotions, to myths and sagas, to rites and ceremonies, to scapegoats and heros, it would point out that a recognition of such features in organizational studies would need to be accompanied by the introduction to organization theory of disciplines formerly remote from it, e.g. linguistics, history, psychoanalysis, anthropology, literary criticism (SCOS 1984).

Behind such a statement would lie a challenge to what has been called the 'celebration of rationality' in organizations. We have been asked to accept that modern organizations really do partake of the legal-rational ethos to which Max Weber drew our attention at the turn of the last century. When Weber wanted to contrast the organizations of industrial capitalism with those of other civilizations he identified their most distinguished characteristic as a belief that their affairs were conducted legally, reliably, consistently, calculatingly, and predictably, magic having been banished from their procedures. He was, however, ambivalent about the extent to which this belief coincided in practice with the rational organizational attainment of reasonable ends, as opposed to the mere adoption of the appearance of rationality.

In pursuit of this claim to rationality, organizational members, and especially organizational leaders, would like us to accept a definition of reality in which organizational conduct is accepted as 'serious business'. Accordingly, the conventions within which organizational affairs are discussed must recognize this: organizations, and especially commercial and business organizations are considered to be utilitarian and formal, operating in a sterile, no-nonsense atmosphere, and managers are expected to display an economic hard headedness which will have no truck with more fanciful notions.

The organizational symbolists challenge this view. They point out that the world of organizations is not, cannot be solely about 'muck and brass', about ends and means, about formal discussions of business strategy within the confines of Weber's 'iron cage of rationality'. This is a partial view of the organizational world, reflecting both the self-image which the *men* of affairs hold of themselves, and the reflection of that image which has been widely accepted in contemporary society.

Of course there have always been some who have raised questions about this self-concerned seriousness. We have already noted that Weber himself was aware that the claims for rationality were fed by the value placed upon rationality in developing industrial capitalist society, so that although the ideology therefore equated rationality with efficiency, the precise nature of this relationship remained open to question (Weber 1968; Albrow 1970). Huizinga also, in his superb dissection of the nature of play, playfulness and games was specially concerned to apply his analysis to the world of business and commerce, taking a view of businessmen as essentially contestants in a game (Huizinga 1970). The business game, like other games, from marbles to gladiatorial contests, was an *agon* enacted within its own enclosed arena. Inside the arena, it would be conventionally accepted that concerns not connected with the game would, for the duration of the play, be suspended or neglected. In their place, an agreed but circumscribed set of rules would define the reality of the game, a reality which would be accepted and sustained by both participants and spectators.

The claims to a wholly rational–technical existence have also been challenged in other modes, by investigators like Donald Roy, who have lifted a corner of the veil of seriousness placed around business by revealing to slightly incredulous readers how the repetitive nature of life in, say, a machine shop might gain a significant portion of its meaning from play and repetitive behaviour, social relations being structured, in one instance described by Roy, around the daily ritual of the theft of a banana (Roy 1960). Other writers have found car workers who take on the roles of characters from the children's television programme, 'Magic Roundabout', or who relieve tedium by making flaming grenades out of balls of industrial adhesive (Beynon 1973); factory managers required to play 'liar dice' at lunch every day (Turner 1971); bakery workers engaged in planned group battles with jam syringes from the doughnut section (Ditton 1979); and coal miners conducting sadistic initiation ceremonies (Vaught and Smith 1980). And, of course, for decades Everett Hughes has been telling us that the technical division of labour generates both a social drama and a moral drama within work (Hughes 1958). In his view, not only do our usual human concerns continue to be felt when we enter a work organization but, accompanied by the obsessional rhythms of organizational activity, they produce events and patterns of relationships which can only be fully comprehended in terms of their dramatic properties.

Until recently, though, the strictures of such writers were not themselves treated all that seriously. Their observations were marginal curiosities, which, if anything, confirmed the irrelevance of the social sciences to real men of affairs. A nod would be made in the direction of the 'informal organization' whenever rationalistic models of formal organizations were discussed on management courses, and some of these matters might be conceded to lie in the province of the personnel department, but little more. In such ways, the worlds of business, money and administration have managed to insulate themselves to a large degree from suggestions cropping up in some of the social sciences that all of their affairs were not governed by a calculating and inescapably rational pursuit of efficiency.

As the nineteenth century public accepted the idea that art was about the depiction of views as realistically as they might be seen through a window, so we have allowed ourselves to be persuaded that organizations are about nothing but the solemn arrangement of work tasks, the following of rules, the making of decisions, and the pursuit of profit, and that all else is irrelevant. As the old view of art was disrupted earlier in this century, so the current growth of interest in organizational symbolism and corporate culture points to the end of an era. Looking anew at the organizational world we can see that it is a sensual and emotional realm, replete with its own ceremonies, rites and dramas. We can recognize, *pace* the accountants, that profit and loss is not the measure of all things, and conformity to rules is not the only notable form of human behaviour. People, social life, language, interactions and interpretations are just as human inside organizations as they are outside.

None of this will come as any great surprise to those who have examined organizations closely, or thought for any length of time about their affairs: the significant difference now is that this point of view is becoming much more widely accepted. It is in danger, indeed, of becoming the mainstream view and the reasons for this are numerous and complex. They include a flagging in the performance of both conventional business strategy and of existing models of organizational analysis. There has been a need to review organizational activities in the face of recession, and the seemingly unstoppable nature of the challenge by Japanese competitors to taken-for-granted industrial beliefs and practices in the west has made managers receptive to alternative explanations of their deficiencies. Along with these changing views has come a willingness to explore what could be called 'alternative' solutions based upon 'culture'. Meanwhile in the social sciences, a widespread retreat from positivism had been underway, provoking a new interest in methods of qualitative inquiry and analysis. Grand theoretical formulations have not lived up to their promises (Perrow 1972) and prescriptions for the construction of organizational strategies have proved difficult to implement, producing a readiness to consider contributions thrown up by alternative modes of inquiry.

As a consequence of this shift in emphasis we are now seeing what we could call, according to preference, 'a hundred flowers in bloom' or 'organizational culture chaos' (Calas and Smircich 1987). Organizations are no longer the sole province of the accountant or the business economist and, since they have ceased to be off-limits, any technique, theory or method previously practised outside their boundaries can now be switched to the inside to offer a novel gloss upon organizational events. Now that it is feasible to probe and debate the multiplicity of meanings which lie behind the official story of organizational activities, a wealth of possibilities has been opened up.

We can consider the ceremonies, the rhetoric, the moral drama, the aesthetic style of organizations. And, just as literary texts, once considered to be merely simple aggregations of signs, have been found to possess endless significance, so organizational behaviour and the scripts, documents and events entangled with it turn out to possess their own 'textuality' which enables them to be scrutinized to an almost infinite degree. It becomes possible to ask what names managers give to their computer systems, and to ponder the significance of their answers. Or to tease out messages about virility and the businessman's self-image from a car-hire advertisement showing a wilting bunch of roses on the seat of a limousine (Linstead and Grafton-Small 1987). Are managerial plans really just instrumental tools, or do they operate as mantras by providing channels of autocommunication for the officials who invent them? (Broms and Gahmberg 1982). Is it possible that the nationalization of the Swedish dental service is proceeding according to an archetypal pattern foreshadowed for us in the myth of Procrustes (Aredal 1986)? Why do female factory workers flirt with new male recruits, only to reject them cruelly later (Konecki 1987)? Are managerial concerns with motivation merely a smokescreen which conceals an unwillingness to recognize that death comes to managers too (Sievers 1987)? What can we discover about managerial thought from an analysis of the rhetoric of take-over documents? Is the directors' boardroom really as functional as it looks or does it smuggle in its own aesthetic in order to transmit messages about its occupants and the way that they would like to be thought about (Witkin 1987)?

And when they fall short of their goals, what kind of rhetoric and emotional responses does their failure engender within the organization (Turner 1971; Schwartz 1987)?

The shift of emphasis associated with organizational symbolism, then, has knocked down some barriers, but it has not yet made way for a new orthodoxy. Most commentators agree that there is a diversity of work going on under the banner of organizational culture and symbolism, and that this diversity is difficult to summarize. The quality of the work on offer is very variable, but firm judgments about this are also difficult to arrive at since the upheavals in the field have been accompanied by a diversity of possible criteria for judging the aims, the potential and the achievements of those who look, in one way or another, at organizations. Several writers (Alvesson 1986; Calas and Smircich 1987) have linked the rise of organizational symbolism with the broader movement of postmodernism taking place in the arts and in other intellectual spheres. In this view the possibility of arriving at agreed standards for the assessment of cultural analyses and related forms of discussion is itself brought into question.

It is clear, however, that the nature of organizational symbols, meanings, social activities and culture are not to be seen as differing in fundamentals from the same kinds of phenomena outside organizations. Organizational symbolism is concerned with symbolic matters which just happen to be within organizations and cultural analyses focus upon matters which are discernible both within and outside organizations.

And even in this formulation, we are perhaps still making too much of the organizational form, reifying it too much. For once we focus upon culture and its symbols and meanings we can no longer confine our concerns to something occurring 'inside' or 'outside' an organization. We are no longer looking at something that an organization 'has', but at the processes that make it possible for an organization to exist at all.

Any fundamental accounts of organizational culture, symbolism, meaning, or interpretations will be likely, therefore, to draw first of all upon general discussions of these phenomena and only in the second place to concern themselves with specifically organizational milieux. To talk about symbols and cultures in particular, it is first necessary to learn about symbols and culture in general. It is perhaps for this reason that many of the recent organizational texts on organizational symbolism and culture read in parts a little like primers in social anthropology for management theorists and industrial sociologists (Pondy *et al.* 1983; Frost 1985). With such caveats in mind, however, it may be useful to try to review some of the issues associated with the new 'license' to study all aspects of meaning within contemporary organizations.

The methods of investigation being pursued within the field of organizational symbolism and culture need to be understood in relation to two distinct types of approaches within the field. On the one hand, the new emphasis upon culture has been seen as something which could be added on to prior traditions of organizational investigation. In this view, symbolism is scarcely mentioned, and culture is seen as one more variable to be added to previous models to improve the efficacy of their predictions. Culture then affects a relatively limited section of an organization's operations. It concerns management activities and those aspects of employee behaviour which are amenable to managerial influence. Accordingly positivistic methodological tools such as questionnaires and attitude surveys can be used to investigate and to quantify such phenomena. This approach, it has been noted (Calas and Smircich 1987), is especially common in cross-cultural inquiries (see, for example, Trompenaars 1985), in an instrumental and positivistic managerial tradition which wants to make sure that American or European practices continue to function when shipped abroad.

By contrast, typical investigations in the symbolist movement are likely to use alternative ways of studying organizations, to be less concerned with prediction and what is seen as instrumentality, than with understanding, with meaning, with interpretation. While questionnaire inquiries are not altogether ruled out, the more likely methods to be used are unstructured or semi-structured interview, or participant observation in one of its variants, supplemented where appropriate by documentary analyses. The raw material for such enquiries needs to be found or elicited; noted or recorded; contemplated; and analysed or interpreted. The earlier stages of this process are those familiar to journalists, anthropologists, ethnographers, folklorists and qualitative sociologists, and the problems associated with them are those of 'fieldwork', the techniques and dilemmas of which are well discussed in the social science literature (Lofland 1971; Burgess 1982, 1984; Hammersley and Atkinson 1983). There have been some methodological innovations, such as requiring people to recall organizational events in the present tense whilst mentally reliving them (Witkin and Poupart 1986), to act out their organizational roles before video cameras (Beck 1987), or to compose their own organizational 'sagas' or 'myths' (Berg 1984), but these changes do not in themselves constitute the new domain of inquiry. The novelty and also the variety of the alternative approaches to organizations lies not in their methods but in their approach to interpretation and analysis.

The methods used and style of analysis preferred can, of course, interact in some ways. The question of where to look for the data and how long to look for it embraces both facets. How much data about a culture is needed for a convincing case to be made? Lévi-Strauss defended himself against charges that he had not carried out an exhaustive inventory of South American myths prior to his analysis of them by arguing that a linguist can work out the grammar of a given language from a remarkably small number of sentences, even partial information being valuable when dealing with unknown languages (Lévi-Strauss 1969: 7–8). Many current cultural studies seem to have tacitly taken a similar approach, implying either that the world of organizational symbolism is so unknown that any sample from it cannot fail to be interesting, or that, like a fragment of a hologram broken off from a larger whole, any small piece of organizational behaviour will embody the total cultural pattern. Both of these positions are contentious. Considerations of 'sampling' may, of course, be rejected by some as being, in themselves, unduly positivistic and thus not of relevance to their particular project.

What catches the attention, then, of the organizational symbolist? First the manner in which things are done – the style of the organization, the rhetoric of managerial pronouncements, the assumptions of the workgroup. It is of interest from a managerial point of view, but also from a more general anthropological one, to see how far managerial attempts to give a company a distinctive style can in fact transform the mode of living experienced by people within the company. Within a particular organization, how is it necessary to speak or write in order to have one's messages recognized as appropriate? The rejected rational-technical form of organizational analysis was one which eschewed any thought of emotions as significant in organizations, except as indicators of deviance or disruption, but organizational symbolists are much more centrally concerned with the sensuous aspects of lived experience in organizational settings. The affective and the aesthetic are assumed to be as crucial as they are elsewhere in our experience, and as important for the understanding of organizational life.

For a number of investigators, to be concerned with symbolism and culture in organizations is to be sensitive to a variety of interpretative processes. These writers take a view of organizational culture which is informed by social anthropology, especially the work of Geertz (1973). Cohen's concern with the symbolic construction of communities is also cast in a form which can be readily transferred from a residential to a work-based context, for he is much concerned with the way in which symbols are used to define group identity, to mark out boundaries and to use symbolic resources to cope with technical and other forms of change (Cohen 1987). Louis suggests that interpretation means becoming aware of the importance of tacit understandings, of difficult-to-detect negotiations, and of other intermittent and intersubjective processes, as well as more accessible physical and linguistic symbols (Louis 1985). There is thus a challenge to devise ways of gaining access to the tacit processes which create, sustain and transmit meaning in organizations.

Organizations and organizational settings are seen as the outcomes of continuous processes of social negotiation. Authority is understood not to operate by decree. Instead, power is seen as a series of bilateral social relationships, which need to be read against a background of prevailing socially agreed assumptions. A precise pattern of compliance will only emerge out of rather complex, delicate and often ambiguous patterns of social interplay in those daily social transactions about authority and deference which are reminiscent of Mary Parker Follett's insistence upon 'power with' employees rather than 'power over' them (Parker Follett 1941). Within a cultural approach, it is thus important to gain a sense of the shared realities which make it possible for organizations to exist and to function (Strati 1986).

With regard to technology and finance, those topics at the centre of the rational-technical image of commerce and industry, they are likely to be regarded, within a cultural approach, as matters which gain all of their significance from the social agreements and socially determined processes of task-related activities within which they have been constituted. These social agreements thus have an independent contribution to make to the support of the roles which members of the organization occupy (Berg 1984; Barley 1986). Budgets are seen not as unchallengeable proofs of the rationality of behaviour in organizations, but rather as indicators of activities which also have social (Hofstede 1980), symbolic, and even 'magical' properties (Morgan 1986), weapons which may be used in battles within the organizational arena.

In a similar fashion, any of the collective activities taking place within an organization may be seen as vehicles for values and beliefs which are important to members of the organization (Morgan 1986). There are a variety of ways of considering this culturally: by looking, for example, at the imagery which surrounds work relationships, at the ceremonies and rituals in which they are defined, supported and celebrated, or simply by asking of a given individual what his or her involvement is with the shared system of meanings found within the organization (Fine 1984).

All of these options are complicated, however, by the likely existence of several systems of meaning within an organization which compete for a member's allegiance. While a lot of managerial writing which takes up the cultural theme tends to assume that organizations have a single 'culture', or that a managerially inspired 'culture of excellence' can be installed in an organization without opposition, those taking a view based upon negotiation will see a complex of subcultures and counter-cultures. In distinctive work-cultures, characteristic attitudes, anecdotes and jokes express identity and preserve the form of relationships with other groups (Turner 1971; Santino 1979), and organizations will also contain several 'systems of symbolic representation' (Aktouf 1985).

Even when the separate traditions within a given organization are not hostile, they will still pass on different sets of values, for the development of a distinctive subculture is an important device for retaining autonomy (Gregory 1983; Grafton-Small and Linstead 1986). Police officers, for example, need to retain discretion to carry out their work on the beat, but police administrators have no interest in protecting such discretion, for they have to deal with public complaints about its misuse (Manning 1977). This difference then persists as a pivot around which cultural differences continue to be organized (Lang 1981; Lynxwiler *et al.* 1983). Or again, Dubinskas has detailed the differences in perspectives and time horizons between the bright young quasi-academic research biochemists in biotechnical or genetic engineering companies and the managers who run them, the latter group having much more limited time horizons than the former, producing another duality of view within an organizational culture (Dubinskas 1987).

Thus to talk of culture is not necessarily to talk of harmony. An organization may contain negotiated cultures but those in different positions in the organization and those with differential access to resources will see the issues and the traditions underlying the negotiation process from competing viewpoints (Riley 1983).

There is a problem, however, running through much of the new literature in organizations in relation to what some have seen as its rather cavalier treatment of established anthropological themes such as myth, ritual and ceremony. Some writers have suggested that organizations support myths, or embody mythical elements in their social arrangements, one of the strongest protagonists of this view being Aredal who makes reference to classical myths in order to gain access to a key which will explain aspects of contemporary organizational policy (Aredal 1987). To sustain such a position, of course, it is necessary to assume that the myths of antiquity embody certain recurrent truths about human affairs which will be re-enacted in contemporary life. Such a view is sometimes justified on psychoanalytic grounds (Tatham 1982; Geneva 1985), the Jungian aspects of such archetypal behaviour even being buttressed by complex and allusive links with aspects of the hermetic tradition (see, for example, Hillman 1980). Other writers transfer patterns of analysis from folklore, asking, when organizational stories, themes or anecdotes recur – who might be the hero or (less frequently) the heroine; what might be their quest or mission; who is the adversary, and so on. Again the assumption must be that there will be a sufficient homology between contemporary life and the patterns of folklore, fairytale and legend to make such comparisons illuminating (Broms and Gahmberg 1982).

The difficulty with such analyses, which we may note here, is not that the processes of story-telling and myth-making do not appear in modern society, for they do. Nor is the problem that the human propensity to create myths has disappeared, for this seems unlikely. The difficulty lies in the social context provided by modern industrial society and modern organizations. If we think of the myth-making capacity as a tendency to humanize the contingent by cloaking it in meaning, we can see that for this facility to create major cultural constructions, a degree of stability over time is likely to be required. The randomness of past migrations, displacements or technical innovations have been absorbed and interpreted socially by being coated with meaning, much as an oyster smooths off an abrasive fragment of sand and turns it into a pearl.

But as the moves in the game of industrial capitalism speed up, so the industrial milieux within which employees and managers operate lose stability and permanence. Many of the anecdotes and stories picked up by the contemporary industrial folklorists who are associated with the organizational symbolism movement (Raspa 1984) seem to be left over from truncated myth-making activities. Given a generation or so of repetition, with the polishing up and smoothing off which would occur within that time, we could then ask about the significance of that which had persisted. Over time, such proto-mythical meaning-constructs would also develop complex symbolic accretions which would link them with other aspects of the culture of those who invented them.

The effects of the habitual transformations, reorganizations and disruptions which are commonplace in modern organizational contexts are compounded by the impact of the media upon all of our relationships. Since we now have the potential to transmit instantly even the most trivial items of style or storytelling around the world at the speed of light, existing myth-making activities are becoming imploded in a society of simulacra (Baudrillard 1985). As a consequence of the interplay of organizations and the media in our society we need to ask carefully how far the significance attributed to myths generated and transmitted orally in pre-literature cultures can be transferred to those fragments of stories and belief patterns which we encounter in contexts which try to stress denotative rather than connotative or symbolic communication. Once invented to meet some immediate communicatory impulse, such creations are likely to be buffeted by forces of industrial ferment which will render their interpretation even more problematic than the interpretation of tribal myths. When Turner first succeeded in filming a ritual performed annually by members of a tribe in Papua New Guinea, the men expressed pleasure that they would not have to repeat that ritual again in future years since they need only show the film (Turner 1969)! Our own ritual processes are likely to be undergoing equally complex adaptations to modern communications technology.

Parallel considerations can be brought to bear upon the assessment of the possible significance of celebrations, ceremonies, and ritual. Organizational investigators have surveyed such forms from the daily coffee break, the office party, and the retirement presentation (Rosen 1985; Turner 1971), to large corporate events (Dandridge 1986), looking at them as sources of solidarity, 'a thread tying all employees together', or as contexts of communication which might generate particular images of the company amongst members.

Simple Durkheimian interpretations of such events, however, do not take full advantage of many developments in anthropological thought. Turner's discussions of *The Ritual Process*, for example, provide a much more fluid and revealing way of considering ritual which does not yet seem to have been applied to the organizational context (Turner 1969). The important property of ritual here is the opportunity which it offers, not to reaffirm the social structure, but to take participants out of structure. If the creative properties of social life occur within the interstices of social structure, the importance of ceremony and *communitas* lies in their propensity to allow members, on occasions, to turn wholly towards each other, crossing the thresholds of their normal relationships with each other and making it possible to change social structure. The opportunities for liminality which might be offered by communion in organizational ceremonies are yet to be explored. Similar observations might be made about the application of structuralist anthropological analyses of the symbolism of ritual to organizational contexts (Leach 1966; Turner 1971).

These deficiencies in the treatment of myth and ritual may be linked with important varieties of approach to organizational symbolism and culture. Many of the current managerial enthusiasts see 'corporate culture' as an entity which can be built into an organization in order to develop high morale and create 'excellence', taking a view of culture which would be regarded sceptically by most social scientists. Even when dealing with matters of some complexity, messages for managers tend to get progressively more simplified and reified as they are packaged to be 'sold' in management training courses or in semi-popular texts. Subtleties have accordingly disappeared in the way that 'corporate culture' is now being increasingly understood so that it is regarded in an oversimplified and static manner. Managers who have been on courses on 'culture' may expect to install a new departmental culture on their first month back in harness.

By contrast, many of the investigators interested in the emphasis upon culture and symbols find an important appeal precisely in the subtleties which make it possible to gain an improved understanding of the full range of human behaviour within organizations. For some, too, this possibility is enhanced by being coupled with a recognition that organizations must rely wholly on the capabilities of all their members if they are to create, sustain and recreate an adequately functioning work culture (Raynaud 1983), acknowledging that the symbols and the culture of an organization must, in the last resort, be sustained by its members.

A fundamental dualism can be said to characterize the field of organizational culture and symbolism, a variety of terms existing to describe this split. Christensen and Kreiner contrast the 'corporate culture' of interventionist managers with the 'culture-in-work' of organizational members (Christensen and Kreiner 1983), while Ott opposes 'pop culture magicians' to the 'honest grapplers' with the ideas of culture (Ott 1984). In one of the most comprehensive and acute analyses of work in this field so far, Smircich and Calas point to a tension between 'dominant' and 'oppositional' views. For them, functionalist, technical, manipulatory approaches, which see culture as a variable, pull against views of culture as a root metaphor, these stressing the cognitive, symbolic or unconscious aspects of organizations (Smircich and Calas 1987). March recently echoed the former view when, in summarizing a set of conference papers, he divided the studies neatly into those concerned with culture as a dependent variable and those concerned with culture as an independent variable (March 1987), a classification which leaves little possibility of making contact with those who emphasize interpretivist or critical views of organizational culture.

Carse, a theologian rather than an organizational theorist, while making some similar oppositional distinctions, offers some interesting asides on aspects of culture. In our discussion above, we have been separating the 'corporate culture' from 'culture in work', separating managerial intentions about culture from that culture which workers (and also managers) weave for themselves while making sense of their experiences in the organization. In a parallel manner, Carse contrasts the 'culture of the boundary' with the 'culture of the horizon' (Carse 1987). Like Huizinga (1970), Carse discusses human activities as sets of games, separating out finite from infinite games. For Carse, finite games are associated with the culture of the boundary – the culture generated wholly within a circumscribed arena. The potentialities for culture creation are then used to aim for an end, for an actuality, rather than for infinite play. And so, after the management course, corporate culture is thought, by those who fail to recognize that the real potential of culture lies in its continuing, never-ending character, to be something which can be specified and then installed. A corporate culture is defined by its boundaries – it is the culture *within* the corporation, and at the boundary there must be opposition, a meeting with hostile forces (see, for example, Mushashi 1974; Ohmae 1982). A corporate culture, intended to engender a company loyalty, must have a belligerent element, since its aim is to embrace everything which it can see. As in Huizinga, this kind of 'finite cage' has an arena, winners and losers. Competitors are necessary to sustain a bounded corporate culture, to keep it clear and distinct and to enable it to pursue its destiny. The inevitable conflict and competition is engaged with those beyond the boundaries, and people are far more attentive to their organization and to its interests when there is danger from such sources.

To paraphrase Carse, corporate theorists are tempted into the belief that they know the story of a company so that they can script its final scene of triumph or defeat. When thinking is bounded in this way, corporate culture transfers possibilities into scripted laws of behaviour within a company, and demands conformity to them. It was for reasons such as this that the writer J. B. Priestley (1934: 78–9) set out his opposition to the idea that a workplace should become the overwhelmingly important element in a worker's life.

In contrast we may offer the notions of symbolism and culture as assemblages of very complex, subtle, and elusive potentials, including the possibility of liminality and the demotic possibilities associated with workers creating their own culture (Gherardi, Turner and Strati, in press). Even for managers, culture in work is somewhat different from the script offered by corporate culture. Culture in work is essentially a creative process, whether the culture-maker is a labourer, a machinist or a managing director. It is potentially the culture of the horizon. Even the dreariest industrial locale can prove on closer acquaintance to be a creative setting, within which may be generated a portion of Carse's 'infinite game'.

For Carse, culture makers are inventors, artists, storytellers, mythologists, makers of possibilities. And those who create culture in work are engaged in precisely these activities. In these aspects of their behaviour they do not produce outcomes, but openings. Whereas corporate culture is to be specified and installed, culture in work is process, it opens forward, and is never finished. For a culture defined by its horizon, rather than by its boundary, Carse notes, the horizon is simply the point beyond which we cannot see. While the horizon itself is not visible, nothing about it limits vision. It opens out into all that is beyond, unrestricted by time or space. It opens up possibilities of moving beyond technical and practical interests to interests which might have an emancipatory quality (Habermas 1970, 1971, Smircich and Calas 1987).

Conclusion

There is no doubt that a new vocabulary and a new set of concerns are invading organizational discussions, for managers, for practitioners in the organizational field, and for social investigators. A luxurious embarrassment of new writing is emerging, but no orthodoxy. After reading numerous overviews of the field, one finds it difficult to summarize the new developments precisely, or in more than the most general of terms. Part of the difficulty lies in pinning down and defining the slippery notions of culture and symbolism, especially since it is easy, and, indeed commonplace, for discussions to slip without notice from static, objectified notions into analyses in processual terms. For some, it is social objects such as values, rituals, myths, or ceremonies which constitute the culture, while for others it is, or should be the process which flows through the creation of these objects or occasions. For similar reasons, it becomes difficult to pin down culture as a dependent or an independent variable: in doing so one loses the essence of culture as a metaphor.

Culture is playful, and while we can explain the products of play, it is difficult to explain the process of play itself. Without play, we are limited in our scripts: with play, original discourse is possible. The importance of the rise of organizational symbolism does not lie in its partial turning away from rationality, with the associated dangers of romanticism (Ebers 1985), or in its delineation of a new field for ethnographers and folklorists to explore, but in the attention which it draws to the manner in which the creative, humanizing, innovating aspects of culture pervade organizational behaviour. Only by attending to these aspects of organizational life can we clarify understanding of the full range of organizational behaviour and realize the full potential of organizational settings as locations for human enterprise.

Chapter six

Ethnomethodology and organizational research: an introduction

John Hassard

Introduction

This chapter has three objectives: first, to review the central principles of the ethnomethodological approach to social analysis; second, to outline the main techniques used in ethnomethodological research; and third, to describe how ethnomethodology can provide insights for understanding behaviour in organizations. In meeting these objectives, the chapter explores research possibilities in the 'interpretive' paradigm of organizational analysis (Burrell and Morgan 1979). It seeks to advance the prospects for paradigm diversity by making ethnomethodology intelligible to the organizational researcher just starting out. As ethnomethodology is frequently accused of being obscurantist, and as many works in this area are difficult for the lay reader, this chapter attempts to decode the more exotic writings of Bittner, Garfinkel, Zimmerman, and others.

What is ethnomethodology?

> We are concerned with how society gets put together; how it is getting done; how to do it; the social structures of everyday activities. I would say that we are doing studies of how persons, as parties to ordinary arrangements, use the features of the arrangement to make for members the visible organized activities happen.
>
> (Garfinkel 1974: 16)

Ethnomethodology is essentially the creation of American sociologist Harold Garfinkel, who established the idea that everyday, commonplace or routine activities are 'accomplished through the competent use of a variety of skills, practices and assumptions' (Garfinkel 1967). It is an approach to social analysis which is grounded in the detailed study of everyday life – it treats everyday circumstances as topics for empirical enquiry, and examines the ways in which people order and make sense of mundane activities, specifically how they make them accountable to others. The aim is to analyse how subjects, through social interaction, make sense of verbal and non-verbal cues ('indexicals' – see Garfinkel 1967: 3–7), whose meaning is dependent on the context of production. Interactions are regarded as ongoing accomplishments in which those involved take recourse to a range of assumptions, practices, and conventions in order to define, sustain and reproduce everyday situations. These practices and assumptions are what the ethnomethodologists call 'methods'.

While it is the writings of Garfinkel and his colleagues (e.g. Egon Bittner, Aaron Cicourel, Harvey Sacks, Don Zimmerman) which are most readily identified with the approach, their work in fact owes considerable intellectual debt to the phenomenological sociology of Alfred Schutz and the symbolic interactionism of George Herbert Mead and Erving Goffman. From the work of Schutz and Goffman, in particular, comes this concern to understand encounters in their own terms, and thus to explain the 'taken-for-granted' assumptions which characterize social situations. In this understanding process, emphasis is placed upon how subjects make use of 'reflexivity' (see Garfinkel 1967: 7–9); that is, how they characterize situations by looking back at what has occurred previously. Here, ethnomethodology borrows two of the main pillars of Schutz's analysis – his notions of 'because' and 'in-order-to' motives – as the basis for a theory of social action.

Indeed, like Schutz, ethnomethodologists are concerned to account for how actions are given *meaning* in the flow of the 'life-world' (Schutz and Luckmann 1974), and especially how actors are constantly trying to make sense of the world and interpret what is happening. From this perspective, social structure, instead of being a hard facticity 'out there' in the external world, is something that is continuously generated within the process of social construction. It is assumed, for example, that lay actors attempt to explain social situations in ways akin to interpretive sociologists. In fact, for ethnomethodologists the attempts by lay actors to make sense of the social world represent mechanisms through which social structure is created and sustained.

Ethnomethodology, therefore, places importance on the common-sense features of everyday life, the chief concern being to understand things that are known to 'anyman'. As Zimmerman and Pollner suggest:

> in contrast to the perennial argument that sociology belabors the obvious, we propose that sociology has yet to treat the obvious as a phenomenon. We argue that the world of everyday life, while

> furnishing sociology with its favoured topics of inquiry, is seldom a topic in its own right.
>
> (Zimmerman and Pollner 1971: 33)

Ethnomethodological research: forms and orientations

> traditional empiricism fails to come to terms with the problems of empirically grounded concepts in the life-world. Concepts are irrelevant unless they are grounded in concrete experiences and unless they refer to the realities of men in their life worlds.
>
> (Phillipson 1972: 146)

Ethnomethodology involves analysing social interaction as an on-going practice. In so doing, studies typically concentrate on either conversational analysis (e.g. Sacks, Schegloff, and Jefferson 1974), or interactions within a particular organizational setting (e.g. Zimmerman 1973).

Douglas (1971) has produced a useful analytical distinction in his discussion of 'linguistic' and 'situational' forms of ethnomethodology. Linguistic ethnomethodologists (see Cicourel 1972; Schegloff and Sacks 1973) examine the use of language, and particularly how conversations are structured in everyday circumstances. They analyse natural language and especially the shared meanings that words have for members of a particular group. They seek to lay bare the network of indexical expressions which give situations their meaning, and make much of the 'taken-for-grantedness' in conversations and of how verbal language conveys more than is made explicit. Linguistic ethnomethodologists demonstrate how much information 'goes without saying', messages being conveyed and understood without ever being verbalized. Garfinkel argues that to comprehend the meaning of statements we need to know not just *what* is being said but *how* it is said; i.e. we must understand the 'rules' participants employ in making sense of verbal interaction (Garfinkel 1967: 24–31).

Situational ethnomethodologists (see McHugh 1968), on the other hand, seek to access a wider range of social activities. Their objective is to understand how participants make sense of, and construct, their immediate social situations. In field studies, situational ethnomethodologists often purposefully disrupt commonplace activities in order to reveal the normative processes at work within them. This is done so as to expose the taken-for-grantedness of everyday situations. The point is made that everyday situations are governed by well-regulated sets of rules, and that these rules serve as meanings through which to stabilize interaction. Although these rules are a largely tacit phenomenon, they nevertheless provide an agenda from which to conduct research.

Through uncovering such practices, situational ethnomethodologists discern how sense is made out of indexicals.

For some, however, ethnomethodology is not just a new approach to sociological analysis, it is actually an alternative to it. Ethnomethodologists often reject formal sociological theory and deny its explanations. Ethnomethodologists feel that orthodox sociology neglects the very phenomena it should treat as problematic. Traditional sociological research is seen to take the phenomena resulting from social processes as given, or else as points from which research should commence. It tries to discover correlations between phenomena without first explaining why these phenomena are of interest. The problem here is that while professional social scientists share everyday common-sense practices with lay persons, and agree with them about the 'proper' problems to be studied, they nevertheless consider lay accounts as faulty and their own as superior. To ethnomethodologists, however, the two are quite similar, as both represent phenomena to be understood in their own right. While lay members and professional sociologists might agree that a certain issue is worthy of study (e.g. bureaucracy, deviance, kinship, etc.), the ethnomethodologist would not analyse that phenomenon in such a hard and 'given' way. Instead, he would treat the 'issue' as a topic for investigation in its own right (see Pollner 1974 on this point). Ethnomethodologists argue that social research should study processes, rather than accept the effects of process as given and proceed from there. Many ethnomethodologists thus strongly resist attempts to locate their work within the bounds of conventional sociology. They dissociate themselves from what they see as the dominant orientation within academic sociology, that of 'constructive analysis' (see Garfinkel and Sacks 1970), and instead confine themselves to understanding the 'awesome indexicality' of everyday accounts. The approach is orientated towards empirical study, and especially to understanding how social actors make sense of common-place events.

However, although ethnomethodology has made significant progress in developing an 'alternative' approach to social analysis, it has nevertheless encountered many problems in so doing. In particular, critics have noted how its empirical output has emerged in rather piecemeal fashion. Yet this is not to say that ethnomethodologists have failed their research objectives: their research has, for the most part, succeeded in documenting social routines in terms of the kinds of typifications, presumptions, and actions upon which such routines are founded. In so doing, this has demanded a logic quite different to that of the Popperian hypothetico-deductive method, as instead a form of ideographic inductivism has been employed. Although referring specifically to the concept of organization Bittner (1974) summarizes the basic premise when he notes:

> The important point . . . is that we must be prepared to treat every substantive determination we shall formulate as the case for exploring the background information on which it in turn rests. By way of defining our task we propose that the study of the methodological use of the concept of organization seeks to describe the mechanisms of sustained and sanctioned relevance of the rational constructions to a variety of objects, events and occasions relative to which they are involved.
>
> (Bittner 1974: 76)

Organizational analysis: Bittner, Zimmerman, Silverman, and Jones

> the meaning of the concept (of organization), and of all of the terms and determinations that are subsumed under it, must be discovered by studying their use in real scenes of action by persons whose competence to use them is socially sanctioned.
>
> (Bittner 1974: 75)

The question remains, then, of how the approach is effected in practice, i.e. what kind of fieldwork do ethnomethodologists do? At its most basic, we can say that their research interests focus upon two main areas: first with analysing the language-forms individuals employ in establishing that the actions of peers are acceptable and understandable (e.g. Weider 1974); and second, with the description of concrete situations in formal (mainly work) organizations (e.g. Sudnow 1973). These concerns often overlap in the final research output (e.g. Silverman and Jones 1976).

The research focus of most interest to us is the description of common-place encounters within formal organizations. Most ethnomethodological studies are in fact of organizations, and the range of accounts is now quite wide; e.g. geriatric hospitals, prisons, welfare agencies, research laboratories, police, abortion clinics, public bureaucracies, and kindergartens. Furthermore, the last ten years have witnessed not only doctorates (e.g. Lynch 1979; Fairhurst 1981) awarded for work in this area, but also the appearance of ethnomethodological papers in mainstream management journals (e.g. Gephart 1978: Fairhurst 1983). Interest in this form of analysis continues to grow, and Garfinkel is presently developing a three-volume manual to assist those wishing to engage in fieldwork (Garfinkel, forthcoming).

As the number of ethnomethodological accounts of organizations has grown, so certain studies have taken on the mantle of landmark contributions, these tending to influence the direction and style of research. This has been mainly where a work has either been the first to discuss a problematic concept (e.g. Bittner 1974), or where the empirical analysis is considered extremely well crafted (e.g. Zimmerman 1971; Silverman and Jones 1976). Through assessing some of these contributions, we will draw out the main theoretical and empirical characteristics of the ethnomethodological approach to organizations.

As Silverman notes, ethnomethodological studies of organizations are concerned with:

> 1 Attempts to examine the ways in which activities and their outcomes are displayed as in-accord with-a-rule such that their sensible character may be recognized, and
> 2 Examinations of the practices and policies through which the features of the real world are provided for in the activities and accounts (both lay and professional) that routinely arise in socially organized settings.
>
> (Silverman 1975: 280)

In denoting these characteristics Silverman is in fact acknowledging a debt to Bittner (1974); who was the first to develop an ethnomethodological treatise with specific reference to organizations. Bittner set an agenda for subsequent field studies, his paper being used thereafter as a benchmark for evaluating empirical contributions. However, although noted for its analytical importance, Bittner's paper is also noted for the difficulty of its style. Therefore, we will try to decode his thesis, the substance of which can be appreciated as outlined below.

Bittner

Bittner argues that in mainstream sociology, organizations are appreciated as 'normative idealizations' or language forms which provide 'a generalized formula to which all sorts of problems can be brought for solution'. He suggests that as organization theory defines organizations as 'stable associations of persons engaged in concerted activities directed to the attainment of specific objectives', then this renders the concept of organization structure unproblematic. Rather than treat organizations as real structures in their own right, he suggests we should, instead, aim to examine the 'sense of organization structure' with which actors operate. For Bittner, the concept of structure is no more than a common-sense typification constructed by individuals for use within particular contexts.

Therefore, to adopt this everyday assumption uncritically, and then to employ it as a basis for organizational analysis, is to engage in a practice beset with problems. Bittner argues that the sociologist who uses the concept so, is in fact using it only as a device for explaining idealized organizational activities. He or she is committing a basic error in that such concepts should be the *subject* of enquiry rather than the tools of analysis. By relying on everyday theories of the world, the sociologist confuses the use of organization as 'topic' with its employment as an unacknowledged 'resource' in the development of explanations. Bittner gives warning:

> In general there is nothing wrong with borrowing a common-sense concept for the purposes of sociological inquiry. Up to a point it is, indeed, unavoidable. The warrant for this procedure is the sociologist's interest in exploring the common-sense perspective. The point at which the use of common-sense concepts becomes a transgression is where such concepts are expected to do the analytical work of theoretical concepts. When the actor is treated as a permanent auxiliary to the enterprise of sociological inquiry at the same time that he is the object of its inquiry, there arise ambiguities that defy clarification.
>
> (Bittner 1974: 70)

Bittner maintains that the characteristic feature of orthodox organizational analysis is its over-reliance on common-sense knowledge of the world. Post-Weberian sociologists are seen to base their explanations on a whole set of implicit assumptions, these serving to build a shield around the subject matter. Indeed, Weber is accused of setting a precedent here, his production of the ideal-type being reliant, primarily, on common-sense knowledge of 'bureaucracy'. Instead of coming to terms with the everyday presuppositions of his analysis, Weber offers a partial account which 'glosses' how competent participants make sense of (notions of) 'hierarchy' and 'office' in the context of their enactment. Bittner suggests that in attempting to formalize a definition of bureaucracy – by way of everyday knowledge –Weber has engaged in a theoretical shortcut. The alternative is to analyse the processes by which competent participants use everyday knowledge of bureaucracy to account for specific activities in particular settings. Bureaucracy has no implicit meaning of its own; it exists only through the socially sanctioned occasions of its use – it does not determine action.

In developing this critique, Bittner suggests that Weber's prime fault lies in being in collusion with those he seeks to understand. As Zimmerman and Pollner note, the position is analogous to a person trying to explain his or her dreams while still being asleep and dreaming – it cannot be done (Zimmerman and Pollner 1971). Bittner notes:

> If the theory of bureaucracy is a theory at all, it is a refined and purified version of the actor's theorising. To the extent that it is a

> refinement and purification of it, it is by the same token, a corrupt and incomplete version of it; for it is certainly not warranted to reduce the terms of common-sense discourse to a lexicon of culturally coded significances to satisfy the requirements of theoretical postulation.
>
> (Bittner 1974: 74)

To replace this form of incomplete theorizing, Bittner advances a method for understanding organization as a common-sense construct. The chief concern is to document the processes actors invoke in constructing the social world. Bittner treats the actor not as a passive functionary, but as a creative author whose competence lies in using the concept of organization to produce rational accounts. Here, the actor is seen to use the concept as a 'gambit of compliance' whereby certain accepted rules of behaviour are inferred by simply *using* the term. Accounts are developed which illustrate how an idea such as 'formal organization' is used as a 'collaborative reference' for establishing the 'stylistic unity' of everyday interaction. Thus competent actors employ the concept as a mechanism for producing order and control. Organization is not treated as an object in itself, but rather as a language-category providing for the object-*like* qualities of social interaction; it is a notion called upon for decoding the 'sense' of everyday activities such as bureaucratic routines.

Bittner's paper (which was first published in 1965) represents *the* major ethnomethodological analysis of the concept of organization. As noted, it has served as the main point of reference for a series of empirical studies conducted during the last two decades. Almost exclusively, these studies have assessed the sense-making strategies of employees in either public services or public bureaucracies (e.g. Bittner 1973; Zimmerman 1971, 1973; Silverman and Jones 1973, 1976; Fairhurst 1983). Researchers have suggested that such organizations are 'constellations of rules' (Fairhurst 1983), the main analytical focus being on how 'competent' actors account for 'rule use'. Organizations are experienced as 'networks of rules of conduct' – networks which define the 'proper' actions to be taken. These rule networks situate the meaning of social activities for actors.

In the wake of Bittner's conceptual thesis, works by Zimmerman (1971, 1973) and Silverman and Jones (1976) represent examples of the empirical ethnomethodological approach to organizations. Their fieldwork focuses on how courses of (bureaucratic) action are contingent upon the relevance of particular rules to particular contexts. These studies illustrate many of the distinctive features of the ethnomethodological approach to organizational research.

Zimmerman

Zimmerman's work, in particular, epitomizes this form of research and provides a template for organizational enquiry. In line with both Garfinkel (1967) and Bittner (1974) he focuses upon the construction of common-sense rationalities, and especially upon how actors in bureaucracies provide for the features of organization structure, and show rule-governed characteristics, in their everyday activities. These processes are well displayed in Zimmerman's most cited empirical papers: 'Record keeping and the intake process in a public welfare organization' (1971) and 'The practicalities of rule use' (1973). Both pieces result from Zimmerman's fieldwork at a district office of a state Bureau of Public Assistance, the former paper analysing the role of the welfare caseworker, while the latter, the role of the receptionist who directs clients to relevant officials.

In 'Record keeping', Zimmerman describes how welfare caseworkers enact 'sensible intake work'. He outlines the decision process that caseworkers employ to help them interpret how much of a client's story can be accepted as factual. Before welfare aid can be given, the caseworker needs to make a decision regarding the 'eligibility' of the client, i.e. in order to justify the decision *vis-à-vis* the official requirements of the welfare programme applied for. Here documentary evidence is crucial, the case record being of particular importance for 'assembling' the world of the client.

In accounting for a client's case, however, the intake worker adopts procedures which both make for, and rely upon, a sense of social structure. The issue is not so much the reliability of these procedures, nor the factual nature of the accounts, but rather the ways in which both *provide* for their 'reliability' and 'factual nature'. The intake worker attempts to assemble the client's case through *post hoc* reconstruction. To this end an 'investigative stance' – an attitude and practice of thorough-going scepticism – is adopted in order to evaluate features which are deemed investigatable (i.e. issues that can be settled by reference to the documentary 'evidence'). Within the interview the caseworker invokes stereotypes of actors and situations in order both to question and assess the truthfulness of the client's account.

In dealing with applicants, caseworkers rely on an assumption of bureaucratic integrity in order to 'bring off' non-problematic situations. They seek to establish the status of official documents as 'plain facts', certain social activities being constituted simply by the process of record keeping. These documented sets of information are treated as reliable and immutable. For the caseworker, the world becomes non-problematic as the case records reflect this presupposition of objectivity. The 'plain facts' position offers no grounds for questioning either the everyday reliability of official documents, or the ordered structure of the world; which in fact they both portray and rely upon. As Zimmerman comments:

> The taken-for-granted use of documents . . . is largely dependent on an ordered world – the ordered world of organizations, and the ordered world of society at large. When simply for taken-for-granted, the features of these ordered domains are matters of mere recognition for which no accounts are called for or given.
>
> (Zimmerman 1971: 350)

Although the majority of ethnomethodological studies of organization are North American (especially Californian) in origin, the tradition of examining accounting practices in public bureaucracies has been continued in Britain, most notably in the work of Silverman and Jones (1973, 1976). Their research succeeds in combining both linguistic and situational forms of analysis.

Silverman and Jones

Silverman and Jones focus on the process of staff selection within a large organization, and especially how power relations are reflected in the forms of language used. Their main concern is how interviews are built around verbal/non verbal exchanges, and in this case how candidates (final year undergraduates applying for junior administrative posts) are assessed by typifications (e.g. 'abrasive', 'acceptable') which 'make intelligible the reasons for known outcomes'. In this study, candidates were found to succeed or fail according to their 'displays of acceptability', the process only becoming problematic when selection outcomes were unknown; i.e. when situations arose in which forms of behaviour to be considered 'acceptable', or the parameters of 'abrasiveness', were ill-defined. The interview came to represent an accounting process driven by the need to make 'authoritative reports' which were themselves capable of being made accountable to others. As a basis for explanation, Silverman and Jones argue:

> an account of any reality derives its rationality *not* from its direct correspondence with some objective world, but from the ability of its hearers (readers) to make sense of that account in the context of the socially organized occasions of its use (and thereby *to treat it* as corresponding to an objective world).
>
> (Silverman and Jones 1973: 63–4)

Thus, from the interview materials:

> we came to the conclusion that 'acceptability' [and 'abrasive-

> ness'] did not picture in a set of possible actions, such that we could predict how any given action would be defined. [Rather their role was in] explaining (but not producing) courses of action. Like 'reasons' in general, they provide a rhetoric through which outcomes are made accountable.
>
> (Silverman and Jones 1976: 60)

These studies by Zimmerman, and Silverman and Jones typify the form of research carried out by ethnomethodologists in formal work organizations. The emphasis is upon treating practical activities as topics for investigation; everyday, common-place events are given the status usually accorded to extraordinary events; and we discover how actors in work settings 'make sense' of their circumstances, and especially how they make their actions (and their outcomes) 'accountable' as rational, common-sensical, and 'in-accord-with-a-rule'. As such, these studies offer an approach to organizational analysis which is far removed from the structured nomethetic accounts typical of 'mainstream' organizational research. Rather than seek to generalize causal relations, they highlight particular activities, and explain how they are created and sustained through the inter-subjective definitions of competent actors. They unravel the complex negotiations which characterize everyday life, and the knowledge and assumptions that underpin the reproduction of 'normal' routine behaviours. Instead of viewing organization as a structure of explicit and accepted prescriptions, they make us aware of conflicting role orientations. They emphasize the creative nature of organization.

Conclusion

This chapter has attempted to give an introduction to ethnomethodology, and to illustrate the type of research conducted by ethnomethodologists in formal organizations. It has reviewed the basic theoretical principles upon which the ethnomethodological approach to organization is built, and has illustrated how these principles are 'operationalized' in empirical studies of bureaucracy. In brief, the chapter has attempted to provide a basic guide for those wishing to consider ethnomethodology as a technique and paradigm for organizational research.

In conclusion, we can say that ethnomethodology is without doubt one of the most original developments to emerge out of the so-called 'crisis' phase in Western sociology (see Friedrichs 1970; Gouldner 1971; Benson 1983). The main reason for this is because it focuses on a set of questions that have been inadequately addressed by traditional sociology, especially those concerning how structured social relations find their way into everyday activity, and how individuals act out their lives 'contextually' according to specific rules of social conduct. Indeed, many ethnomethodologists go as far as to suggest that their concerns are separate from those of academic sociology; for them ethnomethodology is not so much a development *in* sociological analysis, as an alternative to it.

This notion of separate identity has been reinforced by writers who (after Kuhn 1970) suggest that ethnomethodology represents an 'alternative paradigm' to traditional sociological analysis. Notable here are the theses of Bottomore (1975) and Burrell and Morgan (1979), both of which cite ethnomethodology as an interpretive alternative to the functionalist orthodoxy. Ethnomethodology is seen to differ from 'objectivist' approaches in that it refuses to allow for the existence of organizations in any hard and concrete sense. Whilst accepting the *concept* of organization, and especially its use as an accounting practice for making sense of the world, it does not allow for the existence of organizations *per se*; structural absolutism is firmly rejected. Indeed, for the ethnomethodologist, mainstream organization theory is built upon extremely problematic foundations. Organizations are not definite, concrete phenomena, and the organizational world is not a tangible, static facticity. On the contrary, the organizational world is processual; it is based upon the 'intentional' acts of creative participants. Consequently, as the ontology of organization theory is problematic, so too are the concepts upon which the discipline trades (e.g. job satisfaction, organization structure, organization climate); they are merely reificiations. In Bittner's terms, they are treated as technical 'resources' rather than as 'topics' for analysis.

In sum, ethnomethodology offers a unique approach for conducting organizational research. It yields subjectivist, ideographic descriptions of everyday situations through moving closer to the subject matter. Researchers attempt to assess interaction from the perspective of the participant actor rather than the detached (social) scientist. The emphasis is on unfolding social processes rather than on defining social structures. Organizations are considered to have no material existence of their own. Instead they are abstract social constructions whose identities can only be accessed through reference to the 'locations of their production'. Meanings are conferred upon social activities by 'competent' actors – actors who interpret events according to the social context in which they occur. Organizations are sanctioned, and made accountable, only through the interplay of biography, situation, and linguistic exchange.

Chapter seven

Modernism, postmodernism and organization

Michael Power

Introduction

When discussing a concept such as 'modernity', critical attention necessarily focuses upon the boundary or limit of its applicability. One is thereby forced to confront the threshold of other periodizations. Wellmer has drawn attention to the deeply elusive character of the 'pre' and 'post' concept-types which are usually employed to negotiate these limits (Wellmer 1985). He claims that they occupy a marginal location which is hostile to definition. Furthermore, any clarificatory process can be rooted only in contemporary forms of understanding. In the particular case of modernism and postmodernism, the interpretive project is itself bounded by a 'horizon' (Gadamer 1975) that it is attempting to comprehend. It is not merely that we are 'too close' to events to see them as they really are but that there is in principle no privileged standpoint which could give us epistemological security about where we draw the lines that demarcate epochs.

In this paper I wish to speculate, in the hermeneutically tentative fashion outlined above, on the possible meaning of postmodernism for the concept of organization. One of the difficulties confronting such a proposal is to draw from a range of literature which is both abstract and heavily inclined towards aesthetics in a way that is interesting to organization theorists. To address this problem I have opted to concentrate specifically upon the work of two thinkers, Jean Francis Lyotard (1984) and Jurgen Habermas (1972 and 1979). It is not possible using this approach to capture the nuances of postmodernism comprehensively, but it may at least provide a basis for future discussions.

In brief, I wish to sustain a dialectic between Lyotard's postmodernist vision and Habermas's defence of a principle of modernity. The contrast is particularly interesting because the two share much common ground – including a critique of systems theory as they understand it. Elaborating the differences that distinguish them may therefore provide an incisive cutting edge for the issues at stake. In the second part of this paper I provide a general outline of the postmodernist mood in order to set the stage for the specific focus of the third and fourth, where I deal with Habermas and Lyotard directly. The fifth part, the centre of gravity for the discussion, attempts to explicate the meaning of the modernist/postmodernist dialectic for the concept of organization and possible research strategies relating to it. It expresses my views concerning the limitations of the postmodernist motif of 'deconstruction'.

Postmodernism: general themes

In its most stark and general sense, postmodernism stands for the 'death of Reason'. More accurately (and less melodramatically) it is the rejection of a particular model of reason and the various ontological commitments perceived to lie at the heart of it. Such a rejection or 'deconstruction' extends to a number of philosophical sacred cows – the 'unities' of representation, of meaning, of theory and ultimately of the self. Postmodernism is an assault on unity.

Since there is no clear line available to demarcate the modern from the postmodern, the latter comes to express both an 'end' of the former and a radical continuation of it. This inherent ambiguity must be recognized in order to avoid the temptation to make easy categorizations. For example 'modernist' impulses in the visual arts have challenged the concept of autonomous representation. Postmodernism seems to be more radical still, as a continuation of this avant-garde aesthetic without a nostalgia for direct contact with a 'real world'. For example, the postmodernist aesthetic of the sublime is precisely such a conscious withdrawal from traditional concepts of artistic reality. It seeks to make visible the fact that there is something which may be thought but cannot in principle itself become visible or represented. In short, postmodernism rejects the concept of reference as a univocal relation between forms of representation such as words/images and an external world.

Wellmer argues that one must understand postmodernism as a developing modernism (Wellmer 1985). Firstly it is with the work of Freud that the unity and autonomy of the subject are systematically undermined, bringing into view the 'other' within. Yet Freud stops short of a critique of instrumental reason. This is taken up by the theorists of the Frankfurt School who sustain an attack on the whole notion of reason as inherently orientated towards the maintenance of 'order' and control. They offer the haunting image of the 'Dialectic of the Enlightenment' (see Adorno and Korkheimer 1972) as a form of rationality that ultimately recoils upon itself in the pursuit of order and gives rise to disorder. Modernity in this sense is broadly identified with the enlightenment tradition rather than with the late nineteenth and early twentieth century movements in art. Beyond the radicalization of the modern offered by the Frankfurt School lies the critique of meaning and of the subject as the source of that meaning. The postmodernist dynamic makes a further shift to a level of analysis which concentrates upon the rules grounded in practices which precede subjectivity. This is essentially the structuralist attack upon the philosophy of consciousness. According to Wellmer it has the effect of relativizing previous critiques in such a way as to retrieve a 'space' for the subject. However, this space is to be understood in the postmodern sense of action as 'play' and not that overburdened enlightenment notion of free agency.

Viewed in this way postmodernism expresses a project of distantiation from various assumptions of unity implicit in the enlightenment concept of reason. It is a process subject to considerable tensions. For example, within modernist aesthetics there is a theme of 'reconciliation', a hope for the recovery of a relationship with nature. Yet postmodernism simultaneously gives rise to increasing liberation from the natural world and to the splintering of culture into discrete spheres such as science. The energies are released which demand reunification and yet also imply its impossibility. Habermas and Lyotard respond to this tension in different ways, as we shall see.

Habermas: in defence of modernity

Jurgen Habermas is a second generation member of the Frankfurt School mentioned above. In broad terms its members sought to adapt the co-ordinates of Marxism to address the predicament of twentieth century western culture (see Jay 1973; Connerton 1980; Held 1976). The dominant objective of their approach was to confront the increasing power of instrumental reason in organizing social life – 'rationalization' in Weber's sense. The critical task that Habermas inherits is to decode the repressive dimensions of this phenomenon and to realize the emancipation of social agents. The daunting prospect facing a theoretical endeavour of this kind is that the socialization of individuals may be so advanced that there is no perceivable demand by them for the emancipation in question. Where suffering and frustration are not empirically manifest how can 'critique' gain any leverage and purport to speak *for* agents rather than to them (see Geuss 1981)? The general point is reflected at the level of organizations in which participating individuals perceive themselves as functional entities. Their goal is to achieve increased status, remuneration, or (usually) both – motivations which mirror and thereby validate a functionalist approach to the organization as a whole. Critical theory understands itself as an intervention in this self-reinforcing relationship. Habermas's critique of systems-theoretical approaches to the knowledge of social organization is just such an intervention.

For example, in his attack on Luhmann, Habermas questions the analogy between social organizations and biological organisms which inspires that version of the functionalist programme (Habermas 1973). He argues that it is limited in at least three ways:

1 It is not possible to give a non-arbitrary account of the boundaries of social systems.
2 It is not possible to identify a unitary state in which the system sustains itself.
3 It is not possible to identify the 'functional requirements' where there is a plurality of functional processes.

Following Habermas' initiative, it is indeed questionable whether the biological notion of 'survival' as the key system-environment relation can legitimately be projected on to the sociocultural level. To a large extent, modern social organization itself constitutes the environment within which the problem of survival arises, and this process has its basis in history. Luhmann describes the problem for social systems as being that of reducing 'world-complexity'. According to Habermas this in fact boils down to the need to reduce *self*-complexity. The world in question is not external in a simple sense.

Habermas argues that Luhmann's theory projects an over-harmonious integration of motivational forces (at the level of individuals) into the systematic values of the organization. To some extent this vision of harmony is justified since agents take the cynical and pragmatic view of their own possibilities outlined above. However, Habermas maintains that this still represents a scene of crisis or conflict which must be decoded.

Accordingly, Habermas sets out to reconstruct an acceptable systems theory, enhanced by historical reflection. It is this emphasis on 'reconstruction' rather than on deconstruction that marks Habermas out as a modernist. He offers a 'rational reconstruction' of the developmental forces in social organization which depends centrally upon a distinction between the concepts of system and lifeworld. The former bears a family resemblance to Marx's idea of the forces of production. It embraces the material, technological features of social organization and the form of instrumental rationality that constitutes them. In contrast, the lifeworld is that taken-for-granted world which we share as beings who communicate and have values. Habermas's thesis is that social development has eroded the influence of the lifeworld and of the communicative interaction it maintains to guide social evolution.

Systematic values which are narrowly instrumental have 'colonized' the lifeworld. This threatens social reproduction as a whole because it creates a deficit between the level of technological learning and the capacity of the society to organize this knowledge through communication. According to Habermas, this communicative basis of the lifeworld has a rational foundation which has been undermined by functional imperatives of system maintenance. As such, communicative structures essential to dealing with expanding system requirements are prevented from emerging. The imbalance issues in which Habermas calls 'motivations' and 'legitimations' crises. He points to a form of protest in western society today which is class non-specific and defensive as evidence for this. Such protest is more than a self-interested concern for economic welfare.

It is important to note that Habermas's analysis depends centrally upon his theory of communication. The guiding idea is that consensually regulated conflict is the highest developmental phase of societal learning. Extending paradigms offered by Paiget and Chomsky from the level of individual development on to that of macro societal change, Habermas's 'reconstruction' of social transformation expresses a logic of development towards communicative rationality. Forrester has alerted organization theorists to the details of Habermas's notion of communicative rationality in which the idea of interaction is fundamental (Forrester 1983). Strategic actions are always embedded in a framework which has been pre-formed communicatively, and are therefore a derivative action-type.

In the pragmatics of language use, communication thematizes one of four 'validity claims' concerning: the truth of statements, the rightness of norms, the sincerity of engagement, the comprehendability of what is said. Ordinarily these claims are taken for granted and remain unquestioned. As Forrester notes, when a waiter offers me coffee the setting and the speech act is such that I do not question the fact that there is coffee, that the waiter is sincere and so on. Habermas argues that such implied claims may be taken to task and queried in discourse and that this possibility is inherent in language use. Furthermore, it anticipates a resolution of questions/conflict even if in practice this is not feasible. That is to say, it projects an ideal situation of speech free from coercive influence and in which the 'force of the better argument' prevails. For Habermas this ideal is necessarily anticipated in communication and embodies a normative ideal – the recognition of the autonomy of the 'other' as a possible partner in discourse. Though such an ideal may be unrealizable in fact, it nevertheless has regulative force within language.

Habermas's critics believe that many of these claims are defective. Is consensus really a legitimate ideal for all aspects of life? How can it apply to the sphere of personal relationships? Does not the concept of discourse merely reflect an elevation of the cognitive capabilities of individuals – the 'gangstery of intellectuals' as one commentator has called it? However, important as these objections are, Habermas's position is in danger of being misunderstood. He is not idealizing the 'noise-free' and 'fully transparent' society as Lyotard seems to imagine. He recognizes that communication in practice will be subject to many kinds of contextual influence. He is enough of a hermeneutic thinker not to envisage an escape from this. His concern is to provide a theoretical focus for a range of influences regarded as somehow 'systematically distorting', i.e. where the context is one in which the interests of participants are systematically excluded behind their backs.

Forrester alludes to a type of communicative distortion due to personal idiosyncracy such as stubbornness. Influences of this type are always in play and are to be distinguished from the ideological rationalizations of a power structure in which certain kinds of interest never gain access to discourse. Distortions of this type represent the elements of modernity which are (temporarily) at odds with themselves. For Habermas, their realignment is anticipated in the structure of communication itself.

It should be noted in conclusion that Habermas's defence of modernity does not regard technological reasons as such as pathological. In this he distances his position from the strains of Heideggerian Marxism which can be seen in the work of his colleague Marcuse and, to some extent, Lyotard. His task is to reconstruct the elements of a communicative rationality in public life – a task which is simultaneously the continuation and transformation of the optimistic philosophy of the Enlightenment.

Lyotard: the postmodern condition

Lyotard analyses knowledge and makes a distinction between the 'narrative' and the 'scientific' type. The former embraces the legitimizing function that myths and stories have played in traditional communities. The latter represents a break with this such that it abandons metaphysical authority in favour of that of the 'facts'. According to Lyotard this break constitutes a problem in so far as 'scientific knowledge cannot know and make known that it is the true knowledge without resorting to that other, narrative, kind of knowledge, which from its point of view is no knowledge' (Lyotard 1984: 29).

The Hegelian system is the classical instance of the self-knowledge of knowledge. This 'grand narrative', as Lyotard calls it, locates each 'positive' form of knowledge within the development of the life of the spirit. To be located and subsumed within the global process of development is to be legitimated.

According to Lyotard the contemporary problem arises due to a loss of intellectual confidence in the unifying outlook of the Hegelian philosophy. Knowledge and culture have fragmented into a plurality of 'language games' such that science can no longer relate to 'praxis' by virtue of an immanent relation to it within speculative philosophy. The grand narrative of legitimation has dissolved and the self-reflection of knowledge upon its status quo knowledge is now a local rather than a universal affair. Unlike Habermas, Lyotard celebrates this state of affairs without the nostalgic residues of a need for unity.

Lyotard claims that the decline of the enlightenment concept of reason is due less to a simple and balanced splintering of knowledge than to the growing hegemony of one particular form. Like Habermas, he is troubled by the domination of technical reason – 'performativity', as he puts it. The ideal of efficiency and optimal performance which underpins the logic of instrumental reason emerges as an increasingly sophisticated aid to the physiological system. The end of 'survival' refined into a notion of performance guides knowledge rather than a quest for truth and justice.

Lyotard argues that performativity in this epistemological sense extends beyond technical pragmatics and is reciprocally related to wealth and the control of funding for research. Argumentation and theoretical discourse are therefore subsumed within a power structure. Lyotard adds that this is not merely coercive but is able to legitimize itself because it controls what is to count as reality within the processes of verification. This control is one of the systematic barriers to discourse that concerns Habermas. The legitimation is false because it conceals the historical forces that inform the ontological assumption of society as an ordered system subject potentially to cybernetic control. A historical particularity is passed off as a quasi-natural myth.

Lyotard's intention is to mount a critique of the notion of performativity – epitomized for him by the image of the computerized society. At this level there are strong similarities to Habermas's project. Lyotard begins by explicating the implications of performativity for the educational process. In brief, he claims that a self-sustaining system must cultivate performance-satisfying skills among its members. Learning is increasingly reduced to the technical transmission of a stock of knowledge. Teaching can in principal be automated. Agents are drawn into the process by a perceived need to cultivate these 'professional' competencies. Represented here is that process of total socialization that haunted the Frankfurt School of which one of the obvious casualties is the narrative of emancipation. Lyotard rejects any purported reconstruction of the latter, preferring to focus upon tensions internal to the performativity ideal. This style of critique by immanent negation resembles the method of Adorno rather than that of Habermas.

According to Lyotard experimentation by its very nature is not rule-governed. Though lacking in short-term operational value it represents a long term investment with the aim of enhancing future performativity. This tension in the evaluation of experimental freedom has been controlled by isolating the frameworks within which imaginative research may flourish and by monitoring their feedback into the system as a whole. It is in these pockets of research that Lyotard's model of a postmodern methodology takes shape.

Echoing Kuhn's (1970) notion of abnormal discourse and Feyerabend's (1975) idea of methodological anarchy, Lyotard views scientific method as the search for instabilities. New and unpredictable moves are essential for scientific progress and yet are antithetical to the ideal of performativity committed as it is to the environment of a stable system in which inputs and outputs can be controlled. Lyotard seems to argue that new developments in science itself show that the epistemology of systems theory is false. Firstly he interprets quantum mechanics as implying that perfect control over a system is an internally inconsistent idea since increased levels of energy required to achieve perfect knowledge are ultimately disfunctional. He argues that this indeterminacy at the level of microphysics can be generalized to cover the model of bureaucracy. Furthermore, catastrophe theory articulates the possibility that two discrete control variables which have predictable individual reactions to environmental change may jointly lead to unpredictable behaviour. Systems theory therefore has no scientific basis, 'science itself does not function according to this theory's paradigm of the system, and contemporary science excludes the possibility of using such a paradigm to describe society' (Lyotard 1984: 61).

Yet if performativity has no basis in science, it nevertheless possesses a *de facto* pre-eminence in social organization. Lyotard's postmodern conception of scientific method is offered as a negation of it. In particular the notion of 'paralogy' as the creation of new moves and the interruption of consensus is introduced to offset systems theoretical ideas of smooth administration. Thus, for Lyotard, science is the model of an open system which resists and cannot be assimilated to performative unity.

At the end of his essay Lyotard expresses the central issues:

> What is the relation between the antimodel of the pragmatics of science and society? Is it applicable to the vast clouds of language material constituting a society? Or is it limited to a game of learning? And if so what role does it play with respect to the social bond? Is it an impossible ideal of an open community? Is it an essential component for the subset of decision makers, who force on society the performance criterion they reject themselves? Or

> conversely, is it a move in the direction of counterculture with the attendant risk that all possibility for exact research will be foreclosed due to lack of funding?
>
> (Lyotard 1984: 64)

His rhetorical purpose is to distance his position from that of Habermas whose search for universal consensus he regards as ironing out the complexities of the social collectivity. For Lyotard, legitimation is local and consists in permitting the generation of new ideas both at the level of scientific method itself and for social practice. Both these levels are inexhaustible and a politics based on paralogy in Lyotard's sense 'would respect both the desire for justice and the desire for the unknown' (Lyotard 1984: 67).

The concept of organization: consensus and dissensus

How can we meaningfully adjudicate between Habermas and Lyotard in a fashion that has consequences for the concept of organization? In an important sense, both thinkers alert organization theorists to alternatives to the hitherto dominant functionalist approaches. For Habermas the focus is upon the primordiality of the communicative dimension of social organization and the deep commitment to consensual regulation of conflict. This position projects a distinct value orientation concerning the nature of the individual and his/her autonomy. It implies a concept of social organization in the modernist tradition, i.e. it preserves a belief in the enlightenment model of the rational agent. A research approach based upon Habermas's work would reflect these values and this 'critical' stance. It would seek to identify and build upon discursive processes within organizations (see Forrester 1983).

With Lyotard our approach centres upon the indeterminacy of organizational systematic unity. Methodologically, this directs us towards boundaries or 'surfaces' or organizations as scenes of potential instability. The organization is permeable rather than closed. The communicative processes within are localized and have no underlying rational basis. What is crucial is to set up the 'free play' of discursive processes both as a researcher and within the domain of organizational action. For Lyotard the mediation of discourse is a chance affair, whose emancipatory potential consists in conflict, surprise and unpredictability.

These, then, are the broadest implications of the two positions for the study of organizations. The time has come to offer some critical remarks on the differences between them. Both Habermas and Lyotard are dialectical in Benson's (1983) sense since for both social organization is a process, a scene of continuous constitution through the action of individuals. This reproductive process has developed beyond the control of individuals and the ensuing analytical task is to offer some intervention against the sedimentation of certain types of social praxis. But the nature of the intervention for both is different, and hence the nature of their dialectical commitment.

Rorty sets out the contrast as follows: Habermas rebuilds the 'narrative of emancipation' from sources within his two heroes – Marx and Freud. According to Habermas we are committed in a deep sense to being able to distinguish the rational from the non-rational. In this way philosophy and social theory after Hegel remain stubbornly the guardians of reason. Against this, Lyotard respects a suspicion of suspicion, that is, a deeper scepticism about any claim to preserve a 'grand meta-narrative of freedom'. Habermas in turn worries that this position betrays social hope by lapsing into mere context dependency. He is not content to allow localized narratives to 'do their stuff' (Rorty 1985).

While Habermas's more universalistic tendencies have been attacked even by sympathetic critics (Geuss, McCarthy, etc.), Rorty defends his arguments against the 'dryness' of the likes of Lyotard and Foucault. In an illuminating passage he suggests that:

> it is as if thinkers like Foucault and Lyotard were so afraid of being caught in one more metanarrative about the fortunes of the subject that they cannot bring themselves to say 'we' long enough to identify with the generation to which they belong.
>
> (Rorty 1985: 41)

Splitting the differences between Lyotard and Habermas in this way leaves us with Rorty's own Deweyian approach: we need less 'dryness' but no more meta-narratives. However, Rorty also believes that Habermas and Lyotard share a common error. In short, they both take the Kant-Hegel philosophical tradition too seriously. For Habermas the 'end of philosophy' slogans simply over-react to the previous domination of the philosophy of the absolute. For Lyotard modern Hegelian philosophy was an important failure; for Rorty (and, presumably, non-philosophers) it was an unimportant excursus. Rorty's concern to reconstruct the self-image of professional philosophy has a general relevance for intellectual life:

> the attempt of leftist intellectuals to pretend that the avant-garde is serving the wretched of the earth by fighting free of the merely beautiful is a hopeless attempt to make the special needs of the intellectual and the social needs of his community coincide.
>
> (Rorty 1985: 43)

This is a charge that may justly be levelled against Lyotard. It is ultimately hard to distinguish his avant-garde from what might be called a 'high modernism' – the tradition of the negative/revolutionary vocation of art defended by Adorno and others. Lyotard gives no idea of what a postmodernist culture could be like aside from an image of a dynamic with some vague political intent. What he does is to transfer this modernist aesthetic to the methodology of science and technology. The latter's capacity for renewal and change is the new location for the avant-garde. However, he himself raises the spectre of the monopoly of information against which this postmodern methodology as a commitment to 'anything goes' must measure itself. The entrenched nature of this ideology of performativity requires an analysis at the level of political *action* which Lyotard does not provide.

Habermas has a much more developed sense of the political stakes in breaking down the intellectual hold of systems theory. Hence he regards Lyotard as neoconservative. Habermas (1985) also doubts the ability of intellectuals to invent problems as Rorty seems to suggest. The concept of alienation upon which much of his own work is based articulates the general idea of modernity at odds with itself. It is not merely an intellectual mood such as Lyotard's postmodernism which seems to extend to intellectual life alone – the 'free play' of a community which is itself already free. This may be appropriate in aesthetics where postmodernist imagery has its strongest hold, but it will be too blunt an instrument to orientate research into organization, for a number of reasons. Lyotard's dialectic has the effect of creating a methodological montage – superficial in the sense of avoiding an analysis of the structures that hold together, even locally, social action. In contrast Habermas offers a 'phenomenological structuralism' (Forrester 1983). His analysis is concerned to situate the everyday understanding of social agents in relation to the historical structuring of the context in which those experiences come about. He also engages in reconstructing certain key elements of this process with critical intent.

One important characteristic which Habermas and Lyotard share and which may hinder their reception by organization theorists is the tendency to conflate a number of levels of analysis. This in turn makes it harder still to evaluate the nature of the conflict between them. *Prima facie* it is possible to distinguish at least three levels of research as follows:

(a) Substantive socio-historical analysis

At this level the difference between Habermas and Lyotard, modernism and postmodernism, concerns the identification of those structures that each regard as fundamental to social and organizational development.

(b) Normative analysis

While this is intimately related to (a) above, it can be considered in isolation as addressing the question, 'On the basis of what ideals should the transformation of society take place?' Clearly for Habermas the answer is in terms of a liberal-enlightenment/democratic conception of the public sphere as the source of legitimate consensus. In contrast, Lyotard's postmodernism appears to be driven by some form of sceptical anarchism – a more radical liberalism than that of Habermas.

The difference between these value orientations emerges if we consider the suggestion by Clegg and Dunkerley that the 'introduction of demographic principles to organizations may have the dangerous potential of articulating nonindividualistic sentiments' (Clegg and Dunkerley 1980: 517). Habermas's democratic value orientation is subject to internal tensions since the generalizability of the interests of a workforce may be likely to cut across the private, organization-relative interests of profit maximization. Lyotard's amorphous position does not generate these tensions.

(c) Epistemological analysis

Habermas's discursive theory of knowledge and science contrasts with Lyotard's vision of paralogy or anti-method. Both thinkers have a view of what 'science really is' and both are opposed to scient*ism* in its positivistic forms. However, to the extent that both believe that this level of analysis is important in understanding (a) above then they may be guilty of a scientism of their own. Perhaps science as such is not as important an element of cultural change as they imagine. Consequently, the need to draw analogies between science and other aspects of culture is simply one way of looking at society. Clearly the epistemological level of both thinkers is informed by a view of the role of technology as social transformation and as the mediating force between science and society. Unfortunately this role is probably not as well developed as organization theorists would like.

This tripartite distinction does not make it entirely clear how level (a) and level (c) interrelate. The latter is closest to the recognizable concerns of organizational theorists and, in the absence of detailed claims for the significance of technology in determining organizational structure, the epistemological analysis may be of only passing interest.

However, there are strong parallels between the history of epistemology in the philosophical tradition and the more recent social theoretical idea of system. Underlying both is the classical privileging of order over disorder. Such an emphasis on order generates boundary maintenance as a system problem and Robert Cooper (this volume) argues that the *active* nature of boundary maintenance is systematically understated in standard theoretical idioms. Organization, in its most general sense, is the appropriation of order from disorder and the exercise of *power* to overcome the 'essential undecidability' of organizational reality. Yet this continual process is disguised behind a myth of natural order. Cooper draws upon the work of Saussure, Derrida and Bateson as thinkers who view organizational structures as differential and nonstatic. His approach radicalizes the concept of organizational boundary in a way that is highly receptive to Lyotard's central concerns. If the stability and identity of organization rests on the suppression of the 'movement of difference' at the boundary then Lyotard's notion of paralogy is precisely a move to release it and to realize a free play in its place. If classicism is the 'ideology of form', postmodernism is the celebration of formless and undecidable content. It is this normative position more than anything that separates Lyotard from Habermas.

It follows that the 'postmodernist' organization theorist would regard 'boundary maintenance' as the central analytical paradigm. This in turn could have a direct effect upon substantive research. Where for example do organizations end in physical, legal, psychological terms? Who negotiates these limits and how is it achieved? At what point does an organization respond to its non-organizational environment? The problem with these suggestions is that existing organization theorists may say: 'well, we have actually been interested in these issues for some time so calling us 'postmodernists' tells us nothing new'. This is largely true but the contrast between Habermas and Lyotard may bring to view the particular values orientating substantive research, and that in turn may provoke a reappraisal of earlier work.

The 'modernist' organization theorist takes his bearings from the deep-lying modes of consensus which form the basis of organizational coherence. On such a view the role of organization theory is to attend to these structures or 'sedimented selection rules' (Clegg and Dunkerley 1980: 501). This 'depth-hermeneutic', to borrow a phrase from Habermas, identifies the processes by which the relatively impermeable character of organization is sustained. One could say that the modernist is concerned with the formal/universalistic properties of organization.

In contrast, the postmodernist perspective flows from a denial that there is any single, ultimate or deep language game that is uniquely determinative of organizational stability. The organization theorist must be sensitive to the diversity and fluidity of the 'life' of organization and no one model will suffice to orientate research.

This juxtaposition seems to imply that postmodernism is the more empirically sensitive outlook. However, such a method of contrasting it with modernism is misleading since both have their empirical research analogues. The contrast really issues from the level of epistemological analysis unpacked in systems theoretical terms.

Table 7.1 Modernism, postmodernism, and functionalism

	Epistemology	*Social organization*
Habermas (Modernism)	a) Differential logical structure: – technical interest – practical interest – emancipatory interest (Habermas 1972) b) The theory of communication – dialogue as the underlying principle of all method (Habermas 1979)	Social organization as determined by structures of communicative interaction – having a rational basis in principle anticipated in ideal speech
Lyotard (Postmodernism)	Paralogy – the search for instabilities methodological 'Anarchy' – Kuhn (1970) – Feyerabend (1975)	Social organization as an irreducible plurality of language games – generating the problem of boundary maintenance
Functionalism (The plight of modernity)	Instrumental reason orientated towards technical control – Luhmann (1973)	Organization as a closed system Components as functional variables – cybernetic model of social system

Table 7.1 sets out the basic contours of the contrast between modernism, postmodernism, and (with some danger of caricature) functionalism. However, it also gives the impression that a coexistence of viewpoints is possible. For example, Habermas and Lyotard could be said to differ only in emphasis and therefore organization theory is not committed to taking sides.

However, there is a deep source of conflict which, in conclusion, needs to be stated. It concerns the language of 'deconstruction' that Lyotard shares with Derrida and Rorty among others. Deconstructing the false self-understanding of the classical idea of order is one thing. Any particular structuring is not a natural fact but a choice in particular circumstances which may reflect the position of a particular group. It is quite another and more problematic stand to argue from the artificiality of order/structure/boundary to the illegitimacy of any such differentiation. For example, difference in Derrida's sense is a necessary condition of language. Some 'order' or other is necessary, though no particular one may be. The concept of free play as a methodology that rejects a traditional authoritative centre does not fully come to terms with this issue. As a piece of imagery representing the spirit of postmodernism it has a certain refreshing and antidotal legitimacy. Yet it does not, in a way that Habermas does, come to terms with the insight that some deep agreement and structure is necessary to mediate social action and hence all organization. The reduction of Lyotard's vision would be to outlaw all talk of organization in any sense. Perhaps Lyotard would not shrink from this, but one is left feeling that he has taken Kuhn, Feyerabend and recent developments in microphysics far too seriously. The result is not to take seriously enough the substantive terrorism that may intervene to prevent the Bohemian joys of paralogy. At worst one is left with a wholly satirical image of the deconstructionist method, 'The owl of Minerva robbed by later scepticism of Hegel's flight path to the transcendental standpoint notoriously finds itself flying in ever decreasing circles'(Williams 1983: 26).

Conclusion

It is not entirely clear what a distinctively 'postmodernist' concept of organization might look like or what a substantive research programme inspired by Lyotard's methodology might yield. While there is much to question in Habermas's approach he offers a more structured analysis which, even if (despite universalistic intention) only locally valid, is richer in 'critical' content than Lyotard's hopes for paralogy. Postmodernism in this style warns against a particular form of methodological false consciousness and provides a focus upon the concept of boundary as the possible scene of creative instability. But such an anarchistic epistemology fails to provide an account of the relative entrenchment of the organization of consensus and the control of dissent. The method of paralogy as an intervention in the domination of performativity thereby overestimates its own critical power.

The distinction between epistemological and socio-historical commitments, discussed above and reflected in Table 1, is not absolute – the two are reciprocally related – but it helps to locate two relatively distinct levels of analysis. Systems-based theories are both the hegemony of instrumental reason at the level of research (methodology) and an image of administrative control at the level of social organization (ontology). For both Habermas and Lyotard such theories are in some sense false. Habermas looks to richer models of rationality and action to state his case. Lyotard takes up the more radical elements of post-empiricism to make the point that science and social pragmatics are inexhaustibly creative and ruleless.

It was said above that the postmodern condition radicalizes elements of modernity. With Lyotard this subversive potential has its roots in an aesthetic with an uneasy relation to social praxis. The possibility that it may 'fly in ever decreasing circles' is one to which research must be sensitive. I began this chapter by reflecting upon the situation of the interpreter in confronting the dialectic of the modern and the postmodern. We are caught up in the processes we are trying to understand and the use of Habermas and Lyotard illustrates an intellectual dynamic but by no means exhausts possibilities which are always open. Organization theory can draw upon the Habermas/Lyotard debate to redescribe and reclassify current and past research. In true hermeneutic fashion such a taxonomical exercise is also determinative of future ideas. Accordingly the organization theorist is in the ambiguous position of Thomas Mann's hero Tonio Kroger who stands 'between his tradition and his emancipated consciousness, between a world without knowledge and a knowledge without world' (Heller 1958: 77).

Chapter eight

The diabolization of death: some thoughts on the obsolescence of mortality in organization theory and practice

Burkard Sievers

Introduction

During the last few years, the relationships between work, life, and death have become central to my thinking and writing. This obviously has to do with the fact that I am no longer a young man. I have, as C. G. Jung once put it, reached the noon of my life and am beginning now to face its afternoon. Particularly for men, this is a point in time which provides opportunity to contemplate the realities of one's inner and outer world (cf. Jaques 1970). Metaphorically the question is: 'now that I have raised a son, planted a tree and built a house what do I expect from the remainder of life?'

For those contemporaries facing such a phase of their lives the attempt to stay alive may be connected with the painful experience of depression – the result of a loss of previous ideals and visions as well as an increasing confrontation with meaninglessness. As one reaches the zenith of one's life one is confronted with the choice of either doing more of the same thing or starting something different which appears more challenging, fascinating and sometimes even frightening. This is especially so for someone familiar with the search for meaning and to earning his livelihood as an academic. He may have to face the doubts associated with continuing the rest of his life with 'happy science'. Being faced with issues like these one may envy those colleagues who apparently have been naïve enough to perpetuate such a pursuit of happiness, or the few who not only seem able to face the less happy sides of social reality but who, in addition, actively enter a quite different field of work and life experiences; e.g. making musical instruments or breeding sheep.

It is the knowledge that one's own life is getting shorter that heightens the awareness that one day we have to die. In our world the acceptance of this certitude is apparently to be hidden in order to diminish is sincerity and inevitability. As far as modern organizations are concerned, the transition from one's early adulthood into the phase of one's middle adulthood (Levinson 1979) – circa the period of one's early forties – is typically addressed in a curious way. One has to confirm the expectations with which one is surrounded. Energy, competence, success, career, masculinity, and creativity are among the predominant qualities which men during this phase of their lives are supposed to radiate. The fact that in their inner world they may struggle with life in general, and with the possible meaning of their working life as well as with that of their employing institutions, in particular, has to be kept private. Although one may find colleagues in one's institution with whom one can share one's concerns, depression and annoyances, such experience normally cannot be related and transferred to the organizational work and task levels. It is as if this would question the stable state or unduly confuse the intended growth of the organization. As long as survival is written on the banners of our organizations and enterprises, there is just no space for the standard-bearer's potential death. 'The show must go on!'

What I have found increasingly unbearable is the link between the omnipotent fantasies which now characterize organizational development (OD) and the largely phoney managerialist principles upon which the field is based. In the past, although I questioned the subject of my teaching and research I was nevertheless desperately afraid to give it up. Either I didn't know how to fill the emptiness and nothingness which would have been created (Novak 1970), or I was not convinced that what I wanted instead would not frighten more – myself as well as my colleagues, students and clients. It would not be true were I to claim that all these troubles are gone now; but I have learned to trust my doubts. The more I have tried (encouraged by others, among whom Gordon Lawrence both as a friend and a mentor has had the greatest impact) to sail off from the mainstream of traditional social science approaches, and those of management and organization theory in particular, the more I have met others sharing similar concerns and pursuing similar courses.

In contrast with my experiences as a boy scout when, on occasions, I experienced my own incompetence in discovering that a chosen route was obviously not the one indicated by the map, in recent years I have more frequently found that the cognitive maps provided by traditional theories no longer associate with my own experience of working with people in organizations. The predominant images of man, his organizations and their interrelations do not coincide with what I perceive and understand. I have found that, despite their appearances, many of the signs of these cognitive maps are inventions and not discoveries. Some of these inventions appear to be mere defences against a more complex reality. Although they are proclaimed as scientific truths, the majority of them seem to mirror the taken-for-granted fictions and myths of managers and social scientists (who, as their high priests, laud them to the skies). Despite the claim of a recent publisher's advertisement that 'a management text is no place for fairy-tales' (*Academy of Management Journal*, 1986, 29: 876), I have increasingly learned to read them as such – the more so in recent times when the search for excellence has taken on the characteristics of soap opera or musical. Like the Olympic games, the management-orientated organization literature is obsessed with the virtues of 'faster, higher, wider'! To increase an enterprise's size, turnover or profit has become the ultimate surrogate for all meaning and men. Those who in earlier times saw themselves as cast in the image of God have been reduced to homunculi or puppets on a string!

The management of meaning

In our predominant constructions of reality, the members of a work enterprise are subdivided into workers and managers, the latter being interested in the provision of meaning for the former. Those with the task of producing meaning are confronted with a dilemma. Having learned to hide their own search for meaning, and the experience of depression and meaninglessness, they are likely to displace the meaning of their lives into their enterprise's success and survival. The meaning offered by the enterprise then becomes a surrogate to the extent that such meaning is no longer related to the potential experience of death as the anticipatable and final end of the individual members' lives. And the more meaningless this fabrication, the more it displaces any potential experience of, and the suffering from, meaninglessness into the underground of privacy. To question the meaning or to face the meaninglessness of an employing institution becomes an illegal act. The word enterprise more and more becomes a product and a good. According to the 'rules', and consistent with the traditional differentiation of labour, those at the top manage the production process of meaning, which is the duty of those at the bottom to accomplish, regardless of whether they believe it or not.

Unlike the meaning provided in earlier times by such institutions as the church, the state or the family, which unquestionably filled the space of our ancestors' lives, the meaning managed by our industrial enterprises has become a consumption product. The purpose of such a product is to be destroyed so that it can be replaced by the same, or a marginally improved, product. So meaning is treated accordingly. Meaning at the level of the enterprise has to be redesigned, reshaped and replaced from time to time, in order to maintain its appeal and keep its attraction alive. Meaning becomes a kind of metaproduct serving a double function: it is 'the product' through which employees are motivated to produce those products which are sold on the market; and it becomes increasingly identified with the consumer product itself – the consumers themselves participating in this consumption which is limited to the time between the buying and disposing of a product. Typically, employee and consumer are merely different roles for one and the same person – employees *are* consumers. Meaning then appears as a 'paradoxical entity'. It is produced in order to be destroyed to be reproduced and to be destroyed again. This experience represents an advance on the ancient myth of Sisyphus who, every time he had succeeded in rolling the rock to the top of the mountain, only then experienced the pointlessness of his efforts. In Western societies this construction/destruction process has become a simultaneous one. At the same time as an automobile worker is employed for example in producing new cars, he is also 'employed' to destroy his annual car which is to be replaced by the brand-new model. Whereas the ancient circle of production and consumption was related to nature, fertility and reproduction, the present one seems to rely on technology, utility and production – the original concern for life and immortality has been substituted through the mechanics and economics of growth and survival.

In his essay 'On Promethian shame', Anders stated some thirty years ago that man is no longer able to control or transcend the perfection of his products but instead identifies himself with his products, thus becoming a product himself (Anders 1987). This is true of our relationship with our institution of employment, particularly in the way we regard work as an activity provided by work enterprises (Pym 1986) – expressions of the archetype of the 'great mother'. Our larger organizations, the hugh international companies in particular, have reached such a complexity and apparent perfection that no single employee seems able to trust his own capacities for understanding them. These institutions apparently provide themselves with the meaning by which they are to be perceived and understood.

The official shared meaning of these organizations (cf. Smircich 1983) is thus reduced to a commodity on the market, for employees as well as for clients/customers. While a company's history, whether it is the story of Daimler-Benz, IG Farben, or General Foods, ought to account for contemptuous exploitation and annihilation of people, natural environment and resources – and therefore document the parallels with fascism or colonialism of its respective social system – instead it accounts only for past financial achievements and projected future success. The time and costs of people's work life can be accounted like other resources; and as such they have to compete with other goods according to their possible return on investment. The obsession with corporate image, with constructing a glowing identity for the enterprise, serves to suppress its internal chaos, ugliness, madness, and unrelatedness. Such organizational meaning conceals the actual experience of fragmentation, contempt, instrumentalization, and meaninglessness.

It is hardly surprising, then, that tendencies in our employing enterprises towards an instrumentalism and the reduction of people to consumers and goods find confirmation and legitimation in the predominant theories of management and organization.

Symbolization and diabolization

Contrary to such powerful tendencies in organizational practice and theory, there is also increasing evidence of attempts to question and overcome the enduring drift towards meaningless megalomania and the irresponsible destruction of natural and human resources. Now that mankind has proved he can reach farther than the moon and will ultimately be able to create not only animals and crops but manifest himself, maybe we can pose yet again, and hopefully answer differently, the platonic question, 'Just what makes a worthwhile life?'

Among the various attempts to requestion and reanswer such fundamental concerns, particularly in the field of our contemporary organizations and work enterprises, I have found, over the last few years, a method of speculative thought which begins to crystalize around the concept of organizational symbolism. Speculative thought as distinct from mere speculation never breaks, as Frankfort and Frankfort observe, 'entirely away from experience. It may be "once removed" from the problems of experience, but it is connected with them in that it tries to explain them' (Frankfort and Frankfort 1949: 11). As such, speculative thought is much older and much more 'primitive' than what we have come to regard as science, in general, and organization and management theory, in particular. As these authors put it:

> Its main concern is with man – his nature and his problems, his values and his destiny. For man does not quite succeed in becoming a scientific object to himself. His need of transcending chaotic experience and conflicting facts leads him to seek a metaphysical hypothesis that may clarify his urgent problems. On the subject of his 'self' man will, most obstinately, speculate – even today.
>
> (Frankfort and Frankfort 1949: 12).

Organization symbolism represents more of a common concern of some scholars than a new school of social research. It is becoming a metaphor for those attempts to look at the social reality of our contemporary organizations from a wider, 'life-science' perspective. In comparison with the traditional concept of social science, which is devoted primarily to the demythologization and rational explication of social reality, the concept of 'life science' should be regarded as a working concept similar to a working hypothesis. Being in itself an attempt at myth-making, this concept allows us to look at and to explore our attempts at the creation of myths around the practice of work – both in our industrial and in our academic enterprises (cf. Luhmann 1969).

Organizational symbolism, as I understand it in the sense of speculative thought or life science, is the attempt to overcome the widespread tendencies of fragmentation and splitting, both in the everyday practice of organization as well as in the theories through which this practice is supposed to be conceptualized, explained and directed. Organizational symbolism thus may take over the function of a metaphor or become a symbol in itself for further attempts to perceive and to understand our organizations from a more wholistic perspective; i.e. as these are related to surrounding societies, people, their lives, history and attempts of mythopoesis (cf. Frankfort and Frankfort 1949: 14 ff.). Such a focus on relatedness begs the question of why in social analysis cannot a vast range of relationships be perceived, experienced and explained?

For me, this means that in our attempts at speculative thought about people in organizations, two corresponding and fundamental processes have to be taken into account, namely symbolization and diabolization. In our concern for symbols and the related processes of symbolization it is far too easy to lose sight of the ongoing processes of diabolization. By diabolization I do not intend to invoke images of the devil, but to use the word as the Greeks mean it, i.e. in its origins as 'diabellein' – to separate, split or fragment, in contrast with 'symballein' which means to relate, put together, to unite.

As I have tried to describe on other occasions in more detail (Sievers 1984, 1986a, 1987), these diabolizing tendencies in our organizational world and its surrounding social reality are manifold. There is, in addition to the previously mentioned split between those at the top and those at the bottom, the high amount of fragmentation of work which itself is based on an underlying split between job and work as well as between working life and life itself. These social and organizational diabolizations are typically camouflaged and obscured by such concepts as motivation (Sievers 1984, 1986a, 1987b), participation (Sievers 1986b), leadership (Sievers 1987a), and stress (Lawrence 1987). Social science concepts like these not only hide but also neglect the fragmentatized social reality they are built upon. In analogies with symbols, they could be described as 'diabols'. They seem to confirm their inventors' and users' convictions that a broader wholistic perspective neither seems to be possible for themselves nor for the people (and the behaviours) they wish to describe. As such they are based on the unassailable truth that the majority of people, if not people in general, have no further concern than their own individual self-realization and are neither able to comprehend the institutions they live in nor their surrounding society (cf. Lawrence 1979) and therefore they have to be managed by others.

These diabolization processes have found their way into the organization of social sciences. Through the way we are socialized into our academic world, we more or less take it for granted that there are disciplines and theories through which we may conceptualize and understand the individual or the social system. As we have learned to differentiate and to fragmentize our world through our concepts and theories so we cease to be concerned about the fact that we can no longer integrate our experiences (Pym 1976: 687). This leads us, for example, to dissociate totally the splitting and fragmentation processes of our inner world from those of our outer world.

According to the underlying diabolization between man and his institutions, our individual splitting processes seem to have nothing to do with the high amount of fragmentation and splitting with which we structure our social reality. On the contrary, there is much evidence that our private and social attempts at diabolization can be perceived as interrelated, mutually caused and sustained. The inability to hold a coherent view of self, to perceive oneself as a whole person and to be mature (cf. Winnicott 1950) is often enough projected on to the outer social world of our organizations, from whence it is reintrojected to serve as an unassailable explanation for the structure of so-called objective circumstances.

From the work of Klein (1959) and Segal (1964) on infant development and what has become known as a theory of object relations, it seems that our speculative thoughts may be guided towards a further symbolization of the inner and the outer world. While the paranoid-schizoid position in Kleinian theory, with its predominant tendency of splitting, can be understood as diabolization, the repairing and reintegrative attempts of the depressive position equally can be seen as processes of symbolization. The further pursuit of this perspective may contribute towards a better understanding of how the dynamics of the inner and outer world are interrelated, and how difficult it may be to distinguish oneself from others effectively. What so many of us typically refer to as the autonomous individual appears from such a perspective to be quite a friction or a 'diabol' (cf. Sullivan 1950).

The diabolization of death and mortality

Underlying the enormous amount of segregation, fragmentation, and splitting in our organizations lies the fundamental split we in Western societies make between life and death.

So far as our employing enterprises and management and organization theories are concerned, we share the conviction that what work people do is unrelated to their lives and that life in general is no longer connected with death. Collectively we have displaced death from experience. Mortality, once regarded as a constituent part of human existence, has been reduced to a critical episode, a certain point in time, which is supposed to happen instantly, preferably when we are asleep. Death, as Norbert Elias so convincingly demonstrates in his book *On the Loneliness of the Dying*, has become a social event (Elias 1985). Death, like the dead body, has to be isolated and hygienically hidden. As long as we are not unexpectedly confronted by a catastrophic accident, like Chernobyl, the societal displacement of death is the predominant strategy we display to rid ourselves of death and through which we let human mortality fall into oblivion. The fictions we commonly share about our non-mortality are so powerful that they ought to be described as 'con-fictions'.

It is also obvious that through our common neglect of death and mortality, living also loses its frame. For birth and death inevitably give that frame to one's life through which it gains meaning (cf. Bateson 1972; Goffman 1975; Lawrence 1985). By neglecting this frame of life we are mistaking its reality in much the same way as we would mistake a picture as the reality it stands for. By ignoring the frame of a picture, e.g. of a face, a landscape, or a ship, one easily misplaces its meaning into the analysis of the quality of its colours and brushwork.

The institutional methods in use to maintain and to perpetuate this split between life and death are at least twofold. There is on the one hand the split between work and life in the sense that we are increasingly concerned about the quality of working life or a humanization of working life, but with no further regard to a man's or woman's whole life – which dwarfs the time spent in employment. On the other hand, the splitting between life and death is enforced and concealed through the fundamental split in our employing institutions between those at the top and those at the bottom. It seems to me that through the predominant split between workers and managers, mortality as a constitutent quality of human existence becomes extinguished.

In an attempt to understand why participatory activities in organizations, despite widespread propagation, are skillfully avoided or, if attempted, fail, the analogy of Greek mythology comes to mind (Sievers 1986b). Besides the fact that Greek mythology is an ongoing attempt to legitimize the change from the original matriarchy towards the patriarchy as a consequence of the invasion into the Mediterranean peninsula (Borneman 1985), Greek mythology is characterized by another fundamental dynamic, the ongoing quarrel over immortality between the gods and men. Although the gods and goddesses in general were regarded as being immortal, whereas the ephemeral mortals were supposed to end their lives in Hades, this boundary was not impermeable. On occasions, gods tried to kill each other, particularly those who, like Hercules, had been procreated by one of the gods together with a mortal and were preoccupied throughout their 'lifetime' with gaining immortality and a seat on Mount Olympus.

The relationships between gods and the mortals were primarily patterned through extermination, rape or seduction on the one hand and through fraud or hard work on the other. On accomplishing his twelve works, Hercules finally reached immortality, whereas Tantalus and Sysiphus, for instance, tried respectively to defraud the gods of their immortality by stealing nectar and ambrosia, the fruits of immortality, from the gods' dinner-table and by putting Thanatos, the angel of death, into chains. And, as we all know, both Tantalus and Sysiphus failed to obtain for their contemporary mortals a part in this divine immortality. They were finally damned to endure endless torments and never-ending fruitless work.

This quarrel over immortality in Greek mythology offers an analogy for a better understanding of the predominant pattern of the relationship between managers and workers in our contemporary work enterprises. Our enterprises have taken over the function of the ancienne city (Brown 1968; Dunne 1965, 1975). The bigger companies, in particular, tend to symbolize our accepted contemporary notion of immortality. Despite the fact that some of them may go bankrupt from time to time, they are built on the underlying assumption that they will exist forever. Accordingly it is the managers who, by devoting their lives to the permanent growth and survival of the enterprise, continuously try to prove their own immortality. At the same time, those at the bottom, the workers, are defrauded of their mortality as they are converted into production means, tools, cogs, dead-wood, or scrap. And to the extent that workers are perceived and treated like things they are also regarded as non mortals (cf. Ziegler 1982).

Perhaps my argument is too abstract, theoretical or a kind of 'science fiction', so let me illustrate what I am getting at through two recent examples. A friend of mine involved as an organizational consultant in what is typically called a rationalization project (i.e. the dismissal of a certain part of the workforce of an enterprise), told me that he questioned the managers responsible as to whether there were other ways of tackling the situation than just providing some 300 workers with the obligatory compensation and forcing them to join the army of unemployed. When he suggested that this money might be better used to help them in setting up their own business, the answer he got was, 'That is ridiculous! You do not seem to realize that the reason we are dismissing these particular people is that they are scrap anyway. We are happy that we have the occasion to finally get rid of them!' The second example is from the management literature. In his attempt to apply portfolio-analysis to human resources management Odiorne happily labels the workers of the two lower squares of the portfolio as working horses and dead-wood (Odiorne 1984). One is reminded of Boxer, the old working horse in George Orwell's *Animal Farm* (1949). It also raises the question for me of what else can one do with dead-wood but burn it? These two very explicit examples illustrate the high degree of contempt of people (cf. Miller 1981) inherent in many of our contemporary organizational cultures.

From such a perspective it occurs to me that in the Western world, in general, but in the majority of our organizations in particular, we face an increasing diabolization of mortality (cf. Becker 1974). We have somehow diabolized human mortality and displaced it into the atomic bomb. The atomic explosion has become the ultimate threat through which either the vast majority of the world population or mankind in general may be extinguished. We seem to have got used to ignoring our own potential individual implosion which we as human beings carry through the fact that we inevitably are mortal and, therefore, must die. As we are individually and subjectively less and less capable of bearing our own or anyone else's mortality we attempt to objectify our individual mortality into the thinghood of a bomb. We tend to deny the significance and meaning of mortality for our quotidian life via reification.

Objectification processes in our organizations are often linked with diabolization. Objectification can be understood, as Berger and Pullberg put it, as the destruction of the former unity between man and his work or between the producer and his product (Berger and Pullberg 1966). Referring to what I stated earlier about the fundamental split in our organizations between those at the top and those at the bottom, and the inherent tendencies to diabolize mortality in the case of managers into immortality and in the case of workers into nonmortality, it also appears to me that our conceptualization of objectification has to be extended. In addition to the commonly used notion of objectification as alienation or reification, through which people and their subjective experiences are turned into things, there obviously exists a secondary tendency of objectification through which people are turned or turn themselves into gods or, to use a recent example from the debate about organizational culture, into heroes. In comparison to reification, this process of objectification can be called deification. No matter whether the outcome of such an objectification is goods or gods, it exempts men and women from basic human mortality.

Reification and deification are both contrary to symbolization. These objectifications are the processes through which we diabolize mortality and, therefore, lose sight of any meaningful relatedness between work, death and life itself.

Towards a management of wisdom

What, in addition to the obsolescence of death and mortality, is missing in contemporary organization theory is another, related concept – wisdom.

The idea that wisdom could be a meaningful concept in our employing institutions as well as in our literature on management and organization is usually coped with in quite a curious way. It appears as though any traditional notion of wisdom is either totally out of our mind or totally exceeds any human capacity. Instead, we fall back on 'conventional wisdom', which is both an expression and a confirmation of the acquiescent conviction that no way or experience exists beyond the banalities of life. The attempt to reduce wisdom to 'conventional wisdom' is just another attempt at reconfirming the predominant culture of our employing institutions. This culture of dependency (Lawrence 1982) is sustained through a view of leadership which itself can be regarded as a perpetuation of immaturity (Sievers 1987a). This obsolescence of wisdom as a valid notion mirrors to some extent the difficulty organizations are confronted with in their attempts to establish meaning. Although there is an increasing concern to re-establish a notion of meaning in the context of organizational culture (e.g. Smircich and Morgan 1982; Smircich 1983), it is obviously hard to find a position which rivals Peters and Waterman's view that excellent employing institutions have to provide money and meaning for their employees (Peters and Waterman 1982). It is my impression that most of the management and organization literature on meaning is meaningless because it is intended to symbolize meaning against a background of a diabolized mortality. These are attempts to offer meaning to life by simultaneously neglecting its frame through death.

We are also displacing wisdom on a societal level. Instead of regarding wisdom as a human quality which, similar to maturity, potentially all human beings are capable of and which as such can be applied to our social life and work in organizations (cf. Winnicott 1950), we more and more tend to put wisdom into the wheelchairs of those who, because of their age, cease to have a reasonable impact on our lives. However, if one shares the opposite conviction that leadership in our organizations has necessarily to include a management of wisdom, such a view requires reformulating.

I found a statement by Joseph Campbell, the great American mythologist, most valuable in understanding the nature of wisdom. He observes that every human attempt at institutionalization has to take two basic considerations into account: the inevitability of individual death and the survival of the social order. This twofold realization offers us a meaningful image of what wisdom can be about. Bringing wisdom back into our institutions in general, and into our work enterprises in particular, would mean maintaining the dialectical position which holds that while, on the one hand, every member is inevitably mortal, the institution, on the other hand, is supposed to survive and is, therefore, immortal. In comparison to the ongoing attempts to diabolize immortality and mortality, i.e. to split them, wisdom can be regarded as the symbolization of immortality and mortality. To the extent that an enterprise is capable of managing wisdom through its mature members, this means that its leaders are, potentially, agents of wisdom. If a corporate culture contains and symbolizes such a wisdom the leaders of the enterprise could be regarded as mortal agents of immortality (Campbell 1973).

Chapter nine

Chronological codes and organizational analysis[1]

Peter Clark

Introduction

Chronological codes

This chapter exemplifies how the perspective of chronological codes can be used to examine the problems of re-adaption by Western organizations in the face of Japanese competition.

The basic arguments are as follows:

1 the organization sciences are a collection of research programmes and loosely bonded themata which are dominated by a theory and philosophy of time in the singular. This theory requires replacement by the recognition that modern corporations utilize and require a *repertoire* of chronological codes which blends homogeneous chronological codes (e.g. the calendar and the clock) with heterogeneous chronological codes (see page 141);

2 corporations, public and private, differ in the robustness of their repertoires of chronological codes and that robust, multilayered repertoires are essential to long-term survival, especially to efficient innovation;

3 the rigid, homogeneous chronological codes like the formalized timetable and all its variants are only relevant to the most basic forms of collective synchronization, allocation of tasks and scheduling of activities. To an increasing degree there is a requirement for complex individual forms of mutual time-tabling which are exacting in their flexibilities and which operate on a multiplicity of layers;

4 the capacity of a corporation to transform its existing forms of processes and capacities is significantly shaped, both directly and indirectly, by the market structures which have been

designated by the strategic choices of the corporate leadership: socially constructed entrainment to the market;
5 the UK, the USA and Japan differ as societies in the clustering of the chronological codes which shape social choices;
6 the domestic market structures of the UK, the USA and Japan possess distinctive features reflecting the pace and saturation of collective consumer choices. In particular, that the temporal features of Britain and Japan tend to pose contrasting cases amongst the larger, industrial nations.

The perspective set forth here provides a challenging, possibly pessimistic, interpretation of the adaptive potential of many Western corporations. The challenge is to recognize that the existing Western blending of corporate chronologies gives insufficient attention to heterogeneous time reckoning systems, because of the belief that all activity should be planned around the calendar and the clock.

Recent reviews of time and organization studies have rightly sought to heighten the consciousness of researchers and theorists about the temporal dimension, but they have largely failed to situate the current attention given to the role of hours in work and the employment contract within an appropriate theory and philosophy of times in the plural. Consequently, these reviews have failed to recognize the complexity of the overall pressures on orthodox corporate chronological codes which are arising from the pace, flexibility and innovativeness of international competition. Therefore, the paper starts by presenting a theory and philosophy of multiple chronological codes (see page 141). The theory should replace existing conceptions in the organization sciences. The main perspectives in the organization sciences are dominated by time-free theorizing and by cross-sectional designs in which there is time-loss. Temporal conflation is endemic and requires both identification and replacement.

The frame of reference of multiple chronological codes is then applied to an exploration of the thesis that the capacity to adapt by enterprises is strongly impacted by the socially constructed enactment of the market context by corporate élites and by the gradual entrainment to the rhythms and processes of the markets in which the firm has chosen to operate (see page 157). There are crucial differences in the paces of the domestic markets between Britain, the USA and Japan in their speed of saturation, especially with respect to consumer products of cars, white goods, cameras, PCs and similar.

The orthodox theory of organization transitions is examined with reference to the notion of a repertoire of chronological codes (see page 159). Transitions should be distinguished from recursiveness and momentum. Previous work has assumed that transitions are more or less homogeneous across multiple dimensions. However, current research and theory suggests that different aspects (e.g. technologies and buildings) are transformed at different *paces*. Moreover, and equally important, the focus should be upon the chronological codes possessed by those corporations which enter and prosper during phases of discontinuities in sectors. The approach to the analysis of the multiple paces of transition by the Annales School is examined to provide a frame of reference for examining re-adaptation.

Robust corporations (see page 162) are likely to be characterized by possessing complex, multilayered repertoires of chronological codes which enable the parallel working of many different types of activity, each of which has to be resourced, synchronized and scheduled within a market framework inside which strategic time reckoning is by reference to chronological codes whose prime features are heterogeneous rather than homogeneous. Enabling the use of such complex codes will require a development of language games which are specific to one corporation and its strategic choices. The complexity of these new languages cannot be reduced to the eight traits of successful corporate cultures. Nor can the complexity be handled through retreating to simplistic concepts of the market because the paces of corporate strategic decision-making will require anticipation of future price signals. So the mainstream search for the lean corporation which is at the centre of Anglo-American concepts of readaptation is doomed. The complex language games necessary to develop repertoires of future orientated corporate chronologies for the robust corporation will require a focus on multiple language games as the central tool of management. Transitions in existing Western corporate language games seem to be occurring very slowly, possibly too slowly.

Organization sciences: use with care

The Western approach to organization design and to organization transitions has been strongly shaped by the optimism of the founding period of organization studies in the early 1960s. The themata and research programmes of the organization sciences were constituted around the managerial problems of American corporate capitalism (Weick 1969). Consequently, there has been a strong assumption that organizations could be designed and could be changed in the planned directions desired by management. Simplistic yet elegant prescriptions overpowered a concern for description and explanation (Clark and Starkey 1988). Few disputed the postulate of fast, direct change. Inconvenient discoveries of failed innovation were encapsulated and sidelined (e.g. Gross *et al.* 1971).

An exception to this intellectual malaise was Crozier (1964, 1973, 1984) whose analysis highlighted three core themes about corporations:

1. the chronic recursiveness and the inertial politicality which shape the rules of the game within which individual agency is located;
2. the irregularity of short periods of innovation and the durability of long periods of entrenchment and momentum;
3. the difference between American forms of organization and those likely to be found in Europe, especially in France.

Crozier gave an impetus to the development of a descriptive and explanatory reasoning which combined a concern for generalizing with an interest in examining the specifics of continuity and transition. However, that particular direction, also found more widely in Europe than in the USA, did not occupy the mainstream of analyses (see Donaldson 1985).

Since the mid-1970s attention has been increasingly drawn to the rigid, unchanging cultures and structuration of many Western organizations (Abernathy 1978), to the collapse of major innovation schemes (Smith *et al.* 1987), to momentum rather than transition (Miller and Friesen 1984) and to the stability of existing configurations (Mintzberg 1983). These warnings that the prescriptions of planned change were unlikely to be unintended, slow and uneven were largely ignored. So in the 1980s many leading American organizational analysts combined appraisal of existing forms with optimism about ongoing re-adaptation by enterprises for the future. Three examples from the Harvard Business School, Kanter (1984), Lawrence and Dyer (1983), and Abernathy, Clark, and Kantrow (1981), illustrate this tendency.

Kanter exemplified this format with reference to her suggestion that corporate flexibility had been massively and successfully inserted into General Motors. However, by the later 1980s, GM's share of the American market has fallen sharply.

Lawrence and Dyer made a bold attempt to situate the adaptive capacity of American firms in a competitive context. They succeeded in demonstrating an historic capacity of the population of firms in seven diverse American sectors to re-adapt between 1900–1970. From that observation they concluded that there was a structural capacity for further adaptation. This is an awkward conclusion which fails to recognize how the American mass consumer markets are being replaced (Piore and Sabel 1984; Clark 1987).

Abernathy, Clark, and Kantrow concluded their revealing analysis of rigidities in American corporate practice and in the analytic models of the business schools by indicating that an industrial renaissance was unfolding. These three studies exemplify much of the best of analysis whilst holding to a theory of organization transitions which should be used with care – if at all.

The problem of adaptation facing American and European corporations now bears comparison with shifts in the bases of world competition after 1870 from trade to technological science, and their consequences for British firms in the twentieth century.

The attempts to examine the transitional capability of western organizations are rarely comparative across national boundaries. Many studies done by Americans assume that American paces of transition are the benchmark which they and others should follow (DiMaggio and Powell 1983). The general absence of international comparisons, especially between Western and Japanese firms, also reflects the untenable paradigmatic of the organization sciences about the temporal dimensions of the international business enterprise.

Corporate repertoires of chronological codes

This section deals with the contrast between the theory of a singular time used by practising Western managers and by organization scientists from the theory and philosophy of multiple chronological codes which modern science and the humanities increasingly believes is the most convincing and useful postulate. Moreover, this section contends that all corporations require and possess a plurality of chronological codes and that the most strategically significant chronological codes rely on events whose occurrence is more like the irregular formations of clouds than of the regular mechanism of a clock. It is implied that in Western corporations the technocrats of planning and design have given too much attention to clocktime as the solid framework for competitive survival. This section highlights the significance of examining the repertoires of corporate chronological codes.

A singular, unitary time?

Theories of time have passed through two paradigmatic revolutions in the sciences, each of which is highly relevant to the organization sciences: the renaissance science revolution and the modern science revolution of the nineteenth century.

During the formative period of renaissance science the central debate over time may be depicted in terms of the differences between Leibniz and Newton. Leibniz reasoned that time reckoning is constituted by man from constellations of events and is therefore *in* the events. Leibniz argued for the recognition of a diverse plurality of 'chronological codes' or 'time reckoning systems'. In contrast, Newton reasoned that there was a singular, unitary time which is objective and hence independent of man and independent from events. Newton's singular, unitary conception became the everyday meaning in Western Europe and North America. Consequently, time was frequently equated with the metaphor of clocktime as a regular, easily recognized array of processes whose attributes could be readily calculated. The Newtonian conception of a singular objective time is still hegemonic in the organizational science.

The second revolution in the theorizing of time unfolded during the nineteenth century when the sciences developed an 'historical', evolutionary dimension. Modern theorizing, influenced by developments in physics, claimed that time was *in* the events (as Leibniz) and that any set of events could only be apprehended by the observer relative to other events and to the observer. According to this theory of man-made chronological codes there were multiple chronological codes. Moreover, many of these patterns of events were not fixed and regular like the clock. There were in fact two major branches of chronological codes: the homogeneous codes based on the clock and heterogeneous codes derived from natural and social events. Because the patterns of events used as a frame of reference differed between the sciences (e.g. physics, biology, and geology) there was therefore a plurality of chronological codes, many of which were heterogeneous (e.g. the notion of dissipative structures and processes in biology and chemistry).

The impact of the debates from the second revolution in time and their resolution in favour of a plurality of chronological codes has been slow to diffuse to the heartlands of the social sciences and of the educated person. The impact of the theory of multiple chronological codes was more obvious in small enclaves than in the mainstream of the disciplines. Yet there were dramatic demonstrations of the new time sense of multiple and heterogeneous chronological codes in art (e.g. the futurist manifesto) and in literature (e.g. Proust, Joyce, Priestley).

In France, the new theories had more pervasive impacts than in the USA or in Britain – most notably in French sociology (e.g. Durkheim, Mauss, and Halbwachs) which culminated in the complex spectrum of social times proposed by Gurvitch (1964). These developments were complemented by a burgeoning of theoretical work in which temporality was a central problematic (e.g. Lévi-Strauss, Foucault, Lacan). In the 1980s French historiography entered a series of bold attempts to utilize the analytic models of heterogeneous chronologies to give a problem-oriented and analytically driven narrative to historical events. The most visible manifestation of that approach has been the Annales School of historians and the recently deceased Braudel (d. 1987), to whom we shall return later. In France, Braudel and Gurvitch agreed on the heterogeneous character of chronological codes whilst differing on paces at which transitions in different aspects of technology, society and socially structured space might be changing (Clark 1985). Braudel postulated very slow transitions whilst Gurvitch postulated differing paces, some fast, some slow. However, when compared to the image of the pace of transitions currently portrayed in the organization sciences (e.g. Kanter 1984), both Braudel and Gurvitch contend that transitions have long antecedents and much momentum in inertial directions. The systematic attention given to time by French analysts is exceptional.

Outside France, the temporal dimension receives irregular, noncumulative bursts of attention stimulated by insightful, often brilliant pieces of analysis which are frequently cited, yet rarely incorporated into the theories of organizational transitions (e.g. Sorokin and Merton 1937; Moore 1963; Tiryakian 1970; Zerubavel 1978).

The organization sciences are still dominated by the first revolution in time. The most widely accepted philosophical position is the notion of a single unitary form of time which is objective, absolute, homogeneous, linear, evenly flowing, measurable, readily divisible and independent of events. The domination by a single chronological code is massively inhibiting.

Within the organization sciences the élite members of the hidden college whose choice of research programmes deeply influence the direction of the organization sciences as a whole are still utilizing the theory and philosophy of a singular, unitary, objective time against which all events can be periodized and ordered. Consequently many of the recent and large-scale research programmes which claim to be unravelling the processual complexities of innovation in technologies and adaptation have so far failed to address the issue of a technological and organizational process located in plural chronological codes.

This chapter contends that the understanding, description and explanation of organization events requires the use of a plurality of chronological codes. Moreover, careful attention must be given to addressing the problem of the degree to which modern technological and organizational transitions are consciously planned in both highly heterogeneous chronological codes as well as the more homogeneous codes (Clark 1986a).

Heterogeneous codes

Chronological codes may be heterogeneous or homogeneous. Both forms are socially constructed and intersubjectively known trajectories of events which have been selected and labelled because they are anticipated to unfold in a more or less similar sequential manner in the future. These events may refer to phenomena in nature (e.g. clouds, movements of the moon, climate, morphology of flora and fauna) as well as social (e.g. wars, dynastics, dramas) and biographical events (e.g. careers). This section deals with heterogeneous codes and the following section (page 147) examines homogeneous codes.

As indicated earlier, the heterogeneous chronological codes are more analogous to cloud formations in temperate climates in their predictability than to regular devices such as the clypdestra and the clock. Heterogeneous codes are the distinctive cultural possessions of particular societies. There are important differences, for example, between the French and the British (Hantrais, Clark, and Samuel 1984). It follows that heterogeneous codes are also specific to the cultural inheritance of any corporation. The central attributes of heterogeneous codes can be examined along four key dimensions: sequences and signifiers; temporal units; durational differentiation; orientation to the past/present/future.

First, sequences and signifiers. Some codes possess highly defined sequences whose key signifiers are very regular. For example, the Nuer people used events derived from the degree of coupling between cloud formations and the changes in the morphology of flora and fauna to determine the starting points for the two major seasonal transitions of village life (Evans-Pritchard 1940). The use of these oceanological events by the Nuer may be compared with Thomas Hardy's accounts of the problems of forecasting the weather for harvesting in his novel narrating the rise and fall of the *Mayor of Casterbridge* (1902). In practice many sequences of events are irregular and possess multiple branches, only some of which occur on each occasion. Moreover, the events and the key signifiers are separated by durational intervals which are irregular and awkward to determine. Examples of these would include the chronological codes used by psychiatrists and physicians to determine the trajectories of illnesses. Roth shows that in detection of cancer the codes often possess multiple branches in which key signifiers were irregular and deceptive (Roth 1963).

Certain events in the anticipated trajectory are selected as *key signifiers* and *benchmarks*. These signifiers may relate to the climate. Large-scale agricultural societies such as pre-modern China developed highly elaborate signifiers for locating the onset of the monsoons and the major floods which brought water for the rice crops. Wittfogel reconstructed the codes used in the hydraulic societies of Asiatic despotism in which the control of flood waters was so central (Wittfogel 1957). Similarly, there are modern codes in weather forecasting for detecting the possible occurrence of irregular storms, droughts, and similar. The problem of applying these codes before the events was exemplified when in the south of England during October 1987 the most severe storm in two centuries destroyed millions of trees. After the devastation various experts claimed that the signifiers were obvious!

In the heterogeneous chronological codes the anticipated sequences of events are probabilistic. So, constructing the event trajectories involves some recognition that certain events are contingent and these may possess a *contingent periodicity*. In corporations, many of the events which the marketing departments (and their functional equivalents) attempt to interpret when anticipating the future possess a contingent periodicity (Clark 1985).

Second, there are many *temporal units* within heterogeneous chronological codes. Some temporal units are relatively stable, yet the most important units are probably very unstable and highly variable. The stable units include events like 'the time taken to cook a locust' (see Evans-Pritchard 1940). The unstable units will be highly local to specific collections of actors who are most unlikely to be aware of their usage. These units provide a form of temporal differentiation, especially within corporations. For example, many corporations experience uneven periods of demand which are contingent, and so a language of temporal units is developed to designate certain phases (Clark 1985).

The remaining attributes may be examined in reference to the general framework proposed by Gurvitch (1964) and summarized in Table 9.1. Gurvitch sought to provide a language for examining the spectrum of times. The framework should be used to create discontinuous typologies which are only relevant to the description and explanation of events in a corporation at a certain specific phase. Consequently, the same typology of times could not be applied to all phases of a corporation's growth and decline (see Whipp and Clark 1986). Table 9.1. depicts eight broad types of heterogeneous times which can be utilized as a point of departure for specific investigations. We shall return to this framework later (page 154).

The third point to be made is that heterogeneous codes contain shared, socially constructed interpretations of paces and of durations somewhat in the manner set out in the third column of the Gurvitch framework. These durational attributes are rarely examined systematically in organizational studies, yet there is considerable evidence to show that such variations are normal and consequential. For example, American high school life is deeply impacted by the sporting calender and by events like graduation.

The usefulness and the problems of the framework can be explored by taking the case of Western universities since 1965. It might be argued that in French universities the experience of enduring time was transformed in 1968 into a short-phase deceptive and alternating time which was followed by unfolding time, and then by the mid-1970s there was a combination of enduring and erratic times.

Table 9.1. Taxonomy of times constructed from Gurvitch

Type	*Relation of Past, Present and Future*	*Continuity, Contingency and Surprise*	*Duration, Including Pace*
Enduring	Past is projected in the present and future. Remote past is dominant.	Most continuous.	Slowed down, long duration. Present can be quantitatively expressed.
Deceptive	Rupture between past and present.	Discontinuity. Surprise time.	Seems like enduring, but sudden crisis. Paradox. Simultaneously slow and agitated.
Erratic	Present appears to prevail over the past and future.	Uncertainty and accentuated contingency. Discontinuity becomes prominent.	Irregular pulsation between appearance and disappearance of rhythms.
Cyclical	Each is mutually projected into the other.	Continuity accentuated. Contingency weakened.	'A dance on one spot.' Qualitative element strong.
Retarded	Future actualized in present.	No equilibrium between continuity and discontinuity. Contingent elements are reinforced.	Delayed, waiting for unfolding.
Alternating	Past and future compete in the present.	Discontinuity stronger than continuity. Contingency not exaggerated.	Alternating between delay and advance. Qualitative not accentuated.
Pushing forward	Future becomes present.	Discontinuity. Contingency.	Time in advance of itself (e.g. communions in revolt). Qualitative.
Explosive	Present and past dissolved. Creation of the immediately transcended future.	Discontinuity high, contingency high.	Fast movements. Effervescent. Qualitative high.

Source: Clark 1985

The case of British universities has been rather different. Until the early 1980s the universities thought of themselves as being on five-year rolling plans of treasury funding: the slowed down, long duration of enduring time. In the case of British universities the key transition from enduring time to erupting time would be mid-1981 when overall treasury funding to the university sector was shifted downward in an overall reduction by 10 per cent, which was then heavily focused on certain universities which had their financing reduced by 30 per cent. Since 1981 the real values of university funding have been systematically reduced by 1 per cent per annum. The interpretation of duration and pace as enduring is being replaced, although the paces of transition to erupting time is least in the well-established civic universities (e.g. Birmingham and Manchester), and greatest in some of the technological universities (e.g. Salford and Aston) and the redbricks which were upgraded in the 1950s (e.g. Hull and Keele).

Fourth, orientations to the past/present/future have been neglected in organization studies because the future has largely been portrayed in the homogeneous codes of planning and short-run financial accountability (Johnson and Kaplan 1987). However, there is ample evidence that managements develop heterogeneous time orientations and that these are significant to corporate survival. The leadership of all organizations will possess specific combinations of the past/present and future, and these conceptions will incorporate calculations about the degree of risk and contingency in the future. It has been argued that departments of marketing are often key players in the evolvement and use of strategic time reckoning systems (Clark 1985: 56–9; Bluedorne 1987). The orientation to past/present/future will contain organizationally specific predispositions towards the influence of the past relative to the future. The degree of past loadedness in the repertoire of chronological codes in a corporation is very important.

It should not be assumed that attention to the past is the cause of future organizational failure. McMillan, for example, contends that corporate time reckoning in Japan relies on an exquisitely developed informal library containing carefully designated configurations of past events which are used as a frame for comparison to detect sources of difference between the present and the future (McMillan 1985). The elaborateness of Japanese heterogeneous codes in the modern period has been insightfully reconstructed by Smith (1986). In certain Western corporations the significance of macro level events has been addressed through scenario writing and similar exercises. However, it seems that these are rarely integrated into corporate strategy making.

Homogeneous codes

Homogeneous chronological codes possess the following attributes: they consist of an 'objective', singular system containing defined, measurable units of highly stable lengths (e.g. the second and the year) which can be atomistically ordered in a linear and/or cyclical pattern.

The systems can be divided, added, cumulated and subtracted in abstract 'temporal containers' which are free from contingencies and epochal events (see Table 9.2). Perhaps most important, the artefacts which produce homogeneous codes have become smaller, more accurate and increasingly portable, and therefore widely diffused, as systems of maritime navigation and spatial navigation have evolved ever more refined and exacting frameworks. Contemporary transportation and telecommunications systems rely on these codes and assist in their formal production.

Table 9.2. Strategic time reckoning and marketing

	Time periods (seasons)					
Managers' interpretation	*Winter* *1*	*2* *Spring*	*Summer* *3*	*4* *Autumn*	*5*	*6*
Time orientation						
1 present		2A				
2 anticipated		3B ⟶				
3 past		⟵ 1A				

Situational definitions

A = expand production
B = reduce production
(C = innovate new product range: see discussion)

Homogeneous codes are constituted by taking highly regular events as the frame of reference. These regular events include the movements of planets relative to one another (i.e. sideral time and the calendar), the vibrations of a crystal (e.g. the modern wrist-watch), mechanical movements (e.g. medieval town clocks in Europe), or artefacts like the candle burning (e.g. medieval Benedictine monasteries) or the water clock (e.g. China in the thirteenth century). Homogeneous codes provide a highly regular, standardized frame of reference which can be linear in any direction or recurrent and in which the units (e.g. the hour and the week) can be dissected for analysis or cumulated.

These homogeneous codes evolved at two very different levels: the year and the day. Each unit became the focus of attempts to both subdivide the unit into smaller, homogeneous pieces (e.g. the hour and second; the month and the week) as well as to cumulate the units into larger entities which could order the past, present and the future (e.g. the nineteenth century biblical conception of man).

It is now believed that the growth of European towns between the thirteenth and seventeenth centuries provided a milieu for the evolvement of secular homogeneous codes outside the influence of the Christian churches (Le Goff 1980) and that the secularization of homogeneous codes was given a stepwise shift by the founding communities of the USA (Clark 1987). In those settings the notion of an abstract temporal container surfaced and later became formalized within corporations as the temporal inventory (Moore 1963).

There are three main themes which are of relevance:

1 the Western preoccupation with homogeneous chronological codes and with their widespread dissemination (Landes 1983). Homogeneous codes became dominant in the structuration of Western societies, yet there are important differences in their position between the USA and Britain (Gurvitch 1964; Clark 1987). In Eastern societies heterogeneous systems remained more pervasive, although Japan forms an interesting case of the blending of the two forms;
2 linear and cyclical formats were systematically used as frameworks to discover anachronism and to locate events in ordered ways (e.g. geological time and the design of nineteenth century museums). These developments influenced the theories of historical narrative and led to sharp debates between tight analytically structured narrative (e.g. Braudel 1984);
3 the extensive use of planning systems and data bases anchored in homogeneous codes for synchronising, scheduling and resourcing activities within corporations and between interfirm networks.

These three themes presuppose significant transitions in the temporal consciousness of players and of the role of temporal disciplines in work lives and in society. The argument implied in this chapter is that time discipline has become increasingly individuated and internalized through socialization. There are new forms of time discipline, but these forms cannot be adequately understood within the flawed analysis of homogeneous and heterogeneous times proposed by E.P.Thompson (1967), because the analysis misuses anthropological perspectives, exaggerates the British case and fails to address the contested nature of temporal dominance.

First, Landes' comparative investigation of the development devices for the measuring of homogeneous chronologies between Western Europe and China is especially relevant (Landes 1983). Landes, unlike many earlier historians of technical change, does not exaggerate the significance of first inventions, but instead concentrates upon the representative usage of technologies in different societies. Consequently, the issue at the heart of the Sino-European comparison is not so much one of which civilization invented the clock, but to what usage was the clock put and by which strata? Landes contends that clocks and their main variants were typically used in China as decoration for the rulers, whilst in Europe there was a widespread diffusion, particularly amongst the administrative and commercial strata in the towns. These Sino-European differences may be explained by the particular European consciousness about ordered social practices and by the use of the clock to regulate everyday life on an individual basis by the merchant, and on a more collectively regularized basis for certain religious orders (e.g. Benedictines) and for the relatively small number of employed workers in nineteenth century factories (cf. Thompson 1967).

From the sixteenth century onward, western consciousness about the future utilized the calendar and the clock to facilitate an imaginative and abstract leap in everyday language games towards the implicit treatment of the future as:

1 a temporal container of future time which could be allocated in different ways, some of which could be imaginatively apprehended and reflectively examined;
2 the development of idealistic and utopian futures in which existing constraints on time and space were bracketed;
3 the production of secular futures in which economic activity was central as a source of future wealth;
4 the attachment to future projects of estimates of the financial returns to be made to capital.

These conceptions of the future were based upon and compared with broad calculations of how time was 'spent' by various activities. So, by the late eighteenth century leading employers of labour had developed rudimentary human resource accounting systems.

In Western Europe the pattern of evolvement of temporal artefacts was towards portable and miniaturized devices with increasing accuracy. The development of navigational chronometers in the renaissance was a pivotal development for co-ordinating naval-military activity which led to the removal of barriers to merchant trade such as piracy and so facilitated maritime merchant capitalism especially for the Netherlands and Britain (Braudel 1984). Until the late nineteenth century transportation by water (e.g. seas, rivers, and canals) was the fastest, cheapest mode and the development of entrepôts like Amsterdam and London shaped the evolvement of the economic division of labour throughout the North Atlantic and beyond (Braudel 1984).

In the nineteenth century temporal artefacts were used to schedule and to synchronize railroad and telegraph systems. The USA was a distinctive macro market. There was an extensive reliance on homogeneous codes both to operate the American railways and to use them as time buffers for the assembly lines (Chandler 1977). In the 1940s, more refined systems were used as the core infrastructure in the development of land-based American airlines (cf. sea-based states) and the subsequent diffusion of associated chronological systems (e.g. booking). The development of an information-based infrastructure (i.e. rail, automobile, and air travel coupled to telegraph) facilitated the emergence of the most homogeneous and the largest domestic market in the world. In the USA the pace of the market saturation for personal chronometers was very high and provided the key market for the development of templates for organizing large-scale modern forms of manufacture (Clark 1987).

Second, an important usage of homogeneous chronologies occurred with the general search for anachronisms by the careful ordering of social and natural events against the calendar. Modern historiography, itself a product of the mid-nineteenth century was rooted in the uncovering of anachronisms in key legal documents governing the actions of the state and in the relations between states. The contemporary, orthodox notion of history as a discipline with an ordered 'objective' chronology was sedimented and legally legitimated in the renaissance around the time concepts of Newtonian science. Modern history is still deeply shaped by homogeneous chronologies.

Third, corporations, especially twentieth century North American corporations, became the milieu for the production of complex forward-planning systems based on homogeneous chronological codes. Later, interfirm codes were formulated which chained together in an ever-tightening logistical integralism planning systems based on critical path networks. Important temporal innovations occurred in retailing, where prototypical just-in-time (JIT) systems surfaced in the 1920s, initially in the USA. These new systems required the intensive investigation and critique of existing usages of time in different activities and spaces in order to remove areas of temporal porosity. A whole new array of timestudy practices emerged. The origins of the modern developments in time study of individuals (and classes of individuals) have been traced to the introduction of wall-clocks in eighteenth century workshops and in the new occupation of timekeeping. Since then three further lines of development in time study have developed:

1 direct observation and analytical analysis of the components of tasks based on the methods of Taylorism and of the Gilbreths as well as systematic sampling activities;
2 indirect simulation of future and current tasks through the use of

standardized libraries of human movements based on past observations and on film analysis in systems such as MTM. Variants of the MTM systems were used by engineers in Volvo to timetable the famous Kalmar factory;

3 the aggregated analysis of human activity by comparing the rates of output to the time (and cost) of human and machinery inputs.

All three methods have been used extensively, yet the pattern of their usage differs markedly between the USA, the UK and Japan.

In Britain there has been less usage of direct and indirect observation than in the USA. However, for the public sector there has been extensive aggregated analysis of health care, teaching and other activities. The usage of this form relies on having data from a sufficient sample of similar locations which can be compared. Typically, the fastest locations are taken as the future norm. This approach is facilitated by the developments in statistical analysis and data processing. It has been used in the British construction industry, especially in establishing contracts (Clark 1986a).

Corporate usage of homogeneous chronological codes relies on three core concepts and their ideological legitimation by their incorporation into the management sciences (Clark 1978):

- temporal inventories;
- the metaphor of clockwork;
- commodification of time.

Temporal inventories rest on simple assumptions about manpower. It is postulated that labour power is unproblematic and can be transposed in orderly abstractions (cf. Baldamus 1961). The basic formula connects two sets of data: an estimate of the days/hours needed to complete designated activities; and a calculation of the aggregated days/hours of types of labour and types of equipment which the corporation possesses or can gain access to through sub-contracting. There are many variants on this basic formula in manpower and career planning. The usage of temporal inventories has facilitated a very abstract conception of the past/present/future by staff personnel within the technostructures of large corporations. Their claimed expertise has consisted of using homogeneous chronological codes to project past patterns into the future on single time lines. The legitimacy of these approaches to planning the temporal inventory has rested on their perceived rationality as defined by management science. Their adoption and routine usage during the three boom decades after 1945 corrosively created and sedimented a very simplified vision of the future. These systems became incorporated into the chemical industries and the automobile industry. Their increasing role in the US automobile industry is now becoming clearer (see Halberstram 1986; Causmano 1985; Abernathy, Clark, and Kantrow 1983).

Also, whilst the impact of the metaphor of clockwork should not be exaggerated, as in the labour process perspective, neither should the influence of its imagery on corporate planning be ignored. The issue is how the imagery was transposed into corporate practices: for whom, by whom. Western organizations, especially in the USA, have been managed by value systems within which there has been a search for predictability and order by practising managers and business school academics (e.g. J.D. Thompson 1967). The proclivities of the planners created the just-in-case corporation particularly in the automobile industry where the clockwork analogy was applied in a highly focused manner to the assembly line, yet not so rigorously to other areas. Cusumano demonstrates how Japanese car firms (e.g. Toyota) used the analogy in a more embracing fashion (Cusumano 1985).

The commodification of time refers to the attachment of financial values to all periods of labour time and to machine time so that every chunk of homogenized time has its costs. The development of the commodification of time was fully anticipated by Marx who noted that firms whose activities earned less than the average rate of profitability per unit of time were those most liable to collapse. Commodification is at the heart of the human resource management (HRM) perspective. The application of these principles is very uneven. For example, there is clear evidence that retail, particularly fast-food outlets and supermarket chains, have developed practices for the commodification of time which are much more exacting than those which were found until recently amongst teachers and hospital workers (Starkey 1985). Moreover, the very high costs of employing a manager in an expensive metropolitan building and providing him with a secretary are now being offset by encouraging managers to work from home on a time-contracted network system.

The three core concepts of temporal inventory, clockwork, and the codification of time all rest on homogeneous chronological codes. Their specific usage both articulates and reinforces a particular set of corporate values. The existence of specialists who claim expertise in their usage constitutes a layer within the corporation whose agency is directed towards a highly rigid and formalized approach to the future. The simplification of events in the present and their extrapolation into linear futures can be highly problematic.

Strategic time reckoning: lean and robust

This section contends that Western, especially British, corporations have developed a predisposition towards the usage of lean rather than robust repertoires of chronological codes and that lean repertoires conflate the temporal vision of the corporation, especially in enactment of the future. The stringent creation of lean repertoires appears to be successful because of the ablation of segments of corporate activity which are not relevant to the future: creative destruction in a Schumpeterian model. So there has been extensive redefinition of employment contracts to minimize employees' financial rights (e.g. holidays, pensions, cost of retraining) and job rights (e.g. dismissal, tenure). New employment contracts satisfy the position of the employer through offering potential for the speedy use of scarce human resources and their continual redeployment. In Britain these developments are very evident in retail, the tourist industry and in construction. Great attention has been given to these innovations, particularly to the new formalized, time-defined work contracts and to the growth of part-time female work. However, as reasoned elsewhere, it is the robust corporation which prospers in the long run and the issue is how a robust capacity for innovation and efficiency can be achieved (Whipp and Clark 1986; Clark 1987; Clark and Starkey 1988). This section examines robust repertoires of chronological codes with reference to strategic time reckoning and with reference also to the layering of chronological codes in corporations.

It is argued that repertoires of chronological codes steer the core political mechanisms for activating structural poses from the overall corporate repertoire of structural poses (Clark 1985: 59–61). There is a key distinction here between lean and robust repertoires.

A lean repertoire is one in which the steering is set with value systems and priorities which rely heavily on chronological codes emphasizing collective punctuality, formal hours, speed of work and scarcity of time: the homogeneous codes. Flexibility is imposed simplistically. These codes are applied principally to control shop-floor activities at the same functional level so as to homogenize and collectivize activities. Lean repertoires project the future as the highly controllable extension of the present. So there is temporal conflation of the future. Consequently there are very few alternative chronological codes in the repertoire which might be used in managerial language games to detect hidden consequences and surprises (cf. Table 9.2, page 148). In the lean format the usage of formalized individual systems of time management tends to be co-ordinated only through a simple skein of a homogeneous collective timetable.

In a robust repertoire the steering can draw upon a wider, more discriminated and better grounded range of time reckoning chronological codes, especially of heterogeneous codes handling contingency and homogeneous codes. The heterogeneous codes form the solid frame for collective actions and for individual timetabling which might be anchored in individually structured, yet consensually agreed, time planning. Flexibility is valued equally in relation to the speedy usage of scarce temporal resources. Flexibility is actualized through removing structural rigidities and introducing both designed teamwork and focused self-organization with reference to chosen sets of signifying events. Information technology can be used to provide a generalised data base for anticipating future problems, as in the usage of electronic point of sale (EPOS) to reschedule retail outlets (e.g. supermarkets). Robust repertoires are typified by temporal elaboration (cf. conflation), especially in the examination of editing of the mutual interpenetration of the past, present and future. The future will be prised open by referring to diverse examples in the repertoire. Also, the limits of experience will be extended by systematically using scenario writing conjointly with the consideration of analytically structured narrative about past events. These anticipations of the future will involve consideration of the contingencies, surprises, hidden consequences and opportunities posed by alternatives. Overall robust systems are multilayered and flexibly covered so that they embrace and incorporate the technostructure and strategic elites. There will be a complex fabric of nested chronological codes across different functional levels.

In both lean and robust repertoires their enactment and activation will be a political process centering on managerial language games which have implications for both intra-managerial dominance and legitimacy and also for the relations between capital, management and labour.

The differences between the repertoires of robust and lean corporate chronological codes may be illustrated from the case-study of a large European knitwear firm and one of its branch plants. The case-study demonstrates that the repertoire has to be interpreted by certain sets of players. In this case-study the focus is on the interpretations by two sets of marketing experts; one set possessed a robust repertoire and were located at the corporate headquarters and the other set possessed a lean repertoire and were located at the branch plant, Harp Mill (Clark 1985: 56–9; Clark and Starkey 1988). The process of enacting the repertoire (Weick 1969) and its interpretation may be referred to as strategic time reckoning, as distinct from tactical timetabling. In the case of illustration both marketing departments faced a very similar external semi-fashion type of market environment even though their enactments were very different (cf. Weick 1969). The key unit in their analysis was 'the season'.

The marketing department at headquarters was staffed by older, non-graduate men with experience of many seasons of detecting and editing the contingent periodicities in the knitwear industry. They shared and referred to a well developed chronological repertoire of heterogeneous trajectories which were used to encode equivocality in several diverse areas of the environment: the behaviour of customers, new dyes/raw materials/equipment, changes in the weight of clothes preferred by customers, data on disposable income, the use of colours in the media, and so on. The removal of equivocality from the incoming information could be simplified (for our purposes) to three choices about how to define seasonal situations:

- a season for expanding the overall level of production because sales were favourable and it was important to anticipate re-orders from customers;
- a season for reducing production in anticipation of low sales levels;
- a season when the types of garments brought by customers shifts in terms of weight/style/colour and stitch geometry.

Matching the enactment correctly to the unfolding future was very consequential for profitability. If a bad season was correctly anticipated and if that enactment was politically accepted by all of management and by the labour force then management would introduce structural poses for minimizing costs and would activate the role of waste controllers. Moreover, employees knew from experience that there would be little overtime. In this way a season of low sales could be profitable. However, unravelling bad seasons from good was difficult. The greatest difficulty was in anticipating significant shifts in consumer preferences and the capacity of competing suppliers to meet innovative styles.

The strategic time reckoning format of the headquarters staff was an example of the robust repertoire, and its main features are summarized schematically in Table 9.2 (page 148). The format of their system included the assessment of the immediate season as well as the future season, and the continual re-editing of past seasons. Table 9.2 depicts the position in a hypothetical spring season when they enacted the summer as a period of reduced production, the current spring season as one of expanded production and likewise for the immediately previous, winter season. At the period when these men were being researched they correctly anticipated a major shift in consumer preferences and they convinced their colleagues at headquarters of their enactment. At that juncture management began to activate a whole array of dormant roles and structural poses centering on innovation and design. What happened at the branch factory?

At the branch factory the marketing men were younger, more formally qualified (e.g. with college degrees), but less experienced in the seasonal contingencies of the knitwear industry. They had in fact been operating through a period of about fifteen seasons, most of which had been of expanded production. So, when the period of innovation in style began to occur and their sales dropped they encoded the situation as a 'bad season' and its occurrence caused deep concern amongst the workforce, who associated low sales with plant closure. Their failure to interpret the market situation was not recognized at headquarters because such a failure seemed inconceivable and because headquarters was very preoccupied with innovation. When headquarters did recognize the problem it was impossible to activate dormant design roles from the repertoire because the repertoire did not possess them!

Summary

It has been argued that corporations must develop chronological codes which combine, blend and prioritize both homogeneous and heterogeneous formats to create a robust repertoire which is matched by skill in its usage. The case illustration has already introduced the strategically crucial role played by departments whose expertise includes the constitution and enactment of complex, blended heterogeneous and homogeneous codes. Moreover, as indicated, the repertoire plays a central role in the steering of activation/dormancy of roles and the structural poses in which they are clustered. Before considering how these clusters might be transformed it is relevant to consider how they become composed in specific configurations. The next section explores the influence of market entrainment.

Strategic choices, market entrainment and the Japanese case

Of necessity this section must be somewhat speculative because the market dimension has been largely neglected by the organization sciences. The objective will be to demonstrate that the strategic choices made in all corporations about the specific market domains in which they will operate are consequential for the development of the repertoire of chronological codes and of structural poses. The interactions with markets by corporations is mediated by the language games of top management, and the causal interpretation placed on those interactions creates steering rules which soon become deeply sedimented and taken for granted. What occurs may be labelled as socially constructed entertainment to the distinctive attributes of a market domain. Moreover, market domains differ in important respects, especially between the variegated market of Europe and the more homogeneous markets of the USA and of Japan. The role of the North American market – its immense size, the homogeneity in consumer preferences and its high integration

(Clark 1987) – in shaping the recipes for success in American corporations has not been adequately understood (Hounshell 1984; Piore and Sable 1984). Consequently previously successful US templates have been wrongly perceived as the best practice for the future. It is the distinctive pace of the Japanese domestic market which reveals these crucial and consequential differences. Hence attempts to extrapolate on the past adaptiveness of American corporations into the future should be treated with caution (e.g. Lawrence and Dyer 1983).

There are three basic components in the argument:

- strategic choice of market;
- market entrainment;
- the Japanese market.

First, to some extent the strategic debate attacks a strawman because the debate tends to confuse the quite different objectives of prescriptive organization theory with the description of how corporate leaders actually behave; i.e. how they make strategic choices for a specific corporation (e.g. Rover Company) or for a population of corporations (e.g. the British automobile industry – *see* Whipp and Clark 1986). The key aspects of strategic choice are:

- the top decision makers' evaluations of the market opportunities;
- the processes by which top decision makers adapt established strategies in the face of new opportunities and threats.

These two aspects tap the longitudinal relationship between corporations and transitions and influence the environmental rules for success which occur in all sectors at irregular moments.

Also, market entrainment requires careful specification. The notion of entrainment has been borrowed by the organizational sciences from biology. The perspective of entrainment postulates that some of the many endogenous cycles of activity within corporations become coupled to external rhythms of events through the thinking, practices and language games of top executives. So the external temporal signifiers are enacted as triggers to activate internal roles and structural poses (as on page 154). Previous theory and research on this coupling is sketchy and the speculative theorizing of Dill remains highly promising, yet in need of further development. Dill contends that interchanges between the corporation and its external market in the founding period of corporation are significant to the development of longer term adaptive structural poses (Dill 1962). His formulation is probably too deterministic, yet the macroscopic dimensions of markets are likely to embody the parameters of success and failure. The macroscopic dimensions of markets have not been sufficiently appreciated (Clark 1987), especially the significance of:

- what consumers prefer and are willing to purchase;
- the speed of saturation of the larger domestic markets and the significance of this for corporations in their experience of the learning curve and of competition.

It is evident, for example, that after 1700 and until the 1870s Britain was the largest and relatively most homogenized domestic market, and that the features of that market were sufficiently similar to Britain's areas of trading in textiles and cheap material goods. Britain created a maritime-based market system. After 1870 the largest, most integrated and homogenized domestic market became the USA where the revolutions in transportation and in telegraph facilitated crucial innovations in marketing to a set of consumers whose disposable income was enhanced by the cheapness of foodstuffs and other raw materials. It may be argued that the US market was large, homogenized and somewhat quicker in its saturation than the markets faced by British enterprises. Hence US firms were rewarded for moving quickly down the learning curve by the bold use of mass marketing and modern technologies (e.g. Ford).

Rosenberg illustrates this theme with reference to the development of aircraft to reduce land distances (Rosenberg 1982). The USA became the first major land-based economy, though it should be noted that inland and external shipping was an important source of wealth. The perspective of market entrainment would suggest that US corporations would develop cognitions of best practice which were grounded in the specifics of that domestic market and that to a significant extent these were carried abroad where they were less relevant (cf. Chandler and Daems 1980). In that respect US firms developed cognitions within which specific chronological codes were selected and reinforced. Moreover, within the US the changes which occurred in the market over the twentieth century were often accompanied by the replacement of former market leaders by new American firms. An apposite and well-researched example of the demise is the rise and fall of the US paper, the Saturday Evening Post.

Organization transitions: formative experiences and multiple paces

There are three basic issues which require identification and amplification when examining the relationship between corporate chronological codes and transitions in the repertoire of structural poses:

1 the distinction between recursiveness and transitions;

2 the tendency for organizational learning to be shaped by certain formative events and certain cohorts;
3 the differences in the pace with which certain aspects of the enterprise can be transformed – the multiple paces of innovation and exnovation.

In examining these three issues it is assumed that organizations are political systems containing interest groups competing to control meaning systems and the rules of legitimation.

First, recursiveness and transitions. The concept of recursiveness is central to the processual perspective (Weick 1969; Clark 1985a) and it is necessary to examine the notion of process more closely to ascertain its key temporal dynamics.

Most processual perspectives fail to address the issue of recursiveness and its implications. One exception is in the work of March and Simon who demonstrated that thinking and behaviour tend to be compacted into sequences which become habitual for the individual and for intersubjectively organized collective action. These sequences form the repertoire of the organization (March and Simon 1958). However, by relying on the metaphor of the computer March and Simon exaggerated the determinism of the repertoire. In contrast Weick's analysis of the social psychology of organizing highlights the significance of the cognitions which enact and activate the repertoire and also emphasizes the extent to which the repertoire may be forgotten or activated unintentionally (Weick 1969, Bandura 1986). Although there are few empirical studies of recursiveness in enterprises there is little doubting Giddens' (1985) claim that recursiveness is a basic feature of organizational dynamics (Giddens 1985).

So, what are the implications of the repertoire of recursiveness for transitions? The implications are that any transition involves an alteration in existing patterns and that the repertoire has to be altered in either its content and/or the linkages between enactment and performance. Moreover, it follows that many studies which claim that a transition has occurred may simply be observing an aspect of the repertoire which was dormant. This point was illustrated in the previous section with respect to the example of strategic time reckoning in the textile industry. Much of organizational dynamics is recursiveness rather than transition (Miller and Friesen 1984) and there are considerable problems in removing that recursiveness because the existing repertoire of chronological codes is difficult to transform.

Second, the issue of formative experiences in shaping the repertoire of chronological codes requires attention. The relevance of this issue was raised in a comparative study of the long-term role of designers in two automobile firms: in Renault in France (Clark and Windebank

1985a) and in Rover in Britain (Whipp and Clark 1986). In each firm a group of designers came into a position of central power at a particular conjuncture of external transitions in the underlying rules of competition, during which the new political group of designers inserted into the corporate repertoire certain distinctive chronological codes and methods of strategic time reckoning. The Renault case concerns events during the wartime occupation, when a group of designers began to plan a people's car within the framework of resistance to the apparent collaboration of Renault with the occupying forces. This group influenced the transformation of Renault into a socialized firm which was also largely in charge of its own directions. They were enabled to shift Renault's strategic direction from Sloanism to a phase of mass production in the Fordist mode. That group became a cohort extending from design into other areas and embracing a community of workers whose formative experience had been with mass production. The cohort was influential – even into the 1970s – and its predispositions had subtle impacts on the adaptation of the enterprise during the 1970s to the requirements for flexibility in timetabling production. The analysis of cohorts and their influence has been explored in John Players (Clark 1972: 213) and in a forthcoming study of Cadbury by researchers at Aston University, but much further investigation is required.

Third, much previous theorizing in the planned change perspective has implied that transitions occurred evenly across the whole array of facets: the corporate portfolio, buildings, equipment, manpower configurations, hierarchies, power groupings, departmental boundaries, role definitions of occupational groups, underlying attitudes and interpretation of corporate sagas. However, the perspective of multiple chronological codes and of structuration indicates that different facets of the enterprise possess their own distinctive 'time-loadings' and that there are considerable variations between facets in their pace of transition. The theoretical rationale for anticipating variations and hence multiple paces of re-adaptation has been outlined by Gurvitch (1964), and the historians of technological change (e.g. Braudel 1984; Landes 1983). Evidence to support these contentions has become much clearer during the current restructuring of Western capitalism when the disappearance of populations of firms and their replacement by new enterprises has become commonplace. It may be argued that the most rapid transitions can occur through changes in the corporate portfolio, especially in financial exchanges and closures, whilst the slowest transitions seem to occur when incoming new technologies and new forms of organization are introduced. Corporate portfolios can be reconfigured through sales of divisions. In the case of ICI, for example, there has been an extensive shift in the portfolio from heavy chemicals sold in the domestic and European markets to speciality chemicals sold in the USA. These changes have occurred through the sophisticated collusion of interfirm exchanges as well as through takeovers and closures. Shifting the portfolio has been a major feature of readaptation in the 1980s. In contrast there is clear evidence that there have been only fairly superficial changes in the regular contents of activity for skilled craftsmen in maintenance and professional workers in the health industry and in education. Likewise, employers and the state have been able to introduce fast changes in the employment contract, but have found greater difficulty in shifting more deeply held predispositions. It will be worth assessing whether the capacity for exnovation has been more fully developed than the capacity to introduce constructively forms of organization which will give Western, especially British, enterprises a robust rather than a lean capacity to survive (Clark 1987: 378).

This section has argued that a temporally sensitive perspective to transitions is required to disentangle recursiveness from transitions and to provide for a more differentiated analysis of the uneven, irregular paces of transition in different aspects of the enterprise.

Summary

The foregoing examination of the role of chronological codes has attempted to show that these codes combine heterogeneous and homogeneous components and that each is significant. However, it has been argued that heterogeneous codes are central to strategic time reckoning, especially to the adaptive activities of innovation-design, whilst homogeneous codes are more usually focused on the efficiency of planning. It has been argued that the repertoire of chronological codes and the expertise of their activation through time reckoning is specific to an enterprise and is highly consequential for the survival of that enterprise. Chronological codes reflect and shape the ways in which the future is cognitized. It has been argued that the choice of a market for the outputs of the enterprise tends to become a source of entrainment which couples external processes to the development and maintenance of the internal structural repertoire. So, the specific process of the domestic markets of Japan, the USA and of British enterprises constitute different, yet consequential, sources of potential entrainment.

It is worth recalling the differences in the use of chronological codes between the Chinese and the Europeans during the earlier part of this millennium (see page 157). Landes (1983) reasoned that the European concern with homogeneous chronological codes was a significant predisposition of Europeans which facilitated economic growth (Landes 1983). As we move into a new millennium the studies of the complex heterogeneous time reckoning systems used by Japanese enterprises (see T.C. Smith 1986) might be suggestive of how Western enterprises ought to be considering their adaptation to flexible Fordism. If so, the growing preoccupation with individual time management will require considerable revision, yet the capacity to recognize that requirement may be obscured by the absence of access to markets in which the paces of flexible Fordism are currently located.

Part three

Philosophy

Chapter ten

Organization/disorganization[1]

Robert Cooper

Introduction

> Two dangers continually threaten the world: order and disorder.
>
> Paul Valery

Contemporary usage of the concept of organization gives it a formal-functional emphasis and this is no more evident than in that branch of social science we call organization theory. No doubt this is part of the long drift towards the economism of modern institutions so well described by Polanyi in his analysis of the difference between primitive and modern economies (Polanyi 1969). However, the placing of organization theory within the wider field of social organization gives it a significantly different interpretive context in which rational-instrumental behaviour is subject to social or interactional forces. In an early paper on organizational analysis, Gouldner (1959) made a similar distinction in isolating the *rational* and *natural* systems of organization. The main purpose of that paper was to criticize the 'natural' mood for overemphasizing the tendency of organizational members to integrate their activities spontaneously and naturally. Against this view, Gouldner argued that system parts act in accordance with a principle of 'functional autonomy'; that is, far from willingly and spontaneously co-operating with others in the organization, sub-systems seek to preserve a degree of distance from other sub-systems. In what is for us a most telling observation, Gouldner writes:

> Assuming that the organization's parts, no less than the organization as a whole, operate to maintain their boundaries and to remain in equilibrium, then the parts should be expected to defend their functional autonomy, or at least some measure of it, from encroachment.
>
> (Gouldner 1959: 420–1)

What is significant about this comment is the implication that organizational activity is focused on the boundaries between system parts (the 'equilibrium' tendency – a contentious notion, anyway, being derived from and therefore secondary to boundary activity). Organizational structure, writes Gouldner, 'is shaped by a tension between centrifugal and centripetal pressures, limiting as well as imposing control over parts, separating as well as joining them' (Gouldner 1959: 423). Boundaries are thus seen as the loci of paradoxical interactions constituted by the mutuality of 'separation' and 'joining'.

A less explicit concern of Gouldner's paper was to tie the sociological analysis of organization into the still wider context of social and philosophical theory (an indication, incidentally, of Gouldner's own propensity to break down intellectual boundaries). In a footnote, Gouldner briefly casts his discussion of the 'rational' and 'natural' models (the latter now modified to take account of the autotropism of parts) in Apollonian and Dionysian terms respectively (Gouldner 1959: 421). Thus he quite clearly saw the 'rational' model of organizations as an expression of classic control and the modified 'natural' model as a form of romantic freedom. In a later paper, Gouldner carried the discussion further in identifying classicism and romanticism as two 'deep structures in social science' (Gouldner 1973: 323–66). Representing the perspective of order, classicism sees the world in terms of clear-cut boundaries and neat categories of thought which privilege the unities of time and space, the transparency of meaning and the fixity of form. In contrast, romanticism views reality as an 'intrinsic vagueness' in which objects and events blend into one another and thus lose their specific identities; against the universal and permanent, 'the contingent, the changing and local' are privileged; against the average, the special case is raised up; the disorderly is prized over the orderly. Here again Gouldner's subject matter revolves around the function of the boundary in social thought and action. Gouldner's main objective is to assess the pervasiveness of the two perspectives in Continental European and American social science. His character- ization of 'Chicago School romanticism', for example, serves to underline the major differences between the Classic and Romantic modes in social science. What haunts the work of the Chicago School is the idea of active difference located within the boundaries between systems and their parts; the focus of interest moves away from the classic concern with the system *per se* in its ordered unity to the divisions and gaps that constitute the 'between' of systems. The deviant case is not only raised to question the 'logic' and structure of the boundaries between the cases so that, for instance, social roles are conceived as symmetric reversals of each other. Nothing is privileged in this point of view, or at the very least the notion of a privileged system is raised as a 'construction' to be 'deconstructed'.

Gouldner's analysis draws our attention to the role of boundary as a complex, ambiguous structure around which are focused both the formal and informal organizing processes of social life. The boundary emerges as an intrinsically indeterminate medium which requires structuring in a particular order. It is this ordering of an intrinsic disorder that constitutes organization and which prescribes the theoretical recuperation of the boundary concept from its present marginal position in social and organizational analysis.

To comprehend the full significance of this conceptual shift it would be necessary to retrace the history of 'system' as portrayed in the literature of sociology and systems theory where it would not be difficult to show that the concept of boundary has been displaced by the concept of system itself in all its unity.

System and boundary

In the study of systems, social or otherwise, it is often forgotten that representation is a necessary part of the 'knowing' process. We do not experience the things of the world directly, but single out certain of their distinctive or differential features which we then perceive as mappings. In other words, we map the world in terms of significant differences, selecting certain features and excluding others. In this operation our thinking often eludes the actual process of mediation itself and we think and act as though signs and symbols give us unmeditated access to the world, reproducing it as it is without our selective intervention. In the discourse of the social and cultural sciences this art of elision, which suppresses the fundamental operation of the medium in communication, leads us to assume that socio-cultural artefacts can be grasped in themselves and independently of the forms of human communication that actually constitute them.

The analysis of discourse examines this distinction in terms of 'metalanguage' and 'object-language'. A metalanguage contextualizes or 'talks about' an object-language, the relationship between the two being of form to content. The academic language of social science, for example, acts as a metalanguage to frame its object or content which of course is some aspect of social life. In this case the metalanguage implicitly says: 'This is not really social life – it is a way of talking about it, i.e. it is a substitute for it'. But to the extent that this substitute function remains implicit rather than explicit there exists a tendency to regard the metalanguage as the real thing. The metalanguage thus becomes a form of representation which ignores or hides its representing or framing role and which acts like a transparent window which surreptitiously – since the observer is usually unaware of it – shapes what is perceived.

Systemness relies singularly on a conception of unity and unity itself is a product of framing. The frame both includes and excludes and what it includes is subjected by the metalanguage to a process of logical ordering and organization. Typically, what lies outside the system – or more accurately, what is said to lie outside the frame that creates the system – is viewed as less ordered and less unitary than what is included. A privileging of unity and order is attributed to the inside of the system while the outside, presumed to be less organized, is by implication devalued.

Systematic approaches in social science distinguish between the system and its environment and often emphasize the importance of boundary maintenance between the two. It is of course recognized that boundaries may be more or less permeable to environmental influences. The term 'closed system' is used to describe a system that is relatively impermeable to influences from the environment, while 'open system' refers to one which has a high degree of commerce with its context. It is significant that the analysis is invariably couched in binary terms, revolving around the distinction between *system* and *environment*. It is also significant that it is the system that has the boundary and not the environment, i.e. the boundary belongs to the system and not to the environment, which further supports the idea that the boundary serves to frame the system, encapsulating it as a thinkable entity and thus preserving its metalinguistic identity.

Traditional conceptualizations of systems are therefore structured so as to give preference to the idea of systemness, of articulated unity and order. The system (with its boundary) becomes conceptually detached from background or environment and thus takes on a life of its own. This has the effect of diverting attention from the all-important function of the frame. Paradoxically, while the social system is defined as a pattern of relationships, the concept of relationship is its least systematically analyzed feature and this effectively means that we end up with a nepotistic conception of social system. It is, we would claim, the frame which constitutes the relationship between system and environment and consequently it is the frame which provides the key to understanding the relationship between the two. At its most fundamental, the frame is what differentiates between inside and outside and thus must be understood as a structure which produces two mutually-defining points of view. In this context, the system is just as much inside the environment as the environment is inside the system. Whatever point of view is ultimately preferred must be arbitrary by definition. The boundary or frame has now to be conceived not as a static concept, subservient to either term, but as an active process of differentiation which serves system and environment equally.

Within social science itself the study of systems has undoubtedly followed the model of viewing the boundary of the system as a kind of container which holds the system parts together and thus prevents their dispersal. For example, it is clear that Talcott Parsons brings to the study of social systems an acknowledged predisposition (which is itself a boundary or frame of reference) to view systems as *ordered* structures. In *The Social System*, for example, Parsons discusses key concepts such as 'boundary', 'interaction' and 'relation' always from the *point of view* of an ordered, unitary system and not in their own terms (Parsons 1951). Social systems are 'boundary maintaining', differentiating themselves always from the 'environment'. A 'persistent' order (p. 27) pervades the system which is based on the system's 'strains to consistency' (p. 16), 'consistency' itself being understood as 'the logical consistency of a cognitive system' (p. 15). It is thus the 'system', with its correlates of 'logicality', 'consistency', and 'unity', that is privileged. The boundary, placed in a secondary and supplementary role, simply serves to frame (i.e. maintain) the 'system'. But supposing Parsons had decided to subvert this privileged position of 'system' by placing the emphasis on the differentiating or framing functions of the boundary. The whole nature of his theoretical enterprise would have been reversed and not only would he, like Gouldner, have revealed the significant social forces involved in the 'functional autonomy' of system parts but he would have been forced to recognize the primary (i.e. non-supplementary) role of boundary as the source of paradox and contradiction in social life and to relegate 'system' to the secondary and supplementary role. 'System' thus loses its position of centrality in the theoretical analysis and becomes an adjunct to 'boundary' and 'difference' which are then seen as the true problematics of social action.

Much the same sort of criticism could be addressed to the work of Peter Blau. In his work on formal organization, Blau shares the functional-system perspective of Parsons and this emerges especially in his use of the concept of 'differentiation' in organizational structure (Blau 1974). By 'differentiation' Blau means the divisions of labour (specialization) and authority. Like Parsons, Blau is predisposed to viewing organizations within the functional perspective of 'instrumental order':

> The defining criterion of formal organization – or an organization, for short, is the existence of procedures for mobilising and co-ordinating the efforts of various, usually specialised, subgroups in the pursuit of joint objectives . . .although the defining characteristic of an organization is that a collectivity is formally organized, what makes it of scientific interest is that the *developing* of social structure inevitably does not completely coincide with the *pre-established* forms.
>
> (Blau 1974: 29, my italics).

Blau's functionalist orientation then leads him to place the emphasis on specialization and authority rather than on differentiation, i.e. the perceptual centering on 'instrumental order' seduces him into defining structure in terms of *static* differences in role and status and not in terms of the actual process of difference which then of course becomes hidden from awareness and therefore unavailable to analysis.

Like most systems theorists, Parsons and Blau begin their analyses from a position which omits the foundationary step of division or differentiation in social life.[2] Social organization therefore appears already formed. In contrast, attention to the divisionary nature of the boundary reveals that the work of organization is focused upon transforming an intrinsically ambiguous condition into one that is ordered, so that organization as a process is constantly bound up with its contrary state of disorganization. Seen in this way, the mutuality of the organization–disorganization opposition becomes a central issue in the analysis of social organization and social action. It is to this question that we now turn.

System and difference

Organization and information

Social organization may be defined as a structure which relates people to each other in the general process of managing nature and themselves: 'Nature, society and individual human beings are related to each other by the transformation of matter-energy and by the communication of information' (Wilden 1982: 2). In the modern world, formal organization is the main device for transforming matter-energy but when the latter enters the social world it takes on informational character. Thus organizations, in the processing of raw materials, at the same time produce a communicational order which relates their members to each other.

The role of information is to mediate between form and matter, order and disorder; information is a process (and not a state) in which form is made out of non-form. Usually, information is defined in terms of its improbability; the less likely or more unexpected an event, the more information it carries. In a more fundamental sense, information derives its value from the inherent *undecidability* of matter. Mediating between form and matter, information contains a contradiction which is – curiously and significantly – reflected in its etymological affinities with, on the one hand, words of *order* (e.g. in-form, enframe) and, on the other, words of *disorder* (e.g. unformed, infirm); while reproducing materially, information at the same time suppresses it.

Within the social sciences and related disciplines, the concept of information as structure or organization is well-known though it may be construed in different ways (Buckley 1967; Spencer Brown 1969). However, there is general agreement that information is a binary structure based on the idea of division or distinction. The human world is constituted by such divisions, e.g. man–woman, teacher–student, night–day, summer–winter, etc. There are two ways of interpreting such binarity: (a) by placing the emphasis on the two separate terms, or (b) by focusing on the division boundary *between* the terms. We have already suggested that (a) is the dominant mode of perception among systems theorists such as Parsons and Blau. To understand (b) requires that the division between terms be conceived no longer just as a separation but also as a structure that joins terms together, i.e. division both separates and joins. In fact, it is the act of separation which, paradoxically, creates the perception of something that is also whole or unitary. This observation – of fundamental significance in understanding the nature of information or structure – can be more clearly seen in Figure 10.1, which illustrates the separation-wholeness paradox of information. The separate faces of Figure 10.1 share the same profile yet at the same time they repress each other in the sense that the perception of one face is always at the expense of the other. The profiles are thus mutually

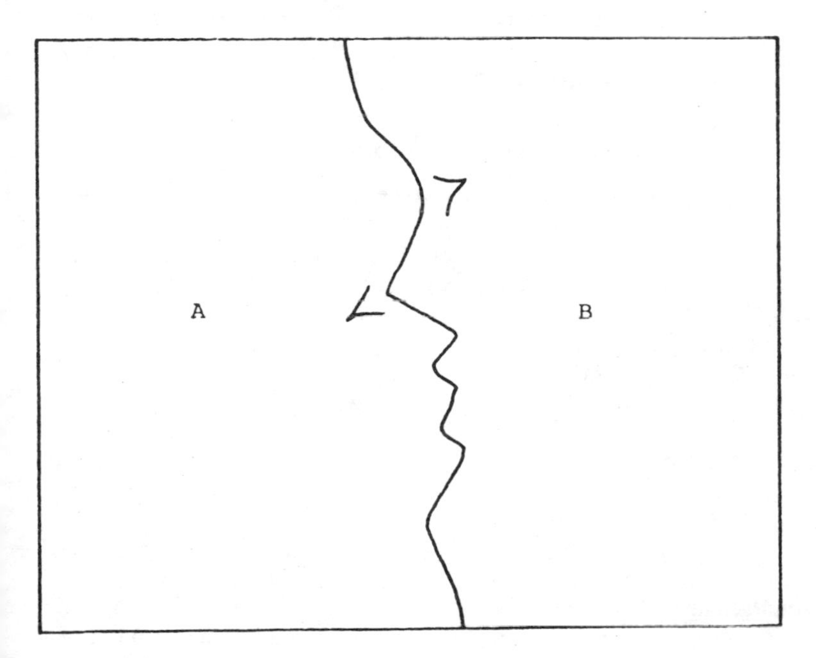

Figure 10.1

parasitic and it is this property which makes them inseparable and their overall structure radically undecidable.

Now no longer a simple binary structure, information appears as the sharing or alternation of a whole between two terms. It is specifically the idea of alternation or reversibility that distinguishes information. Though different, the profiles of Figure 10.1 are also the same in that they are perfect reversals of each other. With this recognition we have gone beyond the common definition of information as merely 'useful knowledge' and have adumbrated its ontotheoretical status.

We have noted that social organization is structured around the communication of information or difference. It is perhaps more usual to express this in terms of the communication of signs, but a sign is merely another name for a difference. The sign enables the individual subject to mark itself off in a social space in relation to other signs – teacher/pupil, doctor/patient, producer/consumer, etc. – but this marking off is subject to the 'mutual parasitism' intrinsic to the boundary between signs. While belonging to neither one side nor the other and therefore being unapportionable by either, it is the boundary which structures the interactions and meaning *between* social actors. The boundary may be shared but it cannot be shared out; it is obdurate and intractable. This resistance to apportionment is a feature of the boundary's intrinsic undecidability. A more systematic characterization may be approached through Saussure's ideas on the 'system of language' and the works of Bateson and Derrida on the concept of 'difference'.

The system of signs (Saussure) and difference (Bateson)

Saussure's *Course in General Linguistics* (1974) provides a framework for understanding language as a structure or system; it may, therefore, serve as a model for all systems of communication, including social systems. For Saussure, language is a system of signs. A linguistic sign is a dual structure made up of concept (e.g. the *idea* of a tree) and sound-image (e.g. the spoken word 'tree'). The concept is called by Saussure the signified, the meaning aspect of the sign, and the sound-image, the signifier. Saussure asserted that signifier and signified are inextricably intertwined. The signified receives the emphasis as the source of meaning, the signifier simply being the vehicle by which subjects exchange meaning. Saussure therefore describes a one-to-one correspondence between signifier and signified.

Later in his analysis, Saussure recasts his earlier interpretation of signification. Signification, he tells us, 'is only the counterpart of the sound-image' (Saussure 1974: 114). But there is a paradox, in that 'on the one hand the concept seems to be the counterpart of the sound-image and on the other hand the sign itself is in turn the counterpart of the other signs of language' (p.114). This point then leads Saussure to argue that language is a system in which each term or sign is defined not by itself but by the presence of other terms from which it is seen to differ so that 'in language there are only differences'.

Clearly Saussure holds two different and apparently contradictory views of language: one that derives from a conception of the sign as the focus and carrier of meaning and the other, located at the level of the language system, which sees the sign as the effect of difference. In the first, the division between signified and signifier is elided despite Saussure's insistence that the bond between the two is arbitrary (and that arbitrariness and difference are 'two correlative qualities') and one can suggest that this is because Saussure, understandably taking a 'common-sense' view of the sign which puts meaning before all else, gives priority to concept over phonetic substance. In this respect, Saussure's concept is the metalanguage to the object-language of the sound-image; the concept contextualizes the sound-image and gives it a place in a seemingly pre-formed world of meaning. Saussure thus provides theoretical support for what is really a semantic conception of language which orders everything according to meaning. But when he moves to the level of the system, Saussure does a complete reversal: the differential features of both signifier and signified are paramount, each linguistic term is a negative product of the other terms. Language is a structure of traces which, when followed, are seen to have no origin but are continually deferred and unfinished just as there is no absolute end to the process of looking up the meaning of a word in a dictionary where one definition can lead on to another, endlessly. Language as system reveals a structure that, far from the positivity and fixity of sign as meaning, is essentially incomplete and without solid foundation, with neither beginning nor end, based on the negative, on what is not. It is the continual deferral of presence that characterizes 'system' as a seriality of differences and which is further elaborated from a different intellectual standpoint by the social anthropologist Gregory Bateson (1972).

Bateson reminds us that we do not experience things in themselves in their full, unitary presence but as transforms or differences of them. The world of form and communication deals only in differences. In the mind there are no objects or events; the mind contains only differences. To talk about things in the mind is to commit the intellectual sin of reification. There is even a problem in talking about *the* mind since this gives the impression of a locatable place, a thing which contains other things. In fact, the mind, too, is difference. Difference, or information, cannot be localized or placed because it is dimensionless:

> It is flatly obvious that no variable of zero dimensions can be truly located. 'Information' and 'form' resemble contrast, frequency,

> symmetry, correspondence, congruence, conformity and the like in being of zero dimensions and, therefore, are not to be located. The contrast between this white paper and that black coffee is not somewhere between the paper and the coffee and, even if we bring the paper and the coffee into close juxtaposition, the contrast between them is not thereby located or pinched between them. Nor is that contrast located between the two objects and my eye. It is not even in my head; or, if it is, then it must also be in your head. But you, the reader, have not seen the paper and the coffee to which I was referring. I have in my head an image or transform or name of the contrast between them, and you have in your head a transform of what I have in mine. But the conformity between us is not localizable. In fact, information and form are not items which can be localized.
>
> (Bateson 1972: 414–15)

A difference, then, is a transform of the world, and 'the mind' records the difference in much the same way as a map records the differences deemed significant by the map-maker. The territory itself does not of course appear on the map:

> What gets on to the map, in fact, is difference, be it a difference in altitude, a difference in vegetation, a difference in population structure, difference in surface or whatever.
>
> (Bateson 1972: 457)

With this insight, it is now more logical to view mind as a structure or circuit of differences; like difference, mind is not locatable but is a process that is immanent throughout a system of differences.

The relationship between information, or difference, and action is effected through exclusion:

> Information, in the technical sense, is that which *excludes* certain alternatives. The machine with a governor does not elect the steady state; it *prevents* itself from staying in any alternative stage; and in all such cybernetic systems, corrective action is brought about by *difference* .... The difference between some present state and some 'preferred' state activates the corrective response.
>
> (Bateson 1972: 381)

In other words, difference leads to action prompted by a negation, by what is not. Information results from selecting one of two mutually exclusive choices which are *a priori* for the subject, i.e. difference corresponds to a dilemma which every message implies – yes or no, this or that, here or there, etc. The action of difference is the selection of one state over another and this is what Bateson means by the 'preferred' state – the lack or absence of the preferred state is what motivates action. Discussing the action of the nervous system, Bateson argues that it is wrong to say that "impulses" travel in axons since the metaphor of "impulse" suggests a hard-science line of thought which will ramify only too easily into nonsense about "psychic energy"' (Bateson 1972: 318). It is 'difference' that travels in the axon – in this case, difference between 'quiescence' and 'activity'. Quiescence and activity have equal informational value:

> It is even incorrect to speak of the 'message of activity' and the 'message of quiescence'. Always the fact that information is a transformation of difference should be remembered, and we might better call the one message 'activity – not quiescence' and the other 'quiescence – not activity'.
>
> (Bateson 1972: 319)

Nevertheless, an act of exclusion does occur and Bateson analyses this in the process of framing. To illustrate the concept of frame, he uses the analogies of the picture frame and the mathematical set. The functions of frames are:

1 To exclude: by including certain messages within a frame, certain others are *excluded.*
2 To include: by excluding certain messages certain others are included.

Now in set theory, as Bateson points out, these two functions are symmetrical and equivalent, being straightforward reversals of each other, but psychologically they are quite separate. The frame around the picture, for example, is really an instruction to the viewer telling him or her to attend to what is within the frame and to ignore what is outside it. Perception of the background has to be formally inhibited and that of the foreground enhanced. In addition, the frame informs the viewer that he or she may not utilize the same rules for interpreting the picture as for interpreting the wallpaper outside the frame. In terms of set theory, those elements inside the imaginary line are defined as members of the same class since they share common properties. Similarly, any message that gives instructions or provides an orientation or direction serves as a frame.

The frame's directing function helps elucidate Saussure's analysis of the signified (the meaning aspect of the sign). Signification rests on the idea of direction, moving in one way rather than another, that is, a selection process is at work which includes certain things while excluding others. Selection at this level is not voluntary but imperative; one is forced to choose one of the differences. It is in this sense that signification 'pre-vents' (ie. 'comes before' as a 'pre-structure') the subject from occupying the *other* position, i.e. each signification is produced by its difference from or opposition to other significations.

From difference to undecidability (Derrida)

Building on Saussure's conception of language as a system of differences, Derrida (1982) has introduced the concept of *différance*. In coining the term *différance* with an *a*, Derrida combines the two senses of the French *différer* – to differ (in space) and to defer (postpone in time) – into 'one designation for what both subverts and produces the illusion of presence, identity and consciousness' (Johnson 1980: 130). Explicating his conception of *différance*, Derrida begins with the traditional understanding of the sign as that which we put in place of the absent thing we wish to be present to us; in this way the sign represents the present in its absence. The sign is thus deferred presence. This classically conceived structure of the sign, in substituting the sign for the thing itself, treats the sign as a derivative of a lost presence towards which the sign carries the subject. The argument that Derrida advances can be said to be essentially against the idea of a fully present reality which we normally consider the world to be, directly and unitarily available to our understanding, and what is posited instead is a world that is continually deferred, postponed in space and time.

The principle of difference, Derrida continues, affects the sign in its entirety, that is, as both signified and signifier. The first implication of this is that the:

> signified concept is never present in and of itself, in a sufficient presence that would refer only to itself. Essentially and lawfully, every concept is inscribed in a chain or in a system within which it refers to the other, to other concepts, by means of the systematic play of differences.
>
> (Derrida 1982: 11)

The play of differences – *différance*, in effect – thus becomes not merely a concept or a word but instead 'the possibility of conceptuality, of a conceptual process and system in general' (Derrida 1982: 11). Briefly, *différance* is that which occasions system and which at the same time lies beyond it. The essential point is that *différance*, just like Saussure's conception of difference, can never be fully grasped in the present since it is an active play that always runs before us. A taxonomic approach to the language system can reveal only an inert statistical and classificatory inventory of linguistic features and would not be able to bring out the essential play of differences, nor would it tell us that these differences are themselves 'effects' of something other than themselves, namely, *différance*.

> This does not mean that the *différance* that produces difference is somehow before them, in a simple and unmodified – in-different – present. *Différance* is the non-full, nonsimple, structured and differentiating origin of differences. Thus, the name 'origin' no longer suits it.
>
> (Derrida 1982: 11)

Since *différance* is ever-active play, it cannot be located in any particular place, which is Derrida's way of characterizing Bateson's idea of information (differences) as a zero form which is not locatable. It may be thought that *différance* can at least be approached but it moves away before being fully caught. As Derrida says, the differences of language are effects which 'do not find their cause in a subject or a substance, in a thing in general, a being that is somewhere present' (Derrida 1982: 11). The differences of *différance* have neither a locatable presence nor a specifiable cause. Like Borges' rediscovery of the ancient metaphor of God and Nature as a sphere whose centre is everywhere and circumferences nowhere, *différance* is a continuous centre that continually divides itself; *différance* is divided presence:

> An interval must separate the presence from what it is not in order for the present to be itself, but this interval that constitutes it as present must, by the same token, divide the present in and of itself, thereby also dividing, along with the present, everything that is thought on the basis of the present . . . . In constituting itself, in dividing itself dynamically, this interval is what might be called spacing . . . .
>
> (Derrida 1982: 13)

If we ask *what* or who produces differences, we couch the question in such a way that we expect an answer in terms of some thing, form or state – that is, some presence. But Saussure reminds us that language (which consists only of differences) is not an effect of the speaking subject but rather that the subject is a 'product' of language, that the subject speaks, is enabled to speak, through the system of differences that constitutes language. It follows that a conception of 'social system' in these terms must dispense with the perception of an interactional structure that is fully given to us in the present; social structure can only become 'present' to us through *différance* which, though it constitutes presence, can never be present. This is a difficult point for us to understand since our habitual forms of thought privilege presence over absence, the positive over the negative. In general, we are given to thinking in binary or polar terms (i.e. not 'differentially') and in privileging one term over the other. Other examples of this bias offered by Derrida are: good–evil, truth–error, man–woman, nature–culture, mind–matter, life–death, where the second term in each pair is regarded as the perverted, corrupt and therefore undesirable version of the first.[3] A hierarchical order is thus set up which prerogates the classical desiderata of unity, identity, immediacy (i.e. spatio-temporal presence) over difference, interval and separation.[4] It should be clear by now that 'presence' (and its component features) is Derrida's way of talking about metalanguage.

Allied to the concept of presence as *différance* (i.e. as deferred presence) is the idea of undecidability, which is Derrida's way of expressing the non-form of information. A certain force or violence is required for the act of separating the decidable from the undecidable. The idea is reminiscent of Simmel's (1950) statement that: 'All system-building, whether of science, conduct or society, involves the assertion of power: it subjects material outside of thought to a form which thought has cast' (Simmel 1950: 357). The concepts of the metalanguage or the frame (which are really the same) are devices for creating undecidability or meaning. An 'excess' always surrounds and surpasses systems which claim to be based on 'decidables' and which are therefore thought to be complete. A simple example is the series of graphic marks on a page – letters, words – which, from the point of view of a metalanguage, are ordered – assembled, categorized and unified – to produce a meaning that transcends the fragmentary, material character of the text. Derrida argues that these material marks *and* the white spaces between them which lend them form are necessary for 'meaning' to be produced yet are themselves without meaning; they are undecidable in relation to the metalinguistic principles brought to bear on them. While being necessary to create the system of meaning, the material text contradicts the meaning system because it cannot be reduced to the decidability characteristic of the latter.

One of Derrida's best-known texts, 'Plato's Pharmacy', analyses the ancient Greek *pharmakon* as treated by Plato in the *Phaedrus* (Derrida 1981: 61–171). Derrida's purpose in this exemplary dissection is to show how philosophy doctors its subject matter in the interests of a privileged point of view; in this respect philosophy simply exemplifies the bias that runs through all tests that assert or look for 'meanings' or 'formalisms'. The word *pharmakon* is intrinsically 'undecidable'; in ancient Greece it meant both remedy and poison, good *and* bad rolled into one. When Plato applies the term *pharmakon* to those he is criticizing (e.g. the Sophists), he intends it in its maleficent sense of 'poison'; applied to Socrates and the Socratic approach in general, which he favours, it means 'remedy'. However, it is less the truth position which

Plato would like to establish that concerns Derrida but the intrinsic ambiguity of the term itself. The 'problem' of the *pharmakon* is that it is the 'medium in which opposites are opposed' and in which one side (site) crosses over into the other (good/bad, inside/outside, etc.) in an ever-active play which brings to mind the 'mutual parasitic' structure of Figure 10.1 (page 173). It is this play or freedom of movement that Plato wishes to stop but which in itself is beyond control, i.e. undecidable.

Derrida elaborates his argument in terms of the inside/outside polarity: 'Apprehended as a blend and an impurity, the *pharmakon* also acts like an aggressor or a housebreaker, threatening some internal purity and security' (Derrida 1981: 128). The 'inside' must fight to retain its 'purity' (this is another way of defining 'self-identity' and 'presence' against the 'impurity' of the 'outside') in much the same way that Plato cleansed 'truth' of contaminating 'error'. The purity of the inside can only be attained, says Derrida, if the outside is branded as a supplement, something extra (an 'excess') not necessary in itself. But the supplement is added in order to complete and compensate for a lack in what is thought to be complete. In order to cure the 'inside' of the 'undesired' aspect of the *pharmakon*, it is necessary to keep the outside out. In this very powerful and fundamental sense, the 'outside' as the undesired supplement plays a necessary constituting rule in the formation of the 'inside' and, far from being a mere accessory, is thus a central feature of the 'inside'. The supplement, therefore, acts as a frame or ground to the content of the inside to which it is marginal. In other words, the supplement supports the privileged 'inside'. But this metalinguistic view of the inside/outside relationship hides a paradox which we have already hinted at in drawing attention to the mutuality or interdependence of inside/outside. Bateson, too, recognizes the existence of this same paradox when he discusses the contradiction inherent in framing where the outside can become the inside and vice versa. To illustrate this, Derrida uses examples from the human body, for its innermost spaces – mouth, stomach, etc. – are actually pockets of externality folded in. An 'outside' is thus seen to be the most intrinsic feature of a system, displacing the inside.

It is clear that the concept of difference provides a way of understanding social systems as contrived devices whose stability and identity rests to a large extent on the suppression of the movement of difference. Especially in the work of Derrida, concepts such as *différance*, undecidability, and supplement 'decompose' or 'decon- struct' the ordered and organized character of social systems to reveal their essentially precarious foundation which founders on the process of differentiation. There are here – and throughout the above accounts – two ways of approaching 'system' or 'organization'. The dominant mode of interpreting and understanding 'system' is by way of a fully present unity, hierarchical order and purpose. We have called this the metalinguistic model whose main epistemological prop is the asymmetrical frame or boundary. In contrast, the work of those writers – Saussure, Bateson, Derrida – who view structures differentially has brought us to an alternative conception of 'system' and 'organization' in which, perhaps at the level of what we might call the infrastructure, we discover an intrinsic undecidability which can only be 'organized' or 'systematized' through an external force that is wholly foreign to it. It is this level which is resistant to order and organization and which we call 'disorganization' or, as in the next section, the zero degree of organization.

The zero degree of organization

Introduced in the social anthropology of Marcel Mauss through the concept of *mana*, zero degree or zero value has been used by Lévi-Strauss to facilitate the understanding of social structure in symbolic or linguistic terms. We may think of zero degree essentially as a state – if this word can be properly applied to such a dynamic concept – of no specific order, organization or direction, a process of undecidability that pervades all social organization. Zero degree is always conceived as an excess to order or meaning, it is always 'more than', it is the overabundance of the signifier in contrast to the 'reduction' contained in the signifed. In his 'Introduction to the work of Marcel Mauss', Lévi-Strauss captures the manifoldness of zero degree in the following words:

> In other words – and taking as a guide Mauss's precept that all social phenomena can be assimilated to language – we see in *mana*, *Wakan*, *oranda* and other notions of the same type, the conscious expression of a semantic function, whose role it is to permit symbolic thought to operate in spite of the contradiction which is proper to it. In this way are explained the apparently insoluble antinomies attached to this notion. . . . At one and the same time force and action, quality and state, noun and verb; abstract and concrete, omnipresent and localised – mana is in effect all these things. But is it not precisely because it is none of these things that *mana* is a simple form, or more exactly, a symbol in the pure state, and therefore capable of becoming charged with any sort of symbolic content whatever? In the system of symbols constituted by all cosmologies, *mana* would simply be a zero symbolic value, that is to say, a sign marking the *necessity of a symbolic content supplementary to that which the signified is already loaded* [our italics], but which can take on any value required, provided only that this value still remains part of the available reserve . . . .
>
> (Lévi-Strauss 1950: XLIX–L)

The surplus or excess of zero degree, or what amounts to the same thing, the signifier, results from the finite, limited nature of the signified which is seen as a lack that must be filled in. It is this surplus or excess that occasions Derrida in his essay, 'Structure, sign and play in the discourse of the human sciences', to conceive of the 'zero symbolic value' of the signifier as play (Derrida 1978). Derrida's essay is worth summarizing in some detail since it reveals the essentially 'undecidable' character of the zero degree.

Derrida's starting-point is 'structure' – let us also add 'organization' – and how we conceive it. Traditionally, structure has always been thought of in a limited way, limited by the idea of it necessarily having a fixed centre of point of origin:

> The function of this centre was not only to orient, balance and organize the structure ... but above all to make sure that the organizing principle of the structure would limit what we might call the *play* of the structure. By orienting and organizing the coherence of the system, the centre of a structure permits the play of its elements inside the total form.
>
> (Derrida 1978: 278–9)

However, the centre 'closes off' the play it has made possible since it excludes itself from the very possibility of play; it creates 'a play constituted on the basis of a fundamental immobility and a reassuring certitude, which itself is beyond the reach of play' (Derrida 1978: 279). In short, this playless centre whose lack of play assures our certainty is another name for *presence* or *meta-structure*:

> It could be shown that all the names related to fundamentals, to principles, or to the centre have always designated an invariable presence – *eidos*, *arche*, telos, *energeia*, *ousia*, (essence, existence, substance, subject), *aletheia*, transcendentality, consciousness, God, man, and so forth.
>
> (Derrida 1978: 279–80)

But modern thought has shaken this illusory edifice and is beginning to substitute for it a conception of centre based on non-presence *différance*:

> Henceforth, it was necessary to begin thinking that there was no centre, that the centre could not be thought in the form of a present-being, that the centre had no natural site, that it was not a fixed locus but a function, a sort of nonlocus in which an infinite number of sign-substitutions came into play. This was the moment when language invaded the universal problematic, the moment when, in the absence of a centre or origin, everything became discourse ... that is to say, system in which the central signified,

> the original or transcendental signified, is never absolutely present outside a system of differences.
>
> (Derrida 1978: 280)

Examplars of this radical shift in thought are Nietzsche for his critiques of metaphysics and absolute truth (for which he substituted the notions of play and sign); Freud for his critique of consciousness, of the 'individualized' subject in possession of itself; and Heidegger for his destruction of metaphysics and the idea of existence as 'presence'. Among the 'human sciences', one area stands out as especially reflecting this epistemological schism, and this is ethnology.

Ethnology, a European science, was born at the point when European culture (which would include political, economical, technical, as well as philosophical and scientific discourses) was forced to stop thinking of itself as the centre of the human universe, the standard by which all other cultures were to be judged. Derrida chooses the work of Lévi-Strauss who, perhaps more than any other social scientist, has concerned himself with self-reflection and self-criticism, with exposing ethnology to the contradictions inherent in its own methodology and discourse. This project is seen perhaps most explicitly in Lévi-Strauss' later work on myths and mythological activity in which he sees his own scientific endeavour as 'mythological' or 'mythopoetical'. The chief characteristics of 'this critical search for a new status of discourse is the stated abandonment of all reference to a *centre*, to a *subject*, to a *privileged reference*, to an origin, or to an absolute *archia*' (Derrida 1978: 286). It is this that is revealed in the analysis of myth. In myth there is no one authoritative reference point or absolute source. For example, in *The Raw and the Cooked*, Lévi-Strauss (1970) realizes that the Bororo myth, which serves as the 'reference myth' for the analysis of all the other myths examined in the book, cannot properly be allotted this privileged referential position since it is simply a transformation of other myths either in the same community or in more remote societies. Because myths are cross-referential in this way, all are equal and hence they collectively refute the idea of one version being paramount for the understanding of all the others. There is also no unity or absolute centre of myth.

The 'differential' structure of myth necessarily precludes it being pinned down to any one position or point of view. Its understanding therefore requires a discourse which has the same 'form of that of which it speaks', i.e. which is itself *mythomorphic*. Traditional scientific and philosophical discourse is therefore inappropriate to the analysis of the zero-degree of myth because such a discourse organizes its interpretation according to the principles of an original, founding source or centre and therefore inflicts a violence on what is intrinsically without a clear organizing centre. Lévi-Strauss thus argues against the idea of a fixed origin that authors – gives authority or credence – to myth. There is no centre, just as there is no subject. The conception of a stable centre is equivalent to the signified whose *partial* nature, as we noted above, creates a lack which must be filled in. This is the nature of play in that it always runs beyond the constraint of the fixed position or meaning; play is another name for zero-degree as it is for myth, absence of centre, and authority (i.e. a determining author).[5]

It is curious that few writers on social systems have explicitly identified the concept of zero-degree or its like. Gouldner we have singled out as one of the rare exceptions, but while his characterization of the 'deep structure' of Romanticism institutes the notion of zero-degree it lacks the rigour that 'structuralist' (or 'post-structuralist') thought has added to it. It is also curious that of the thinkers cited by Gouldner as representative of this tendency in social science, none has really put his theoretical or conceptual finger on the definitive properties of zero-degree. Gouldner's exemplars of the counter-classical position are only hazily aware of the nature of the phenomena they are trying to express. It seems to us that Gouldner's case could have been significantly advanced by using the sociological insights of Georg Simmel, which, strangely, he completely neglects.

Simmel's theoretical position, especially his so-called 'theory of forms', is remarkably similar to the concept of zero-degree. Simmel's attack on the classical position echoes the critique of classical 'presence' that we find in Lévi-Strauss and Derrida. 'Classicism .... is the ideology of form, which regards itself as the ultimate notion for life and creation' (Simmel 1965: 21). The classical approach, based on the assumption of a privileged centre, is a 'closed system [which] aims to unite all truths, in their most general concepts, into a structure of higher and lower elements which extend from a basic theme, arranged symmetrically and balanced in all directions' (p. 21). Against this, Simmel argues that form, although necessary as a categorizing device, is partial, temporary and cannot exhaust (i.e. fully comprehend) the infinite nature of the raw material of life (Simmel 1980).[6] This means that no one form can occupy a privileged position, hence differentiation becomes the definitive mark of form, as in Derrida's deconstruction of the classical 'centre' which becomes 'decentred'.

What is perhaps more relevant to our present purpose is Simmel's use of the concept of 'play'. Social structure is not a simple set of categorizations for Simmel, but a 'play' of relationships which is seen in much the same way as Derrida's conception of play. Let us remind ourselves that play as the movement *différance* is that which is always 'more than' a specific form or meaning; that which cannot be contained or limited. Play is that which is supplementary to form. In his analysis of the role of secrecy in social life, for example, it is clear that Simmel understands the secret as a process which supplements or compensates for the lack of play in formal structures (Simmel 1950). The essence of the secret society, says Simmel, is autonomy or freedom. The autonomy indicated here is differential to the larger, more encompassing system from which a desired property is missing and which the autonomy seeks to supplement. As a sociological variable, autonomy is the movement of *différance*, of which secrecy, as Simmel suggests, is one of the major social expressions:

> The employment of secrecy as a sociological technique, as a form of action without which certain purposes – since we live in a social environment – can simply not be attained, is understandable immediately. Not quite so evident are the attractions and values of the secret beyond its significance as a mere means – the peculiar attraction of formally secretive behaviour irrespective of its momentary content. In the first place, the strongly emphasized exclusion of all outsiders makes for a correspondingly strong feeling of possession. For many individuals, property does not fully gain its significance with mere ownership, but only with the consciousness that others must do without it. The basis for this, evidently, is the impressionability of our feelings through *differences*. Moreover, since the others are excluded from the possession – particularly when it is very valuable – the converse suggests itself psychologically, namely, that what is denied to many must have special value.
>
> (Simmel 1950: 332).

Here Simmel couches his analysis in terms of the inside/outside distinction; those excluded are placed outside and are thus *without*, i.e. they lack something in relation to those included. Simmel's equating of secrecy with autonomy, emphasizing as it does the ideas of inclusion and exclusion which mediate between the two, helps extend Gouldner's earlier mentioned analysis of organizational boundaries and the process of functional autonomy (i.e. the 'play' in the system which is beyond so-called 'rational' control). For Simmel, secrecy illustrates the infinite, unfinished character of social life, which not only refuses the fixity of a determined form, but which also transgresses it. As an expression of zero degree, secrecy is a subversion of the known and formal term, a movement beyond that which can be publicly observed and hence organized; the secret – like the sacred with which it shares an ancient etymology – derives from an inviolable exigency to preserve what is expunged in every form, namely, the reversal or counter-form which constitutes every boundary and which here is expressed in terms of play or freedom.

Zero-degree is thus a theoretical condition of no meaning, no form, of absolute disorder which one might call the primary source of form or organization, if the concepts of 'primary' and 'source' did not call to mind the sense of an absolute origin which was itself organized. The disorder of the zero degree is that which is essentially undecidable and it is this feature which energizes or motivates the call to order or organization. Order/organization, stemming as it does from undecidability, cannot in any ultimate sense be based on a natural 'logic' or 'rationality' but is realized only through an 'externally' imposed determination which effectively means 'force' or 'power' in one or more of its thousand guises.

Organization and the therapeutic function

If zero degree is an excess, a surplus, a supplement, if it is always 'more than', then order and organization must necessarily be a reduction, a deduction, 'less than'. In a parenthetical remark in his article, 'Structure, sign and play in the human sciences', Derrida (1978) draws attention to this distinction in a specially interesting way. Commenting on Lévi-Strauss's use of the term *ration supplementaire* (supplementary allowance), the 'economic' reserve of the zero degree which has to be 'shared out among things according to the laws of symbolic thought' (Derrida 1978: 95), Derrida suggests that this is the origin of the concept of ratio itself (reason, reckoning, rationality).

The relevance of this remark for understanding social action may be grasped by retracing part of our earlier argument (see page 172) which couched social behaviour in terms of the action of differences. We showed there that 'difference' was essentially a reversible structure which we illustrated through the 'reversible profile' of Figure 10.1 (page 173). The 'ratio', or 'sharing out', discussed by Lévi-Strauss and Derrida is here the reciprocal sharing (not specifically a 'sharing out', as we indicated) of the same space (actually the zero degree) which is intrinsically resistant to division, i.e. is undecidable. To solve this problem, social systems have to organize themselves to as to deny the existence of undecidability by erecting systems of 'logical' and 'rational' action. Without elaborating this point, we believe that a related argument exists in the work of Herbert Marcuse. In his essay 'Industrialization and capitalism in the work of Max Weber', Marcuse reinterpreted Weber's concept of 'rationalization' so that, instead of rationality as calculable efficiency, it was seen as a form of unacknowledged political domination which serves to privilege the interests of particular groups (Marcuse 1968). In an exemplary move, Marcuse also reveals the extent of Weber's own 'will to power' when he points out that Weber himself recognized his own commitment to the concept of 'rationality', thus admitting a limit (we would say a 'frame') to his conceptual scheme:

> [Weber] defined himself as a 'bourgeois' and identified his work with the historical mission of the bourgeoisie; in the name of this alleged mission, he accepted the alliance of representative strata of the German bourgeoisie with the organizers of reaction and repression.
>
> (Marcuse 1968: 208)

In declaring his frame of reference, his metastructural position, Weber invalidates rationality as a transcendent product of scientific thought and shows that it too 'takes sides'; in doing so, Weber implicitly recognizes the differential character of social structure in which formal rationality is further supplemented by the framework of domination:

> Precisely insofar as this formal rationality does not go beyond its own structure and has nothing but its own system as the norm of its calculations and calculating actions, it is as a whole dependent, determined 'from the outside' by something other than itself.
>
> (Marcuse 1968: 214)

We would like to suggest (as Marcuse himself does in various writings) that rationalization as domination is dependent upon the mastering or control of the surplus or supplement that characterizes the zero degree in all social systems and that this essentially involves controlling the metastructure and the metalanguage. In another essay, 'Aggressiveness in advanced industrial society',[7] Marcuse recognizes this same process when he associates what he calls 'surplus-repression' (essentially, the incorporation of the supplement or excess of zero degree into a privileged and preferred point of view) with the 'management of language', providing examples of communicational domination that vividly demonstrate for our own time Plato's similar appropriation of the *pharmakon* (Marcuse 1968). But all this can be summarized in the thesis that social power (authority, law, organization) is the forcible transformation of undecidability into decidability. We illustrate this thesis in the organizational context by means of a fictionalized account of several real-life incidents which occurred in the British and US navies nearly two hundred years ago, contained in Herman Melville's *Billy Budd, Sailor* (1970).[8] This is the story of a young sailor on a British man-of-war in the year 1797. Falsely accused of mutinous plotting by the devious master-at-arms, John Claggart, Billy, unable to answer the charge because of a stutter, impetuously strikes Claggart dead in front of the ship's captain, Vere. The captain, a just and honest man with much sympathy for Billy, convinces his fellow-officers that under the circumstances – Britain is at war with France and there have been other mutinies – Billy must hang. Undecidability constitutes the warp and woof of the story: Billy is fair, innocent and harmless but he kills; Claggart is evil, mendacious and pernicious but he dies a victim; Vere is wise and honorable but he is directly responsible for the hanging of a man whom he feels is blameless. Billy is a simple believer in manifest meanings and the transparency of signification: 'To deal in double meanings and insinuations of any sort was quite foreign to his nature' (Melville 1970: 327). He cannot comprehend the possibility of there being a discrepancy, a perversion, between covert structure and overt meaning. Claggart, in contrast, a believer in the discrepancy between structure and meaning, personifies ambiguity and duplicity. Claggart accuses Billy of duplicity, of being other than he seems. Billy's denial of this through the striking of Claggart actually proves the very duplicity he denies. Action demands the resolution of this contradictory network and this of course is left to Captain Vere who makes his decision on the basis of political and historical circumstances (not unlike Weber's reasons for supporting formal rationality) to preserve the traditions of 'lasting institutions'. Melville clearly sees this organizational problem in terms of the mastery of difference and in a short passage that recalls Saussure's equation of arbitrariness and difference ('arbitrary and difference are two correlative qualities') and Derrida's proposition that *différance*, especially in social life, is always attended by a certain 'violence', comes to the heart of the issue:

> Who in the rainbow can draw the line where the violet tint ends and the orange tint begins? Distinctly we see the difference of the colours, but where exactly does the one first blendingly enter into the other? So with sanity and insanity. In pronounced cases there is no question about them. But in some supposed cases, in various degrees supposedly less pronounced, to draw the exact line of demarcation few will undertake, though for a fee becoming considerate some professional experts will. There is nothing nameable but that some men will, or undertake to, do it for pay.
>
> (Melville 1970: 397)

Vere 'draws the line' with reference to the requirements of the established institution. Even the ship's chaplain is enjoined to render and thus to gloss the exercise of 'violence' in the name of a superior 'presence':

> Bluntly put, a chaplain is the minister of the Prince of Peace serving in the host of the God of War – Mars. As such, he is as incongruous as a musket would be on the altar at Christmas. Why, then, is he there? Because he indirectly subserves the purpose of the cannon; because too he lends the sanction of the religion of the meek to that which practically is the abrogation of everything but brute Force.
>
> (Melville 1970: 398–9)

Melville shows that the undecidable can only become decidable through the practice of power and 'violence' and at the same time reveals authority as an institution which can only eliminate violence by elevat- ing it into the ultimate authority. Domination occurs here in many guises, not least of which is the control and mastery of the metalanguage necessary to rationalize and justify the point of view of organized authority. Melville completes his story with a graphic example of the domination of *différance* through an account of the Claggart–Budd affair which supposedly appeared in an official naval chronicle of the time:

> On the tenth of the last month a deplorable occurrence took place on board HMS *Bellipotent*. John Claggart, the ship's master-at-arms, discovering that some sort of plot was incipient among an inferior section of the ship's company, and that the ring leader was one William Budd; he, Claggart, in the act of arraigning the man before the captain, was vindictively stabbed to the heart by the suddenly drawn sheath knife of Budd.
>
> The deed and implement employed sufficiently suggest that though mustered into service under and English name the assassin was no Englishman, but one of those aliens adopting English cognomens whom the present extraordinary necessities of the service have caused to be admitted into it considerable numbers.
>
> The enormity of the crime and the extreme depravity of the criminal appear the greater in view of the character of the victim, a middle-aged man respectable and discreet, belonging to that minor official grade, the petty officers, upon whom, as none know better than the commissioned gentlemen, the efficiency of His Majesty's navy so largely depends. His function was a responsible one, at once onerous and thankless; and his fidelity in it the greater because of his strong patriotic impulse. In this instance as in so many other instances in these days, the character of this unfortunate man signally refutes, if refutation were needed, that peevish saying attributed to the late Dr Johnson, that patriotism is the last refuge of a scoundrel.
>
> The criminal paid the penalty of his crime. The promptitude of

> the punishment has proved salutary. Nothing amiss is now apprehended aboard HMS *Bellipotent*.
>
> (Melville 1970: 407)

In this example – which, along with Plato's manipulation of the *pharmakon*, could claim to represent Orwellian 'Newspeak' apparently before its time – authority and reason work through language to marginalize that position which threatens their institutional sovereignty. At the same time an illusory unity of England is created which represses the conception of difference, the unitary system being sustained overall by the symbolic purging of corrupt forces from a 'pure inside'. Efficiency is aligned with good against evil, which at the same time is a stigmatum for undecidability. What constitutes the *apparent* logic of authority and reason is the figurative language of rhetoric at work in the metalanguage and it is the insidious movement of such language that carries out the 'force' or 'violence' that is necessary to formally organized systems.[9]

Marcuse's most systematic critique of rationality is contained in *One-Dimensional Man* (Marcuse 1964) which focuses on the management of language as a significant process in the creation of systems of technological rationality. In this book there is much to suggest that Marcuse was aware of the undecidable character of social relations, especially in his suggestion that cognitive concepts have a transitive meaning, i.e. an excess of meaning over and above the particular, operational referent. The purpose of technological rationality is to repress the essentially ambiguous nature of social symbolism and appropriate it in the name of authority and reason by 'cleaning up' undecidables such as the *pharmakon*. Marcuse maps out a similar role for applied social science in industrial society, e.g. 'The elimination of transitive meaning has remained a feature of empirical sociology' (Marcuse 1964: 114). Although not an issue which Marcuse addresses, we are inclined to suggest that the so-called elimination (one could also say domination) of transitive meaning is part of a more general urge for the elimination of the uncertain or undecidable and that this desire is most conveniently 'satisfied' through power.

In the social sciences, such certainty (i.e. decidability) would seem to be more realizable through social power, that is, the development of social science in society is likely to depend upon the development of a validating relationship between the social scientist and the dominant institutional power in the society. We believe that this suggestion is implicit in Marcuse's critical analysis, especially in his condemnation of 'operational thinking' in social science. Despite its claim to objectivity, operational thought is not in any sense different from any other means of generating 'information' since it is necessarily subject to a selection process, i.e. something undecidable has to be made decidable. What enters the selection process and structures the decidable is of course power in some form or other. This essentially is Marcuse's thesis. He demonstrates it with several examples from sociological research, one of which is the 'classic' study of the Hawthorne Works of the Western Electric Company. In this study, says Marcuse, operational thinking served to manipulate workers' complaints against management by reducing the 'excess' meaning contained in such vague indefinite terms as 'the washrooms are unsanitary', 'the job is dangerous', 'rates are too low', etc.

A worker, 'B', complains that the piece rates on his job are too low. An interview reveals that B's wife is in hospital and he is worried about the medical bills. Transitive statements of wide generality are thus translated into functional form. Marcuse details the general movement from undecidability to decidability:

> 1 'Wages are too low'. The subject of the proposition is 'wages', not the particular remuneration of a particular worker on a particular job. The man who makes the statement might only think of his individual experience but, in the form he gives his statement, he transcends this individual experience. The predicate 'too low' is a relational adjective, requiring a referent which is not designated in the proposition – too low for whom or for what? This referent might again be the individual who makes the statement, or his co-workers on the job, but the general noun (wages) carries the entire movement of thought expressed by the proposition and makes other propositional elements share the general character. The referent remains indeterminate – 'too low, in general' or 'too low for everyone who is a wage-earner like the speaker'. The proposition is abstract. It refers to the universal conditions for which no particular case can be substituted; its meaning is 'transitive' as against any individual case. The proposition calls indeed for its 'translation' into a more concrete context, but one which the universal concepts cannot be defined by any *particular* set of operations (such as the personal history of the worker B, and his special function in the plant W). The concept 'wages' refers to the group 'wage-earners', integrating all personal histories and special jobs into one concrete universal.
>
> 2 'B's present earnings, due to his wife's illness, are insufficient to meet his current obligations'. Note that in this translation of (1), the subject has been shifted. The universal concept 'wages' is replaced by 'B's present earnings', the meaning of which is fully defined by the particular set of operations B has to perform in order to buy for his family food, clothing, lodging, medicine, etc.

> The 'transitiveness' of meaning has been abolished; the grouping 'wage-earners' has disappeared together with the subject 'wages', and what remains is a particular case which, stripped of its transitive meaning, becomes susceptible to the accepted standards of treatment by the company whose case it is.
>
> (Marcuse 1964: 122–13)

Marcuse is at pains to show that the particularization involved in this brand of operational thinking is also the 'partialization' of the problem, that is, it involves the selection of a point of view which favours – is partial to – one of the parties. As such, it requires the suppression of *différance* and the substitution of 'presence'. Marcuse, in a most revealing phrase, describes the Hawthorne research as having a 'therapeutic function' in which an 'unrealistic' excess of meaning is abolished. This observation assumes a special trenchancy in the context of Derrida's analysis of Plato's similar 'therapeutic' operation on the *pharmakon* in which an undesirable 'excess' has to be excised. The therapeutic function is the purging of the 'bad' which threatens the system's internal purity and security and it is this function that Marcuse sees as fundamental to the conceptualization and practice of organization. The therapeutic function serves the process of rationalization in which social structures are ordered, organized and made decidable always at the boundary line between opposing forces, between inside and outside, good and bad. The redefinitions of 'problems' that Marcuse notes in the Hawthorne study are really reappropriations of the ambiguity which characterizes the boundary. But it is more than the simple idea of control of one party by another. Essential to it is the therapeutic function by which the 'controllers' can purge themselves of the 'bad' side of the *pharmakon* by locating it 'out there', in the 'other', leaving only the purified 'good' inside. Power thus assumes a kind of morality, the expression of the war between good and evil, between the essential and the parasitic, so establishing a hierarchy not merely of simple position but of worth and centrality. The struggle for the 'superior' position necessarily requires the 'support' of an 'inferior' position inasmuch as the latter is what defines the former. The boundary as the line of *différance* is the combat zone between authority and non-authority; in itself, the undecidable. To appropriate the undecidable is to claim a certainty on 'information', which is to say that knowledge is power.

Organization and the normalizing function

In its most fundamental sense, organization is the appropriation of order out of disorder. In our analysis, we have tracked this process through the concept of information from which order is extracted as form and disorder refused as non-form. In Saussure and Bateson, order is a result of the directing function of the sign or frame which itself is an active and continuous process of selection based on the principle of inclusion/exclusion. In Derrida, the action of order in systems of communication is revealed as a struggle between the decidable and the undecidable. In other words, Derrida places the selection of order from disorder in a context of power in which language (by which we mean systems of communication in general) becomes the very object of the conflict. It is necessary to understand that, viewed in this way, language and speech are not merely the vehicles for the expression of conflict but become the objects to be appropriated, as our exposition of Marcuse's work suggests. Language is not rooted in the object *per se* but in the active subject which wills and energizes the object into existence. Derrida calls attention to this will-to-power as an antagonism between the pure and the impure,[10] between the certain and the uncertain; the selection of information is dramatized as a therapy of power.

To understand more clearly this conception of the 'active subject', let us recall Saussure's view of language as a 'system of differences' in which the speaking subject is a product of the language system rather than its producer; this is equivalent to saying that the subject is actualized by division or information and, far from being a self-sufficient and unitary structure, is identifiable only in terms of its differences from other terms in the system. Furthermore, these differences are inscribed as social marks upon the human subject's material body and property; this is how the subject is enabled to 'speak' to other differences in the system. Since the subject's realization of itself is so utterly dependent upon the mark of difference, it would be more correct to say that the subject *is* difference.

Now, we have seen (Figure 10.1 and related discussion) that differentiation includes an area of mutual parasitism from which the binary terms of difference have to disentangle themselves in order to gain the certainty of identity. Since these differential terms *are* the subject, the quest for certainty (or purity) of knowledge is also a quest for self-certainty and these two processes cannot be separated; hence the deep involvement of the subject in the act of knowing, for in purging the object of knowledge of 'error' or uncertainty the subject at the same time purges itself of any doubt about its own self-identity. The equivalence of subject and difference is thus distinguished by *order* in a dual sense: an 'external' order which organizes differences into a system of lawful relationships and an 'internal' order which is a command to the subject to rid itself of 'error'. Here we have the mechanism which explains Derrida's 'therapeutic' in which power emerges in the division of the subject and finds its *métier* in purification; thus power cleanses.[11]

A familiar objection may be raised that the concept of the therapeutic, whose aim is to heal and make whole, is appropriate only to the medical and physiological order and not to the social order which is an entirely different domain. But this misses the essential point that it is order *per se* and not its particular content that necessitates the corrective and restorative function of 'therapy'; it is an exigency of the process of understanding itself, necessary for the subject's own conceptualization.

In an incomparable study of therapeutics in biological and social systems, Canguilhem has shown how the concept of organization developed in the nineteenth century through the normal–abnormal opposition (Canguilhem 1978). The normal became an object of study initially through a concern, both practical and theoretical, with pathology, disease and, in a more general sense, with 'error' and the 'incorrect'. Both correct knowledge of the systems as well as their correct administration required an understanding of their correct norms and these were to be discovered only through their inversions in the abnormal. What is right and acceptable in a system is therefore based on an inclusion/exclusion principle which maintains the 'purity' of the inside by keeping out 'impurity'; understanding is really a curative process.

It would not be difficult to show that the scientific interest in norms and normalization which began in the nineteenth century was correlated with the problems of administering the large populations that accompanied the rise of industrial societies at that time. It was found that problems of great scale could only be effectively understood and managed through a systemization of linguistic, legal, sanitary, industrial and other norms as well as the deviations from these. The norm became a formalized tool for dealing with aggravated differentiation. Canguilhem traces the development of normalization in France from the formalization of rules for the correct usage of the language by the State's grammarians in the seventeenth century, which enabled the identification of linguistic mistakes in terms of difference from the norm, through the establishment of the metric system at the end of the eighteenth century, to the technological and administrative norms appearing in more recent times (Canguilhem 1978: 145–88). The norm functions as the basis of order, not only ordering the system to restore normal state in cases of deviation but at the same time providing an order of knowledge for the system to conceptualize itself. The norm is therefore to be seen as a conceptual and perceptual necessity rather than a mere means of survival.

As a result of Canguilhem's analysis, the concept of formal organization has to be read in a new light and its component features of division of labour, administrative centralization, standardization and rational planning – now innocently understood as the rational expedients of modern administration – have to be seen as instruments of a process of *technological normalization* motivated by a therapy of power. It will help at this point to recall our earlier discussion of traditional approaches to social systems, especially Blau's functional view of organization as an 'instrumental order'; in that approach the emphasis is placed on the 'instruments' which enable effective goal attainment; for Canguilhem, the 'instruments' are secondary to the 'order' which they have to create. In other words, the nature of the 'object' is different in the two approaches: for Blau, the object of formal organization is a utilitarian product or service; for Canguilhem, normalization is the object in which the system must realize itself. Mass-produced items are perhaps the clearest examples of objects that are standardized according to the system's norms; as such they are materialized expressions of the system's need to conceptualize itself: adapting a conceit from Lévi-Strauss (1966) we may say that the mass-produced goods of industrial society are good to think with and not merely good to consume.[12]

In Canguilhem's analysis, objects do not have natural and translucent lives of their own but are products of intense and complex social labour, imbued with normalized meaning and value. In contrast to the functionalist coherence of traditional systems theory based on an implicit metalanguage which excludes the subject from knowledge of its own involvement in the production process, Canguilhem directs attention to an object-language which works on the boundaries of systems, revealing each boundary as a gap that resists order and where every object has to be earned against an anti-object, a norm against an ab-norm. Since we have seen that the boundary as a differential term *is* the subject, Canguilhem's analysis necessarily includes the human subject in the object-language where it acts through a 'will-to-cleanse'; in other words, information, subject and certainty are coterminous in every system of production. When we apply this consideration to the study of formal organization as a system of academic production we are obliged to recognize the same processes that Canguilhem notes in the making of an 'object', that is, the complex process of social labour embodied in the actual instruments of investigation and which *precedes* what is in this case a theoretical object. But the instruments of investigation are normally regarded as supplementary (in Derrida's sense) and therefore external to the object. The purity of the object's 'inside' can only be attained, says Derrida, if the 'outside' is branded as a supplement that is not necessary in itself. But Derrida also shows, as we have noted, that the supplement is added in order to complete and compensate for a lack in what is thought to be already complete.

It is in this sense that the statements of that discourse which we call 'organization theory' are supplementary, for they represent the 'organization of organization', that is to say, that as texts *on* organization they are themselves 'organized' according to certain normalized criteria (often called scientific and/or academic) so that it becomes impossible to disentangle the content of organization studies from the theory or methodology that frames it. By this logic each statement about system or organization is not merely a piece of information about a particular subject matter but – significantly – the statement 'produces' what it denotes. As an agent of supplementary production, the text includes itself in the structure it seeks to analyse and understand, thus creating undecidability. In a differential system, which by definition can guarantee no certainty, the lack of surety forces theory to invent the means of its own realization. It is this desperate insight that motivates the thought of the writers we have examined here and which links their varied approaches, from Gouldner's probing of the practice of theory to Marcuse's dissection of the theory of practice.

Chapter eleven

Person, role and organization: some constructivist notes

Roger Holmes

In this chapter I shall attempt to answer one problem by posing myself a second. The first problem I shall ask myself is what an organization 'is', the second, quite differently, is how it is possible for the concepts of role and person to be combined in the same universe of discourse. I shall address myself to this second problem (at some length) and then return to the first. The reason for my adopting this somewhat unusual procedure should become clear as the argument progresses.

So now to the first question: what do we, can we, understand by an 'organization'? Is there such a thing as a prototypical organization – a kind of Platonic idea which embraces, however abstractly, what an organization 'must be'? A term which can refer to a concentration camp, a car hire firm, the Lord's Day Observance Society or a Train Spotters' Club is clearly a very accommodating term – so accommodating that its being granted any kind of delimited identity might be thought to represent a victory of optimism (or presumption) over the inconsequence of the everyday. Be this as it may, I shall try (as I have already mentioned) to answer this question by setting myself a further one – namely the problem of resolving the relationship of those two primal organizational phenomena – role and person.

Role and person, I shall argue, present logical and ontological difficulties in their simultaneous use (however compellingly, a full description of the phenomena at issue would require their simultaneous presence), and further – and this is important – these difficulties cannot be reconciled unless a very major step is taken. This step is none other than the abandonment of the theory of knowledge – empiricism – which has dominated (with unparalleled success) scientific work for the last 350 years. In its place I will suggest a different approach to the knowable – an approach known as 'constructivism' (associated, particularly in psychology, with the name of Jean Piaget). Constructivism, I will argue, can reconcile the concepts of role and person, and hence, by extension, the problem of what an organization 'is'. Throughout this discussion the argument will be abstract. Abstract but not irrelevant – at least to the problem I have set myself. Indeed, amongst other matters, I hope that this chapter will show the importance of general background consideration for our appreciation of the ordinary and the clear-cut. I will begin with the second of our two problems – the logical and the ontological irreconcilability of the terms 'person' and 'role'.

The logical irreconcilability between the personal and the social lies in the way people and roles are defined. People are defined in what I shall call an 'independent' way – that is, on their own, separate from their surrounding context (in psychological terms, the figure is defined independently of its ground); roles, though, are defined in a 'relational' way – that is, in terms of their context (in psychological terms, the figure cannot be defined independently of its ground). The person is independently defined since, in defining – in saying what is being referred to – a person, no reference need be made to that person's surroundings – the person is the same person wherever he may be (in this chapter the male embraces the female); a role is relationally defined, though, since in defining – to say what is being referred to – say, a foreman, other roles must also be mentioned. Thus one cannot talk about the role 'foreman' without referring to the role 'worker', the role 'manager' – and a whole host of other roles.

It is clear that these two kinds of identity (I shall use the term 'identity' to refer to anything – concrete or abstract – that is being discussed) cannot be combined in one universe of discourse. They cannot be combined because it is in the nature of independent identities to stay the same despite surrounding change, whereas it is in the nature of relational identities to vary with surrounding change (the role husband can be changed by the role wife without instituting divorce proceedings, the role foreman can be changed by the addition of other roles – personnel managers, time and motion officers, and so on). How can one integrate the independent with the relational when the relational has no enduring existence?

There are other differences as well. Independent identities, being independent of their surroundings, can move (movement implies the enduring in the transient) but that which changes with change of context cannot move – all 'movement' here is a change of state; again, independent identities having clear edges (the point where the enduring figure and the transient ground meet) can either be or not be – there can be no thing there – they are therefore refutable. Not so relational identities. With relational identities the defining context can itself maintain their identities. Thus, if we take the numbers 1 and 0 (numbers are an extreme example of relational identities, all numbers depend on each other for their definition), the number 0 can give as much information as the number 1 (a reading of 0 on a thermometer can give just as much information as a reading of 1 – or –1); or, in a different context, there can be unfilled positions in an organization. Relational identities need not be refutable since the framework in which an identity is set can ensure its continued existence.

So much for the logical incompatibility or personal and social identities; the ontological difficulty lies in this – if it is assumed that the person is the most elementary unit of discourse (and the social in some way describes the phenomena that exist when groups of people come together), then the role must be the creation of people – it must be a 'social construction of reality' where the 'social' is constructed by the people concerned (firms can be registered into existence by humble individuals and firms can be declared bankrupt – by less humble functionaries).

If this is true, then we should expect the social to be less 'real' than the people who comprise it. But the social is not less real than the people who comprise it. Not only is the wider society manifestly 'there' (and can remain so in its own right – at times, it would appear, against the wishes of large numbers of its members) but the role – that elemental piece of the wider society – can be more real than any individual member who fills that role.

Discussion of the real is always inconclusive (i.e. is, in the last resort, emotional response disguised as existence-in-itself – but then that applies to the whole of ontology), but we can note here that an individual can be transformed in others' – and his own – eyes by assuming the role, say, of king (and not just king – foreman, school prefect, having a PhD – nothing, however humdrum, it would seem, can stem our imputations of significance) and equally transformed back to insignificance on his losing that role – once Richard II had been stripped of his kingship, he was left with but an echo of his past to save him from clean death.

This preeminence of the role over its incumbent is obviously a 'good thing' in the sense that society could presumably not exist in any impersonal way (that is, in its own right, over and above the people who constitute it) without it. Despite this desirability, though, it poses a problem in the very nature of its existence. For it relies on a form of attribution of reality associated with the ontological argument for the existence of God. This was first put forward by St Anselm, an Italian who was Archbishop of Canterbury from 1093 to 1109. The argument can be condensed as follows: because I can think of a most perfect being, that being must exist. That being must exist because if it did not exist it would be less perfect than if it did (for, remember, I can think of a most perfect being). Therefore God – who is the most perfect being – must exist.

This argument can be shown to be based on the assumption that, just because one can envisage that which is greater than oneself (i.e. 'the most perfect being' one can think of), therefore, the greater being must exist – for how could the lesser be the creator of the greater? The greater must exist in its own right. The similarity with the formal role should be clear – because I can envisage a role which is more important (real, etc.) than I am, then that role must exist in its own right.

This argument is generally held to have been disposed of by Kant, who pointed out that, just because one can envisage something, it does not necessarily mean that what one envisages is true – just because I think myself to be the President of the United States does not necessarily make me so. What is really interesting about this argument is that it has had – at least amongst philosophers – a very tenacious life indeed; Descartes revived it, Leibniz took it seriously, and, to those who are not persuaded of all the Master's teaching, it would appear to have a post-Kantian revival with Hegel.

Leaving aside the logic of the argument (which must, in my view, remain inconclusive – those who accept it can always retort that those who reject it have no idea what 'that which is greater than oneself' really is in the first place – and where criteria are privileged, discourse must end), it can be shown (and I shall attempt to show later) that, at base, the issue is psychological. The argument has had such a tenacious existence not just, as noted, because it is ambiguous, but also because it rests on an enduring psychological presumption – namely that we assume we can envisage that which is greater than ourselves and, further, that we assume that that which we assume to be greater than ourselves must therefore exist.

However, more of that later. All I wish to point out at the moment is that, if we confine ourselves to a somewhat less than transcendental level – and so have to forgo the escape clauses with which the transcendental is so generously endowed – then the arguments against the ontological argument must surely hold. And that means that if we consider the person to be the most primitive unit of society, and if we then see the role as the creation of the person in society, and if we then further see the role as somehow more important than the person – then we are behaving in a logically illegitimate way. (And the same holds if we take more than one person – numbers in themselves cannot lend ontological distinction.)

This is my second irreconcilability between the personal and the social. On two counts, logical and ontological, the personal cannot be the basis of the social.

But what, then, can be done? The personal and the social must be reconcilable; we are, and supremely so in organizations, simultaneously people and positions whatever the sophists may say. Indeed we are, and our dual position is not only real – it can be shown to be logically reputable, to boot. Provided, though, we make a major sacrifice. If we make this sacrifice then the problems we have met with here – and indeed other problems – are over. But the sacrifice we have to make is very major indeed – it is no less than the abandonment of the independent as the basic unit of discourse.

This is a major step. Not least because abandoning the independent is logically disreputable, and – perhaps worse these days – involves an attack on empiricism. It is logically disreputable in the sense that it makes logic impossible. Logic – and the use of reason – depends on the identities at issue having clearly defined meanings, meanings that do not change as one moves through discourse (the word 'definition' itself implies a limit – the original meaning is 'to bring to an end' – 'de', and 'finire' – to finish); if one withdraws from the restricted ('finished') independent and moves to the echoing relational as the basis of discourse, all precision is lost: and one can neither accept or reject where there is no precision.

Thus logic will be lost, and if this chapter were to practise what it preaches and abandon the independent it, too, would be rendered – provided that that is not too presumptuous a term – incoherent. Worse, though, if possible, is on the way. And that is that the abandonment of the independent as the basic unit of discourse involves the renunciation of the approach to knowledge – empiricism – which is in direct accordance with our immediate apperception of reality and, further, which has been so successful that it has transformed the world.

Thus the abandonment of the independent would not only render me incoherent – since precise definition would no longer be available to me – it would also violate what we all most value in our appreciation of outer reality; and it would – and by the same token – challenge head-on the most successful attempt at gathering and using knowledge the world has yet known. It would be presumptuous to consider such presumptuousness merely presumptuous. And yet I will abandon the independent as primary, and – what may be worse for some – I will do so by using that which I proscribe – the independent in discourse. I will leave it until later to show how – or, indeed, whether – I can extricate myself from the absurd situation in which I find myself.

I shall begin this somewhat hazardous resolution of the problems I have set myself by describing the nature of empiricism. Empiricism is the theory of knowledge that stresses the primacy of sensory facts – we should heed what our senses tell us, not what faith would have us believe (as in the case of religion) or what our reason insists must be the case (as with Plato). As an effective force in the modern world, it can be taken to date from the early seventeenth century, when Galileo turned his telescope on Jupiter and saw that Jupiter had moons. This was crucially important since it challenged head-on the Aristotelian assumption that there were only seven moving bodies in the skies. This odd fact might not be thought of to be of too much moment, but it mattered at the time because the assumption that there were but seven moving bodies in the skies had been integrated into a comprehensive cosmology. This cosmology (that of Aristotle) reflected an epistemology – assertion of the knowable – that had been elaborated by Aquinas and adopted by the Catholic church. Galileo, by showing that there were more than seven moving bodies in the skies, had presented a direct threat to the established orthodoxy.

This stress on observation was successful and led to a steady withdrawal over the centuries of the teleological and the transcendental (both part of the Aristotelian approach) as reputably established cause. And with the loss of the teleological and the transcendental, man, relying on his limited senses, busying himself with the details of his mundane life on this planet, has transformed his mundane life on this planet. This achievement – of importance to those who value the mundane (i.e. this life) – has been made possible by the adoption of empiricism. And empiricism is based on the primacy of the independent.

Empiricism is based on the primacy of the independent in three senses. (These three senses are not mutually exclusive in their definition but are distinct enough to warrant being taken one at a time.) In the first place, it asserted that the facts that were observed must be independent of one another. Each of Galileo's moons was separate both from each other and from the environment (which was, after all, why they could move), and this separateness has been the empiricist's ideal ever since: the facts must speak for themselves in their clarity (even if their clarity is that there is no clarity; where there is a clear – obvious – lack of clarity or a mess, that mess must be acknowledged). To be 'circular' in one's definitions – not to define identities in a distinct way – has been the empiricist's mortal sin ever since.

In the second place, empiricism is based on the independent in that it insists on the total and final exclusion of (i.e. separation from) the knower from the known: the known must speak with its own voice and be in no way a reflection of the person who knows. Its very origin lay in its assertion of the irrelevance of the knower – whoever looked down Galileo's telescope, be he the Pope himself, would see Jupiter's moons – and the individual has been banished from the known ever since: to 'contaminate' one's data by influencing what one sees has also been an empiricist's mortal sin. (It is indeed the same mortal sin as the earlier one just mentioned – this one, too, involves a form of circularity.)

Thirdly – and subsuming the first two senses in which empiricism is dependent on the independent – it can be shown that empiricism depends, for the ordering of its data, on criteria that stand outside the content of discourse and adjudicate upon that content. (This third form of the independent subsumes the other two since in the long run, nothing whatsoever that is less than the absolute whole can be expressed without criteria.) Thus, in order to say that that which is before one is a 'chair', one must first have a criterion of what a chair is; in order to say that 'this chair is bigger than that chair', one must first have a measure that is independent of both chairs and that can apply to both; in order to say that the chair is 'real' and not 'imaginary', one must have before the event a distinction of the objective and the subjective that a particular instance of a chair must meet (a real chair would be objective and an imaginary chair would be subjective); and, finally, in order to say 'if chair A is bigger than chair B and chair B is bigger than chair C, then chair A is bigger than chair C', one must, before the event, have established logical necessities which always hold and which can be applied to particular cases.

Thus empiricism is wholly based on the primacy of the independent – the independent defines its separate, non-circularly defined facts, the independent asserts that the knower is separate from – and does not contaminate – the known, and the independent provides the empiricist with the criteria which allow the identification of fact, the attribution of objective reality and the use of logic. Without the independent there would be no empiricism.

And without the independent there would not have been the success of empiricism. For, just by observing what is there – how the identities which are being studied vary under varying circumstances, the empiricist has established the existence of consistent sequences – or 'causes' – in nature, and thus allowed him to control nature. In short, empiricism has won mastery in his domain. And we have all been his beneficiaries. Thus, in asserting that the independent should lose the primacy of its status, I am not only rejecting that which makes articulate and precise discourse possible, I am also threatening at its base the most successful attempt at dealing with the known the world has yet seen. Surely a challenge to its primacy must smack of hubris.

And yet I shall abandon the independent as primary; and I shall do so because of the fate of the theory of knowledge – empiricism – it made possible. Where empiricism – which is but the application of the assumption of the primacy of the independent to the study of identifiable phenomena – fails, the assumption of the primacy of the independent fails too. And empiricism fails at the very moment of its success – at the moment where it establishes cause.

Empiricism has, as we have seen, transformed the world by establishing cause – thus enabling us to predict how identities will behave in varying circumstances. This has been one of its great strengths (empiricism – with its clear cut distinction between objective and subjective, etc. – not only feels right, it is successful too!) but this, for all that, is its undoing. For in establishing cause – the marriage of the past and the future – we undermine the independent.

The independent cannot tolerate the past for, if the independent is consequence, it ceases to be independent. This has always been recognized for the third (and most important) of the three forms of the independent on which empiricism is based – but it can be shown to hold for the other two forms as well. The third form of the independent was that of certain definitional, ontological and logical criteria, criteria that allowed us to order the world. These forms of the independent must be, to be criteria at all, outside causal reality, acting but not acted on. It was for this reason that Plato, with his theory of ideas, placed definitions in heaven where they could define – without being influenced by that which they defined. (Why should we believe a definition, if that definition can itself be acted on? – it is like expecting a judge to be impartial when we know that the judge is open to the influence of those over whom he is expected to adjudicate.)

This resort of placing criteria outside causality has lasted down to this day: those brought up on the orthodoxies of the Vienna Circle were taught that there were three forms of ontology (not that the word was used) – facts, values and tautologies ('tautologies' embraced *inter alia* the extended criteria of mathematics and logic). This tripartite division (where criteria in the sense that I have just discussed were hived off and placed among the tautologies) was not argued; it was given, flatly. Can any self-respecting theory of knowledge rely on so arbitrary a base?

But then empiricism – or any theory of knowledge based on the independent had no choice. It had no choice since any theory of knowledge that did not argue that independents existed *a priori* would lose those independents. We have already seen how this would be with abstract criteria (abstract criteria had to be outside causality to be criteria), but it can be seen even more vividly with the second form of independence insisted on – that of the observer and the observed.

If the subjective–objective is caused, the subjective–objective distinction (the distinction between observer and observed) ceases to hold. It ceases to hold since now both observer and observed are consequence of that which is not themselves (since nothing can explain itself) and, the distinction, being derived, is not final: being derived it must without begging the question – be derived from a common source, and those who share common origins cannot logically be distinct.

This unsatisfactory nature of distinction between observer and observed was seldom raised – it was just assumed that knower and known were 'obviously' distinct; and the same can be said of the first form of independence on which empiricism was based – that of one sensory feat from another. Here the impossibility of the independent having a causal, ordered past comes vividly to the fore – for how can we study the psychology of perception (on which most of the empiricist's non-circularly defined facts are based) without begging the question? How can we study how our eyes work without using our eyes, without using the very organ whose validity is at issue? The exercise is either logically impossible or, if admitted, disastrous. It is logically impossible if we insist that the ground of discourse cannot be the object of discourse (i.e. that the base line cannot be questioned) and it is disastrous if we allow it to go forward and then treat sight as a consequence – for if that is done then sightedness being a result of something other than itself (since, to repeat, nothing can explain itself) could not just be the result of what is seen: 'what is seen' would be shown, *inter alia*, to have a neural-chemical base – and so to be no pure reflection of 'what is seen'.

But where, having rejected the *a priori* nature of the independent (and the theory of knowledge – empiricism – that based itself on that independent) can the various forms of the independent come from? They cannot, as we have seen, come from any coherent past – time solves nothing and our coherent past, just as our present, would need its imported criteria to make sense.

To say that the coherent is based on the coherent is, to repeat, to beg the question. But what can we do but beg the question? We have already seen that the independent *a priori* is necessary not only for empiricism but also for coherence. Thus, without the independent *a priori* we are reduced to incoherence. Well, so in a sense, we are. This brings me to a hard statement that not everyone will like – at the basis of coherence must lie non-coherence, a total non-coherence where nothing can be recognized or said. At the basis of coherence lies a mystery, a mystery which can never be explained – but which nevertheless explains.

That the unexplained should precede the explained may sound odd. But is it? We come into the world we know not how: that we should be alive at all cannot be explained to us – and if we ourselves should emerge from non-coherence, why should not the world around us, the world we seek to explain? Are not the knower and the known in any event confounded? How can we know of ourselves if we know nothing but ourselves? And are we not ourselves – in our very existence – the cause of there being anything outside ourselves to know?

'Oh, but we all know about copulation and reproduction' – but only after being alive do we know about them; being alive comes before any awareness whatever. By definition, nothing can be said about the basis of our awareness; it must remain unresolved. Given this necessary mystery that underlies, it is difficult to see where this paper can go: in attempting to reconcile the personal and the social, I have reached a dead end.

In the most important of senses this is true – nothing can account for the unaccountable and, by our very physiological base, we are dogged by a mystery which can never be escaped. In a less satisfactory sense, though, we can, meretriciously relying on graded hindsight, make a couple of observations (and, if these prove unsatisfactory, we should expect no more.) These observations are about the nature of the merging coherence.

First, about the nature of the primal mystery or non-coherence: one thing can immediately be said about it – it is reflected in us by a sense of certainty. This is not the certainty of those who have achieved mastery of detail, it is the necessarily mysterious certainty that precedes all articulated awareness. It is the certainty of physiology – a certainty rooted in the constants of the body, a certainty that cannot envisage the existence of doubt. Doubt is quite a complex state of mind – it involves being aware that there could be something of which we are not aware. Such sophistication is not possible at the precoherent level.

To attain an awareness of ignorance we must first be aware of at least the possibility of further knowledge. And how can we do that, except by learning of such knowledge? Nowadays we can be aware of our ignorance of black holes – but only because their existence has been pointed out to us. Indeed, some may feel that this regenerate ignorance can be taken too far – whole acres of possible ignorance are now regularly presented to us by science: surely such opportunities for ignorance have gone far enough.

Sadly, we live in an informed age. But then there is always the pre-coherent persuading us there is no need to know, a pre-coherent that has its own distinctive awareness. This is the second point that can be made about the physiological basis of our awareness – it is reflected in one sense of freedom. Our sense of freedom is a non-rational absolute. It is there, before the event, denying the need for delimited coherence; our sense of freedom is indeed the inherited physiological speaking in the blind certainty of that which *knows* before all knowledge. We can no more shake off our sense of freedom than we can lose those other physiological inevitables – our sense of pleasure and our sense of pain. So much for the nature of the primal non-coherence – it is certainly most aware of itself when it feels free. We now come to the nature of the emerging coherence.[1]

So much for the non-coherent that precedes the coherent. We now come to the problem of how such non-coherence translates itself into coherence; or, put another way, how the criteria (definitions, measures, ontological assumptions, logical necessities, and the rest) which inform (i.e. grant form to) the coherent psychological (as opposed to the precoherent physiological) known, derive. In one sense, as we have seen, we cannot know – any more than we can know where we ourselves (the basis of all we know) come from – but in another less satisfactory sense at least the possibility of escaping logical absurdity may be presumed.

Not, though, if we heed the empiricists. Empiricists, as we have seen, totally beg the question by assuming *a priori* the very independent criteria whose emergence is at issue. Most strikingly of all they assert a subjective–objective ontological split and then further assert that the latter and only the latter is the proper basis of the known. The approach that we can consider, though, without total logical disreputability is that of constructivism: and constructivism is, in psychology at least, the brain-child of Jean Paiget.

Paiget's approach will only be given briefly here – enough to show the bones of his account. This account has the very great merit of not assuming coherence *a priori*. Paiget can contemplate a primal non-coherence, because Paiget (who starts from a biological base) assumes that the pre-coherent deed underlies awareness. Constructivism inverts empiricism in that it takes the physiological activity of the organism rather than the psychological self-evidence of the independent as *a priori*: the physiological-merging-into-the-psychological replaces the absolute subjective–objective distinction. With Paiget there is no question-begging assumption that the known underlies the known – rather the known is the consequence of that which is not itself – the deed. By acting on the world (i.e. by being alive) we become conscious of the orderliness of the world; by acting on the world we achieve awareness of the independent.

This approach – the replacement of the self-evident by the deed – involves an inversion of the normal course of science. Instead of starting with the unchanging and the self-evident and seeing the growth of knowledge as charting the vicissitudes of such self-evidence (how unchanging water, for instance, turns to steam or ice under certain conditions), Paiget takes pre-coherent 'change' for granted and then seeks to describe the emergence of the self-evident. In other words, he describes the emergence of that which *inter alia* allows us to define, measure, use logic and the rest. 'But the use of logic involves tautologies and tautologies are outside time.' Yes – that which is outside time, once arrived at, may nevertheless have its base in time.

But how can such emergence be charted? It is, by definition, absurd – the pre-coherent cannot account for the coherent. This is true, but one avenue is open to us – to observe the emergence of (what we now accept as) the coherent through the cessation of (what we now accept as) the non-coherent. And this is what Paiget did.

Very similar to Freud (who, it will be remembered, studied, for example, slips of the tongue and used such slips to illuminate the unconscious ground of conscious awareness), Paiget noted children's mistakes (as measured by later standards of coherence) and how such mistakes diminished with the passing of time. In this way he showed how children gradually became aware of that which, with later hindsight, can be seen to underlie coherence – the unchanging. Thus Paiget studied the growth of the ability to see, for instance, a rattle as being 'the same rattle' when viewed from different angles; the ability to see two objects as being of the same size despite one being close at hand and the other further off; the ability to recognize a circle as a circle, even though it strikes the retina as an ellipse: throughout he is concerned with the derivation of the basis of empiricism and coherence – the unchanging, the independent. (And, being derived, we can never say that our awareness of the unchanging is complete.[2])

Paiget plotted the emergence of the psychological coherent from the physiological pre-coherent; the invariant – or the independent – is the basis of coherence and Paiget plotted the growing ability of the child to see the same and so to recognize. What, then, are the consequences of this emergence? These are of the first importance and the rest of this discussion of role and person will depend on them. They can be looked on as of two kinds – those concerned with the known and those concerned with the knower. I shall begin with the known.

Two of the points here are necessary and one is contingent. The first, necessary, point is that the growth of the awareness of coherence must result in a more complex appreciation of what I have called the 'independent' and the 'relational'.

The reader will remember that at the very beginning of this paper I distinguished between that which was defined on its own, independent of its context, and that which was defined in relation to its context (a chair is an example of an identity independently defined and the number 3 is an example of an identity relationally defined). Now it is fairly clear that these two sorts of awareness must emerge simultaneously – one must have the independent even in the relational, or all relationals would be the same (this interplay of differences and similarity is clearly seen if one compares two different octaves in music – these octaves, which are relations, are both similar to, and different from each other) and, conversely, all independents, as Hegel saw, must – unless one is going to take a very hard Plato line – have a relational context.[3]

This brings us to a second – and also important – necessary point about the known. This is that knowledge, being learned, must be someone's learned, someone's knowledge. There can no longer be a question (if Paiget is given any credence at all) of there being any objectivity in its own right: public knowledge must have a private base.

Given its importance – and our total inability to escape its conclusion – it is perhaps surprising that this inescapable conclusion is so readily escaped. Many and devious are the ways we cling to an outer ontology or substance (to use a new forbidden word). One point, though, although tangential, may perhaps be made. (This is the contingent point I said would be made about the known.)

It remains a 'fact' (i.e. that which defies logic but cannot be escaped) that, once a child becomes aware of a necessary similarity (that a chair is still the same chair, for instance, seen from in front or behind, or that 2 and 1 is the same as 1 and 2), he becomes not only convinced of its inevitability – but incredulous as to how he or anyone else could ever have doubted it. (We have met this point before in a somewhat more high-powered way. As we have seen, logic and tautologies were considered self-evident and so, in some sense, as external and outside time. It did not occur to these exalted intellects – from Plato to the Vienna Circle (twentieth century apologists for empiricism, no less) that that which is deemed eternal *once it exists* may nevertheless have its roots in time.)

This gives a third kind of certainty – not the physiological certainty that insists before awareness, nor the fallible 'certainty' of those who hope they have mastered previously defined detail, but what I shall call the 'achieved certainty' of those who believe unquestioningly in the sensory and logical constants of which they have become aware.[4]

So much for the implications of an emergence of the coherent on our assumption of the known: first, if the coherent emerges, then the relational and the independent must, despite their logical independence, define each other in a complex way; second, all knowledge must be someone's knowledge – and there can be no objectivity in itself. This last point is the less easily recognized because, for whatever reason, those constants that we do achieve insist upon their inevitability and bind what we can see.

We now come to the implications of the emergence of, as opposed to the eternal self-evidence of, the coherent for the knower. The basis of this has already been alluded to and can be stated in a short sentence – awareness of the coherent is awareness of what the knower cannot help. Awareness of the coherent, therefore (to the extent that it is achieved), diminishes our sense of power and freedom, lessens what Freud called our 'omnipotence of thoughts'.

To the extent that we become aware of the coherent – that it is a chair in front of us, that the chair is bigger than another chair, that two chairs and one chair is the same as one chair and two chairs, that there is a difference between the chair outside me and the chair that I imagine in my own mind, etc.– to that extent we must acknowledge the existence-in-itself of that which is not ourself. That this should be so – that awareness of the coherent is the awareness of what the knower cannot help – has always been the firm plank on which empiricism rests; empiricism pointed to the coherent evidence of the senses, a coherence that could not be denied – even the Pope had eventually to acknowledge Galileo's moons.

Having discarded the subjective–objective distinction and discussed the way in which our growing (psychological) awareness modifies our physiological absolutes, we are now in a position to resolve the difficulties attendant on the concepts of role and person. I shall take them in turn.

The first difficulty was the logical non-reconcilability of role and person – roles were relationally defined and persons were independently defined: roles were being defined by their relations with their surround (the role of foreman being defined by the specific relations with managers, specialists and subordinates) and persons were defined on their own, independent of any surround (people can, after all, change their surround and stay the same people – people can move).

These are now reconcilable because, having shed empiricism and the mandatory primacy of the independent it asserted, role and person can have a common base. Independent and relational emerge, as we have seen, *pari passu* – one can never, as we have seen, have a relationship without an independent (or all relationships would be the same) and one can never have a non-related independent (unless one adopts Plato's ideas in their full timelessness).

This fusion at their base of the independent and the relational – both of them reflecting the physiological deed, emerging through its own activity into awareness – accounts for something that may have struck the reader – namely the unsatisfactoriness of this distinction. This unsatisfactoriness, we can now see, is based on the very definition of the terms themselves. As has been noted, we cannot have a purely independent definition; each needs the other and neither alone could have any existence (for each would be too abstract).

This messiness of definitions – a messiness which only Plato with his ruthless abstraction was prepared to reject (and which presents empiricists with endless, and ultimately unresolvable, problems of circularity and which presents all of us, since both the relational and the independent are necessary but only the independent is refutable, with the limits of the knowable) becomes immediately comprehensible once we assume that any distinctiveness a definition may have is a consequence and so a matter of degree.

Thus the logical difficulty is reconciled by arguing that the relational and the independent emerge *pari passu* from the pre-coherent, each being as emergent or psychological as the other. Not so the ontological difficulty – the difficulty that roles were simultaneously the creation of man and yet superior to man: for how could the inferior be the source of the superior? This difficulty can also be resolved by invoking the constructivist, *a priori*, physiological–psychological distinction (as opposed to the empiricist subjective–objective distinction) and by seeing the person as more 'constructed' and so less important, 'real' or (the word I shall use from now on) 'numinous' and the role as less constructed – and so more important, real or numinous. And why should the role be considered to be more numinous than the person? Very simply – because the role is more abstract. The abstract and the physiological are curiously linked, for the abstract, even as the physiological, finds itself apart from that bias of psychological coherence, 'the haphazard randomness of the everyday' – the abstract is above it even as the physiological is beneath it. This is indeed how matters of high value are linked to the physiological – they are linked by their non-haphazard, non-random natures. It is happenstance and contingency which wrench us from preconceptions and significant thoughts: and thus *les extrèmes* of the physiological and the transcendental *se touchant* – neither can be challenged.

All this depends, of course, on seeing the physiological as the ground of the numinous. But why should it not be? I have already argued that the physiological is the seat of certainty – the certainty which manifests itself to us in our sense of freedom; is it any contradiction, then, to see the physiological as the seat of the numinous as well? It is surely tempting to see the numinous as but the sense of freedom contemplating that which is not itself. The numinous is, like our sense of freedom, but a persistent relic of our physiological absolutism – just as we preserve our sense of freedom despite our ever-growing awareness of the inevitable, so too do we preserve a sense of the absolute – despite our ever-greater grasp of the contingency of circumstance. The numinous, as we should expect from that which has a physiological base, is but, to repeat, emotional response disguised as existence-in-itself.

This may be thought somewhat fanciful, but, whether or not the reader gives credence to the notion of the abiding physiological being the basis of the real and the significant, it should be fairly clear that once one posits a physiological base to awareness, then the possibility of the physiological presenting us with its own reality – a reality which has none of the qualities we associate with our everyday psychological awareness (which are bound in space and time and in no way necessarily Significant or Numinous) – should not be ignored. Why should we seek the Deity in heaven when our bloodstream will do?

And our bloodstream, as bloodstreams are wont to, is persistent: a moment's thought should make it clear that the attribution of significance and reality to the abstract is a very common thing indeed. Thus some people, whether or not they intend it, in effect consider the word to be more important than its referent ('The Divine', I have heard say, 'is rightly so called.'); again, connotations may, in the eyes of some, come before denotations and metaphors may – to those who really want to extract significance from the yet undelineated – at times appear to precede the humble cases they supposedly illuminate. (And then must consider how we idealize, how we invest with 'unreal' qualities, such as abstract existences as nationalism and religion. Surely the power of such cloudy existence far outruns in primitive force any explanation in terms of consequential identification.)

This stress on the tawdry, latter-day numinous cannot be logically faulted – for, once the independent ceases to be the basic unit of discourse, the independent must be derived; and where the independent is derived – and so does not define itself – no antecedent, however deluded in hindsight, can be excluded. We cannot even exclude what is being suggested here – that the ontological difficulty can be resolved by assuming that it is God (or the physiological) who has an idea of us.

So much, at some length, the resolution of the difficulties presented to us by the simultaneous existence of role and person. How can such a resolution help us with the first problem this paper addressed – what an organization can be said to 'be'! In what way can that amorphous identity 'organization' (which can reflect all things from a concentration camp to a train spotters' club) be illuminated in its definition by the abstract discussion we have just enjoyed?

Well, the problems of the nature of the amorphous identity which is an organization can be illuminated ('resolved', as we shall see, is much too ambitious a term) in the same way that the problem of role and person was illuminated: by abandoning the empiricists' distinction between objective and subjective – of which only the former is the proper business of science – and replacing it with the constructivists' distinction between the physiologically and the psychologically known – where the latter is an emergent consequence of the former.

The guiding assumption of an empiricist, as we have seen, is that under no circumstances can circularity be permitted – the objects discussed must be defined independently of each other (or how can we be sure that we are discussing one thing rather than another?) and the objects discussed must be independent of the person who discusses them (or how can we escape the influence of the transient private subjective in our search for the enduring public objective?). However great the logic of this position (and it is total – if there are no clearly defined identities there can be no conclusive logic) it does mean that all phenomena are thereby necessarily classified as either subjective or objective and the possibility of a half-way house between the two cannot be tolerated, since half-way houses are necessarily circular (if something can be seen by B but not by A – presumably a half-way house – can we not just as well say 'It was there because B saw it' as 'B saw it because it was there'? It is only the clear cut which can be argued not to be circular).

Thus anyone approaching the nature of organizations from a conventional empiricist position must assume that either organizations are 'objective' – in which case they are 'really there' in the same way that rocks and trees and sunsets are 'really there' or that they are 'subjective' – in which case they are not 'really there' but have the same status as value judgements and the fantasics so beloved by psycho-analysts. There is no third possibility. Given, then, that organizations must either be objective or subjective – there is nothing else they can be – then organizations are necessarily objective. They are *there*, aren't they? At least we agree – all of us – on that. Given, further, that they are 'there', they must be identifiable as themselves – or otherwise they could never have been considered to be 'there' in the first place. To an empiricist, a rose is a rose and must be.

Thus has the problem of the nature of organizations arisen. It has arisen because it has been assumed from the start that organizations must be ordinary objective phenomena. All this is changed if we abandon the empiricist's subjective-objective assumption and if we adopt the constructivists' physiological-turning-into-psychological approach instead. If we adopt the constructivist approach, logical rectitude and lack of circularity are not demanded *a priori*, they are seen as consequence of a process which witnesses the emerging clarity of the identities at issue – at least to the extent that they are emergent (there is no reason in principle why identities should be logically respectable).

In other words – and this is the central point – with the constructive approach our awareness of phenomena can have a history. This is crucial, for where there is a history there is there the possibility – totally denied by the *a priorist* empirical approach – of different pasts; and where there are different pasts there can there be different presents – and not all awarenesses need be alike. Indeed there could be an infinite number of different awarenesses, each variously physiologically or psychologically based. Thus we could have (and do have) awareness very close to our primal physiological sense of freedom – such as when we sense the existence of 'power' in others (power being our sense of alien freedom) again we could have semi-coherent numinous awareness (as with certain forms of poetry) and then again more or less psychological awarenesses, stripped of supporting, *a priori*, self-confidence – as with the pragmatic constants used by science. This list is sketchy and inadequate – the point at issue is that awareness could in principle be of differing kinds, each form of awareness being variously maintained.

This is one of the consequences of awarenesses having a history – they can be on a gradient reflecting different points along the physiological–psychological continuum; there is, though, a second and even more intractable consequence, namely that different individuals may hold different assumptions as to what a particular phenomena 'is' (if I may use that question-begging word).

This, again, is not a problem with empiricism. If a rose is a rose and must be, then there can only be one apprehension of each phenomenon, the apprehension which reflects what the phenomenon in question 'is'. With the constructivist approach this is not the case – our apprehension of the outside world is 'constructed' as a result of our acting on (and being acted on by) that world – and there is no reason in principle why we should all share the same relationship with – or the same awareness of – our environments. Where definitions are constructed there may be definitions variously constructed.

This possibility of differences in apperception between people is particularly important because awarenesses may not just be on a physiological–psychological continuum but, quite differently, may be of different kinds: they may reflect what we can call 'natural' and 'social' realities.

Natural realities are such things as rocks and trees and sunsets – all of which have already been mentioned as being the sort of things empiricists consider to be 'really there'. A man could have an awareness of such phenomena (presumably) even if he had passed his life alone. Not so with social realities. Social realities have already been introduced at the beginning of this chapter when I discussed the status of role. Roles, it will be remembered, were, quite unlike rocks and trees and sunsets (though the contrast was not brought out then), the creation of people, a 'social construction of reality'. Other social realities, also social constructions of reality, are such phenomena as languages, laws – and organizations. Languages, laws and organizations are also the creation of man and those who were brought up alone could have no idea of what such realities might be.

The natural–social reality distinction is closely related to the physiological–psychological continuum, but is not identical to it and the differences between these two must be brought out. Perhaps the easiest way to do this is to look at a form of social reality we all have had experience of and which, indeed, dominates our lives, namely the state.

In a state we find social reality which embraces lesser social realities, which in turn embrace yet lesser social realities – and so on. (Thus a state embraces a government which in turn has within it ministries, which in turn have within them departments.) These social realities are maintained by causes – causes which are imposed (and not, as with natural realities, discovered), and then presided over by a brooding, abstract identity which blesses or proscribes the causes which come within its ambit. This numinous identity, for numinous it is (indeed it is the ultimate source of the numinousness of roles), is called 'authority' and the causes which are imposed are called 'powers'; powers which, if blessed by authority, are held to be 'legitimate' and which, if rejected by authority, are deemed to be 'illegitimate'.

Even this briefest of overviews of a complex social reality shows us how much closer it and the parts which comprise it are to the physiological than to the psychological in their derivation: thus the notion of power is, as we have seen, our notion of freedom (itself of primitive physiological origin) given outer form (your power is my freedom); the notion of authority whose presence is the determinant of permittedness in powers is patently physiological – authority could well be that which those stronger than ourselves revere. Nothing could be further removed from the articulated inconsequential of the psychological everyday.

Thus the main elements of a state – the notions of power, authority, etc. – are of physiological origin. Towards the beginning of this chapter I observed that the fact that the role (another necessary element of the state – consider the position of prime minister, civil servant, etc.) was held to be of a higher order of existence than – and hence conferring a higher standing to – its incumbent, was presumably a 'good thing', in the sense that society could presumably not exist in any impersonal way without it: we can now see that the entire acceptance in our minds of the abstract-inescapable which is at the base of our ability to construct wider social awarenesses – that is, social awarenesses which extend beyond the lives of those who embody them – depends on the primitive physiological basis of our ability to know.

But the state does not just exemplify the primitive preconceptions of men (far too primitive for them to be refuted in any ordinary way). The state is also maintained by the energies of men – without people to enforce law, the law will decay. Authority must inform the desires of men for authority to be maintained; and even then this may not be enough. Authority can also be attacked from outside – by those who proclaim their loyalty to (i.e. support of) a rival source of legitimacy (or authority). The state owes its existence to the desires of men quite as much as it does to the primitive awarenesses of men.

Now the state is but an organization – albeit on a large and articulate scale, and what goes for the state also goes for such humbler associations as a car hire firm or the Lord's Day Observance Society – these too will have their positions, authority and legitimated power –

and when we come to describe what an organization 'might be', all of that which has been described above must hold.

At least to some degree – presumably the aura which legitimizes the authority of a car hire firm is not necessarily as pronounced as is the aura which illuminates the existence of, for instance, a convert of Carmelite nuns. This appeals to a degree, though, but further complicates any possible definition of what an organization might be. For now, if we look at organizations soberly in the light of what has been said, a truly daunting prospect presents itself. We see an association of men which comprises identities of conflicting logical status (as with person and role), which is presided over by what one takes to be a pale shadow of the Holy Ghost – i.e. authority (or, if that does not please, by a direct consequence of the physiological basis of apperception), which, further, against all conceivable empirical demands, is both created and maintained by the energies of men, men who can create their own causality (the 'legitimate' power with which roles can be endowed). Such a phenomenon can clearly not have any ordinary definition.

Well what kind of definition can it have then? Is anything at all possible? Before answering this question we could ask another, somewhat similar, one. Namely, how is it that organizations have been considered a unitary variable – as 'one thing' characterized by distinctive properties – in the first place? And the answer to this question is easy (at least if one accepts what has been said in this paper so far) and satisfyingly paradoxical – organizations are considered to have consistent properties because, the ultimate bathos, they share the same name: the name, in other words, is the determinant, not the servant, of reality. This may be thought ridiculous but it is not physiologically ridiculous: words are abstract and can be endowed with physiological self-evidence (i.e. certainty) through their very abstractedness. It was for this reason that I argued that the abstract role could carry greater ontological significance than the more humble – i.e. the more clearly recognized – person; that connotations may at times be thought to be more important than denotations; that metaphors may appear to precede the humble cases they supposedly illuminate – or what we should deem such cloudy existences as nations, religions – and organizations – to 'be'.

But, admitting all this, must we therefore be mute? Are we allowed to make no statements as to what an organization 'is'? And the answer in a way sums up this paper – for the answer bears upon the nature of definition, empirical and constructivist definitions not being the same. To an empiricist, definitions are based on what our senses tell us. They are therefore *a priori*, the basis not the consequence for the known. If one sees a cup before one then the cup is identified as itself by having been seen as itself. Cups, at least as a ground for knowledge, are what they look like. That complicated things may subsequently be said about cups is neither here nor there – that which a cup starts by being, it in some final sense remains. A cup is a cup and must be.

Very different is the constructivist definition. Constructivist definitions are the result, not the ground, of the ordering of the world – we arrive, through our relationship with the world, at the basis of the definition – namely the unchanging. There is no anchoring here on the insistence of the senses. A cup looking like a cup and proclaiming itself as distinct is but one, albeit vivid, example of an achieved invariance – an invariance in no final sense distinct from those other invariances (to the extent, of course, that they are invariant) – the awareness of classes, criteria and those generalizations in science we call 'laws'.

'The awareness', be it noted; with constructivism, to repeat, 'public knowledge must have a private base' – a private base that need not in every case be the same. Awareness, being achieved, need not be identically achieved.

Given this, then, can we say what an organization 'is'? And the answer is, in any immediate, *a priori* sense, 'no' – any more than we can finally define anything else at all, for that matter.

Does this mean, then, that we should abandon any hope of identifying those constants which an organization might be held to embrace. Not at all: with the constructivist approach, awareness of the unchanging, the enduring (the basis of a definition which sums up but does not presume to assert) is the consequence of our 'construction' of that awareness – of our acting on the world and, we hope, deriving from such action categories which will reflect the world. Organizations will progressively be more defined as more is learned about them.

One final point must be made. Empiricism has come under attack in this chapter – but only as ontology – the presumption of what things 'are' – not as method. The empiricist method – the gathering of information and the eliciting of generalizations therefrom – is the only way we can legitimately advance our knowledge. We certainly cannot do it by analyzing the 'essence' of – the 'real existence behind' – our definitions (our physiology will see to that), we can only do it by gaining such incidental, local awareness that enables us to achieve the only hope of enjoying knowledge we have – the ordering of events which proves repeatable. Both the believer in the transcendental and the asserter of the empirical try in their different ways to present us with self-sufficiency – the numinous which justifies itself and must not be explored, the sensorily self-evident which is the unquestionable ground on which we must build our knowledge. To a constructivist, all awarenesses are on probation and no awareness is final: our awarenesses are achieved and it is presumptuous of us to assume that we can achieve no more.

Chapter twelve

An alternative to paradigm incommensurability in organization theory

John Hassard

Introduction

In recent years the literature of organization theory has been replete with assessments of its paradigmatic status. We have seen numerous works analyzing the study of organizations by reference to alternatives to the dominant 'systems' paradigm. The identification of new paradigms candidates has, for many, signalled a state of crisis – the orthodoxy being undermined by communities who claim to solve 'puzzles' (Kuhn 1970) which the systems approach is incapable of addressing (mainly concerning change and conflict). These developments, in what may be termed the 'sociology of organization theory', have been predicated on Thomas Kuhn's history of science, with elements from the *Structure of Scientific Revolutions* (SSR) thesis being used to justify descriptions of community structure. Here, Kuhn's seminal concept of paradigm has been *the* medium for depicting the developmental progress of organization theory as 'poly-paradigmatic' (Lammers 1974).

However, despite the wealth of material generated by this process, use of the 'conventionalist' philosophy of science (e.g. Kuhn, Hanson, Feyerabend) has all too frequently been superficial. Kuhnian theory has been used as the analytical basis for works demonstrating scant awareness of primary principles. Concepts from conventionalist philosophy have been used in ways inappropriate to standard debate. In particular, in organization theory few concepts have been employed as inconsistently as that of paradigm. This concept, originally the centrepiece of Kuhn's argument, has become progressively devalued, so much so that a once-powerful notion, resemblant, in one sense, of the *Weltanschauung*, is now employed at all levels of analysis, being substituted freely for terms such as perspective, theory, discipline, school, or method. Indeed, when commentators talk of an 'individual's paradigm' (Parkes 1976), this illustrates the lack of discrimination.

In this chapter I wish to address issues central to this 'paradigms' debate. I will assess some logical problems emerging from commentaries depicting paradigms as incommensurable, and discuss the questions this raises for the communication of ideas in organization theory. Although the chapter will present arguments relevant to developing inter-paradigm understanding, it will not, however, review the many Kuhnian schemes offered (e.g. Friedrichs 1970; Ritzer 1975; Burrell and Morgan 1979; Pondy and Boje 1981). Reviews of this literature are readily available elsewhere (e.g. Eckburg and Hill 1978; White 1983; Lincoln 1985). Instead, the chapter will tackle deeper issues, and assess the correspondence between paradigm models and the *philosophical* principles upon which they are founded. It is argued that only by returning to the original philosophies (of science) on which these ideas are based can we discover, firstly, if original principles have been interpreted correctly; and second, if they have provided a sound basis for mapping the paradigm terrain of organizational theory. Analysis will show how current paradigm schemes are not only based on a truncated reading of Kuhn, but also that their logic is ambiguous when we confront issues of scientific communication.

To address these problems, we first return to basics – to Kuhn's descriptions of science and thus to the concept of paradigm.

Elements of Kuhnism

The widespread reputation of Kuhn's 'Structure of scientific revolutions' (1962 and 1970) has resulted from his claim that traditional wisdom in the philosophy of science does not equate with the historical evidence. Kuhn's suggestion is that dominant theories of scientific practice – whether inductivist or falsificationist – are incompatible with the facts of how science has actually progressed. Falsificationists, however 'sophisticated' (Lakatos 1970), are methodologists whose ideas are never met. Scientific practice is never realized in Popperian terms, and as such, 'no process yet discovered by the historical study of scientific development at all resembles the methodological stereotype of falsification by direct comparison with nature' (Kuhn 1962: 77).

For Kuhn, the everyday reality of science is more akin to the lifecycle of the political community than to the dictates of formal logic. Theories portraying science as the linear accretion of verified hypotheses are completely rejected, as instead Kuhn speaks of discontinuous periods of normative and revolutionary activity. He claims that the history of science has witnessed numerous upheavals in which accepted wisdom is replaced by a new way of seeing, this process serving to change fundamentally the basis of a science's reality concept. Indeed, the degree of change is such that the standards, concepts and procedures of the post-revolutionary approach are totally incompatible with those of the pre-revolutionary consensus. For scientists, this change experience is akin to the appreciation of a new *gestalt*, the process being similar to religious conversion. When science changes, a new approach emerges based upon the fresh dictates of an alternative community structure, the new tradition, like the old, being what Kuhn terms a 'paradigm'.

For us, it is Kuhn's likening of paradigm-change to the instant transformation of the gestalt-switch which is important; for this argument seems to deny any possibility of communication between paradigms. As Kuhn states, during periods of revolutionary science, 'scientists do not see something *as* something else; instead, they simply see it' (Kuhn 1970: 85). Kuhn argues that a change of paradigm allegiance cannot be based on open debate as there are no logical arguments to demonstrate the superiority of one paradigm over another. As the new paradigm is incommensurable with the old, there is no resource to an independent arbitrator or mediating third party. Indeed, there can be no logical demarcation of the supremacy of one paradigm over another, for their advocates hold fast to separate sets of standards and metaphysical beliefs. Being a proponent of a particular paradigm means one can never concede to the premises of another – the findings of a rival paradigm are not acceptable. For Kuhn, 'when paradigms enter . . . into a battle about paradigm choice, their role is necessarily circular. Each group uses its own paradigm to argue in that paradigm's defence' (Kuhn 1970: 94). Rival paradigms cut up the world with different standards, different assumptions, different *language*. In sum, 'the normal-scientific tradition that emerges from a scientific revolution is not only incompatible but often actually incommensurable with that which has gone before' (Kuhn 1970: 103).

This analysis has made a considerable impact upon organizational sociology. As most commentators argue that the social sciences are polyparadigmatic, this suggests that communication and debate are impossible – paradigms are based on assumptions which are in fundamental opposition to those of their rivals (Burrell and Morgan 1979). This, however, has led to a contradiction. For while analysts argue that paradigms are exclusive, and that scientists tend to remain locked within their paradigm-learned perceptions, many also claim that we need researchers who are 'specialists in more than one paradigm' (Pondy and Boje 1981). This has meant that in virtually all of the paradigm models available there is confusion over this issue of incommensurability. In the best-known scheme, that by Burrell and Morgan, references to inter-paradigmatic communication are typically awry (Burrell and Morgan 1979). While initially there is a firm assertion that their (four) paradigms are, 'mutually exclusive . . . they offer different ways of seeing' (p. 25), later there is oscillation between Giddens' view that 'some *inter*-paradigm debate is also possible' (Burrell and Morgan 1979: 36), and the subsequent equivocal statement that, 'relations between the paradigms are best described in terms of "disinterested hostility" rather than "debate"' (Burrell and Morgan 1979: 36). Burrell and Morgan are, of course, not alone here, for the problem is rife throughout the literature (e.g. see Friedheim's 1979 critique of Ritzer 1975; and the review by Eckburg and Hill 1978).

Therefore, to accomplish progress on paradigm mediation we need to resolve these basic contradictions. Not only do we need an awareness of what the paradigms of organization theory are, but we require a rationale for mediating them. In other words, we need a thesis capable of confronting the relativism of the incommensurability thesis. To achieve this we should go beyond a basic sociological reading of Kuhn.

Main problems: incommensurability and relativism

Kuhn's original position, in attacking the proposition of theory-independent 'facts', seems to deny the possibility of objective choice between paradigms; i.e. there can be no 'good reasons' for preference of a new paradigm as such reasons will always be paradigm-dependent. For Kuhn, 'the competition between paradigms is not the sort of battle that can be resolved by proofs' (Kuhn 1962: 47). Therefore, in Kuhnian theory the two traditional pillars of science – objectivity and progress – are seemingly lost. Not only are we bereft of a means of evaluating competing paradigms rationally, we appear deprived of any way of comparing them at all – we see different worlds through different paradigms. This position appears a relativist one – it seems that while scientific theories change, such change cannot signal progress. As Kuhn has said, 'like the choice between competing political institutions, that between competing paradigms proves to be a choice between incompatible modes of community life' (Kuhn 1970: 94).

These problems of relativism were central to the contributions collected by Lakatos and Musgrave (1970) – or the literature commonly known as the 'Kuhn-Popper debate'. For us, the central issue lies in Popper's attack on Kuhn's use of irrationalist symbols, i.e. Kuhn's descriptions of dogmatic scientific activity. While Popper's well-known suggestion, in *Logik der Forschung* (1968), is that there is a necessary place for dogma – in that we must not reject theories too soon or their power will never be realized – he later qualifies this (Popper 1970) to suggest that it is a totally different conception of dogma to that presented in *The Structure of Scientific Revolutions* (Kuhn 1962). In Kuhn, science is characterized by the proliferation of a *ruling* dogma which exercises hegemonic control for lengthy periods. In periods of so-called 'normal' science the (Popperian) tenets of real debate are inaccessible. Popper argues that Kuhn's images of 'puzzle' solutions within a common framework, while appealing, do not match up with fundamental, rational principles. Thus, 'the relativistic thesis that the framework *cannot* be critically discussed is a thesis which can be critically discussed' (Popper 1970: 56). Kuhn's restrictiveness is seen as misplaced because alternative frameworks are not inconceivable. In Popper's famous statement:

> I do admit that at any moment we are prisoners caught in the framework of our theories; our expectations; our past experiences; our language. But we are prisoners in a Pickwickian sense; if we try we can break out of our frameworks at any time. Admittedly, we shall find ourselves again in a framework, but it will be a better and roomier one; and we can at any moment break out of it again.
>
> (Popper 1970: 86)

A comparison of frameworks, and thus critical discussion, always remains possible. What in Kuhn is regarded as an impossibility should better be regarded as a difficulty.

A major watershed in this debate was the withdrawal of the 'later' Kuhn (1970; 1970a; 1977) from the 'exclusivist' incommensurability thesis, as instead he begins to talk – albeit tentatively – of communication. Whilst rarely acknowledged in organization theory, this later Kuhn finds it increasingly difficult to hold on to the incommensurability thesis. Indeed, when distancing himself from Feyerabend (Feyerabend 1970), he insists, 'where he talks of incommensurability *tout court*, I have regularly spoken also of partial communication' (Kuhn 1970a: 232). Whereas Popper (1970) vigorously argued that even the most incompatible languages could be made translatable, Kuhn took refuge in the argument that, ultimately, there are crucial differences in *meaning* which are beyond access; i.e. we can only translate up to a point before we are forced to compromise between incompatible objectives. As Kuhn notes, 'Translation. . . always involves compromises which alter communication; thus, 'what the existence of translation suggests is that recourse is available to scientists who hold incommensurable theories. That recourse need not, however, be to full restatement in a neutral language of even the theories' consequences' (Kuhn 1970a: 268).

While for paradigm mediation we note that this position is still not satisfactory, it is, nevertheless, now far removed from the grand isolationism of the instant-paradigm thesis. Indeed, the new position *does* attempt to offer a way out of hermeticism – notably through Kuhn's remarks on nature. Kuhn now argues that there *is* an objective sense in which a new paradigm is better than the one it replaces (Kuhn 1970a). The crucial factor is this role he finds for nature. While Kuhn originally documented how, for example, Einstein's paradigm replaced

Newton's because it was able to solve any problem equally well or better, he also maintained that this paradigm change did not signal a closer approximation to truth. This led to cries of relativism as the whole question of progress was brought into question. In 'Reflections on my critics' (1970a), however, Kuhn attempts to remedy this situation by suggesting that, for the linear paradigm changes of the natural sciences, scientific problems are not exclusively determined by paradigm forces, but that *nature* exerts a paradigm-independent, factual world bringing forth problems for solution. Kuhn notes that,

> 'no part of my argument . . . implies that scientists may choose any theory they like so long as they agree in their choice and thereafter enforce it. Most of the puzzles of normal science are directly presented by nature, and all involve nature indirectly. Though different solutions have been received as valid at different times, nature cannot be forced into an arbitrary set of conceptual boxes'.
>
> (Kuhn 1970a: 263)

Therefore, by applying Kuhn's original thesis, organization theory has failed to acknowledge the important qualifications made to this argument. Indeed, these later reversals signal, for Shapere, 'for better or for worse, a long step toward a more conventional position' (Shapere 1971: 708). Kuhn's later articles herald almost a *volte face* over this central question of incommensurability. Instead of arguing for exclusive paradigm-determination of meaning, he now advocates not only the seemingly progressive influence of nature, but more concretely, certain overlaps of paradigm meaning (i.e. 'shared everyday vocabularies' which serve to isolate 'areas of difficulty in scientific communication', and which subsequently illustrate 'what the other would see and say when presented with a stimulus to which his own verbal response would be different' (Kuhn 1977: 202). Indeed, this process leads to a position whereby competing scientists

> may in time become very good predictors of each other's behaviour. Each will have learned to translate the other's theory and its consequences into his own language and simultaneously to describe in his language the world to which that theory applies.
>
> (Kuhn 1977: 202)

For our purposes, however, these later more orthodox statements do not offer a deep enough explanation of how we may retain a sense of relativity whilst also allowing for inter-paradigm understanding. Although in his later works Kuhn argues for 'partial' communication, there is much equivocality as he oscillates between 'persuasion' and 'conversion', 'translation' and ' isolation' (Kuhn 1970a). For the goal of paradigm mediation, Kuhn fails to go far enough towards a form of analysis which would retain paradigm identity whilst offering an alternative to hermeticism; i.e. a form that would allow a dissected world to be explored. Such a position, 'sustain[ing] a principle of relativity while rejecting relativism' (Giddens 1976: 18), would present analytical openings for those who argue that organization theory holds a plurality of exclusive paradigms. As the majority of commentators, including Kuhn, take the social sciences to be pluri-paradigmatic, this would offer a basic rationale for those currently advocating 'multi-paradigm enquiry' (e.g. Ritzer 1975; Burrell and Morgan 1979; Pondy and Boje 1981; Morgan 1986).

In seeking such a position, we will move away from Kuhn and toward the 'later' Wittgenstein, and signally his concept of 'language-game'.

Analytical openings: the 'later' Wittgenstein

We have noted how Kuhn's attack on traditional positions stressed the failure of positivist propositions to recognize that what we choose to regard as knowledge is essentially inseparable from the time and culture within which scientific decisions are made. Kuhn argues that such positivist positions are erroneous in that they fail to grasp their own relativity and dependence on cultural values. The point is not that a particular scientific position is inevitably sociological, but that each position (or paradigm) gains separate existence through learning of its own language; or, put simply, the way in which it beholds the 'world'. While as Stuart Hampshire suggests, 'we cannot step outside the language we use, and judge it from some ulterior and superior vantage-point' (Hampshire 1959: 192), so for Kuhn, 'the proponents of different theories are like the members of different language-culture communities' (Kuhn 1970: 205).

For Kuhn, then, as for the later Wittgenstein, there is considerable recognition for the ways that language can cut up the world, and thus of Wittgenstein's notion that the meaning of words is dependent upon the given 'form of life'. In Kuhn, the scientific community is bound largely by the presuppositions it holds, such premises, in turn, providing the rules which specify the perceptual limits of problems and solutions. Language erects the boundary encircling what scientists think and therefore do. Although this position may seem deterministic, we will argue that Wittgenstein's thesis is less so. Indeed we will suggest that it approaches a middle ground between the extremes of relativism and absolutism which can alleviate many difficulties arising out of Kuhn's 'strong' incommensurability thesis (Kuhn 1962).

Fundamental to Wittgenstein's 'later' arguments is this notion of the impossibility of separating language from the human *milieu* of its location (Kenny 1973). Indeed, the 'Philosophical Investigations' (1953) are, for many, levelled against his Tractatus thesis that words in an utterance are in some way mutually related to the objects for which they stand. In the later works, language is a social activity expressive of human needs, a means of communication within the world and not merely a reflection of the order of the world. As Wittgenstein suggests, 'the term "language game" is meant to bring into prominence the fact that speaking of lan- guage is part of an activity, or of a form of life' (Wittgenstein 1953: 23).

The concepts of 'language-game' and 'form of life' are, however, like paradigm, rather elusive. In the 'Blue and Brown Books' Wittgenstein states:

> I shall in the future again and again draw your attention to what I call language games. These are ways of using signs simpler than those in which we use the signs of our highly complicated everyday language. Language games are forms of language with which a child begins to make use of words. The study of language games is the study of primitive forms of language or primitive languages.
>
> (Wittgenstein 1958: 17)

Word language, then, is activity, and not merely a static and abstracted sign structure. As Disco puts it, 'when language is *spoken* there is a speaker and, usually a listener . . . here we have a language *game*, language in use, the production of meaning'. As such, any other conception of language 'must accede to the charge that it has de-contextualized the symbol system. It has removed from the semiotic structure the *behaviour* in which it is, *aborigine*, embedded' (Disco 1976: 270).

The middle ground we mentioned is forged through Wittgenstein's thesis that language is both a *product* of human activity and a *producer* of meaning – and thus of new forms of human action (Phillips 1977). Here we witness a dialectic between language as a producer of new meanings, and as itself dependent on conditional 'facts of nature'. Wittgenstein does not wish to propose that facts of nature wholly prescribe language, nor on the other hand to advocate that facts of nature are entirely the products of our language. Instead, as Phillips notes:

> while he [Wittgenstein] gives many examples of imaginary peoples with forms of life different to that of our own, and therefore, with such basically different conceptions of the way things are that they can be said to live in a 'different world'; this is not the case for the world in which *we* live. Of course, there are different language-games among us, but there are certain facts of

> nature which have a priority over all language games. In other words, nature has something to say, but it does not determine what we can say.
>
> (Phillips 1977: 84)

Wittgenstein, then, seeks to infer an infrastructure of species-specific possibilities delimiting the conceptions that can emerge – a form of life expressing both the grounds for language and the limits of such possibilities. Nature, itself, however, is not limited to our form of life, for there remains another domain of elements with which we interact and which, in so doing, delimit our language; i.e. the unanalysed ways in which 'the world is'. Such a world is made sensible because the language within which such thought is cast offers no ground to question its material basis. Any such rejection would hold recourse to a solipsist position.

By drawing upon Giddens' proposal of the conceptual correspondence between language-game and paradigm (Giddens 1976), this analysis can accommodate our questions about incommensurability and relativism. These problems can be addressed by reference to the dialectic of language and nature; i.e. the argument through which Wittgenstein seeks to undermine deterministic explanations whereby either one *causes* us to act. By illuminating such a tension, Wittgenstein avoids adherence to the relativism evident in Kuhn's work and, indeed, in much of the sociology of organizations.

The language-game of everyday life

The central feature in this relationship is Wittgenstein's chief distinction in the field of language-games; i.e. that between what he terms the 'everyday language-game' and other technical and special language-games. The everyday language-game is our first basic language. It is the first language we accommodate; our first years of life are characterized by the quest to assimilate the natural structures of the everyday language-game. We learn to speak, to ask questions, to discriminate between waking and dreaming. Thus, such an elementary framework forms the bedrock for our later linguistic acquisition and for the later accommodation of special language-games; it is the basis for language, and thus of what we can possibly think (Disco 1976). As the everyday language-game is the very basis of thought then it needs no justification – justification is but a special language-game. However, Wittgenstein gives caution, in that 'what we have . . . to do is to *accept* the everyday language-game; and to note false accounts of the matter *as* false. The primitive language game which children are taught needs no justification, attempts at justification need to be rejected' (Wittgenstein 1953: 200). Indeed, as Phillips notes:

> the everyday language-game constitutes the very rock bottom of our knowledge and experience. It would simply make no sense to ask whether it is true (or false), for there is no transcendental criterion – which would have to stand beyond or outside our language – by which such a judgement could be made.
>
> (Phillips 1977: 88)

Therefore, we are left in a position in which 'the everyday language-game has . . . an epistemological and ontological primacy. It interpenetrates and shapes as well as contextualising all other language-games played in a society' (Disco 1976: 277).

It is this interpenetration of the everyday language-game into all other language games that is important for us. Technical language-games can be seen as discrete and bounded but for differing purposes. While we have a language-game of science, we also have other language-games cutting up science – like physics, biology, psychology, sociology, etc. – with further interpenetrations coming from games such as theorizing, calculating, testing, etc. None of the latter is discipline-specific. On the contrary, all overlap with other technical language-games in seeking to make sense of some bounded portion of everyday life – thereby constructing language-games suitable for such understanding (Phillips 1977). Although such special language-games can develop, there is always, however, basic interpenetration; i.e. a necessary recourse to the language-game of everyday life as the foundation for all special languages. Thus we can only learn the language-game of organization through use of ordinary language which, as we have said, is beyond justification (albeit what we say within a special language-game is not).

While metaphysical models, and especially the 'shared models' of Kuhn's 'disciplinary matrix' (Kuhn 1970), can be equated with community-bound language-games (Giddens 1976), we have also noted how other language-games – such as calculating and testing – while themselves bounded, nevertheless overlap with other technical language-games in making sense of the world; notably here the scientific world. Thus, while the language-game of 'truth' may be ascribed through intra-paradigm and intersubjective consensus – the consensus theory of truth – the language-games employed in its justification do not necessarily exist in such a relativist vacuum. Language is, after all, employed by humans while partly dependent on certain 'facts of nature', and as such, rests on constraints that are prior to the conventions of Kuhn, Hanson or Feyerabend.

We have noted how technical language-games have ultimate recourse to the metalanguage which underlies them – the everyday language-game. Thus, the everyday language-game establishes not only the possibilities of what we can *think* but, with regard to perception, similarly of what we can *see*. Although the limits of what we can see are set according to the metalanguage of our form of life, within such bounds there may be an almost infinite *set* of possibilities – the natural limits. Such a line of analysis underpins the solutions to paradigm mediation advocated by Maruyama (1974) and Phillips (1977), who both reject the grand isolation of Kuhn and Feyerabend, whilst similarly objecting to arguments such as Popper's for breaking out of our frameworks at any time (Popper 1970).

This account can therefore be removed from charges of pure relativism. It can suggest ways of undermining the 'strong' incommensurability thesis through recourse to the dialectic of nature and the everyday language-game. It offers analytical openings for retaining relativity whilst rejecting relativism. This analysis, in stressing the interpenetration and overlapping of technical language-games, begins to overcome the hermeticism inherent in the use of paradigm in organization theory. It thus offers analytical openings towards paradigm mediation.

Coda: towards paradigm mediation

This reading of Wittgenstein argues that as our perceptual limitations are so empirically established, then the rules and conventions of our 'metalanguage in use' allow us to deal not only with a present language-game, but also with a new language game into which we may be *trained*. Here, the emphasis is not on a sudden gestalt switch occurring which allows us to see the light, but rather, as Watkins argues, on there being established perceptual arrangements which facilitate a transfer of allegiance (Watkins 1970). Phillips, for example, has cited Kohler's faces and goblet drawing to explain the impossibility of appreciating the goblet if one only has knowledge of faces, because 'unorganized experience cannot order perception' (Phillips 1977: 111). It is, therefore, mistaken to talk of such instant switches of allegiance, and indeed Phillips has argued for a concept of 'seeing as' (the ability to reflect between seeing 'this' and seeing 'that') as an intermediate step, and foil, for the incommensurability thesis. The Kohler drawing is, of course, often cited in support of the theory-dependence of observation – notably by reference to Hanson's (1958) work. However, as Phillips stresses, this is not so much an argument for incommensurability *per se*, but represents, instead, an excellent example of how two language-games can be straddled at once. The learning of what faces or goblets are allows not simply a transference from the goblet to the faces: it permits us to *see* faces, *see* the goblet, or even *see* the Kohler drawing. All are experiential states, all transferable, and all capable of reflection.

For Kuhn, a scientist working under one paradigm cannot entertain another – that is, until the conversion experience which changes his whole world view (Kuhn 1962). Watkins (1970), Shapere (1971) and Phillips (1977), however, all question the logic of this instant-paradigm thesis. For them, unorganized experience cannot order perception. If we can be trained so as to comfortably straddle two paradigms, then, as Giddens suggests, it should not be too difficult to apply the logic to paradigms (Giddens 1976), especially as scientists sharing a paradigm are, as Kuhn states, sharing 'language' (Kuhn 1962). As the rules and conventions of our 'metalanguage in use' serve to explain each special language-game, then in turn the interpenetration of language-games such as theorizing and testing can be used as the basis for explaining, and teaching, other special languages. Practitioners in different paradigms share ordinary language as well as much technical language. Although this is far from complete, it is the basis for training into future possibilities and realizing 'seeing as' – that is, the understanding of two language-games or paradigms. This is not, however, through recourse to a theory neutral observation language, but to the everyday language-game holding ontological and epistemological primacy – the dialectic of nature and language.

Epilogue

This form of analysis, then, offers analytical openings for those wishing to address issues of paradigm incommensurability in organizations. In particular it outlines a more robust thesis for dealing with problems of paradigmatic mediation. Although many writers on organization proclaim the advantages of 'multi-paradigm research' (Burrell and Morgan 1979; Pondy and Boje 1981; Morgan 1986 etc.), none has yet offered a satisfactory account of paradigm communication. This reading of Wittgenstein offers a way forward.

Part four

Epilogue

Chapter thirteen

Post-paradigm enquiry

Denis Pym

> All the natural world hardens into the mechanistic image and nature so perceived is nature adrift, waiting to be put to the use man sees fit. For Newton the celestial spheres comprise a machine; for Descartes animals become machines; for Hobbes society is a machine; for La Mettrie the human body is a machine; eventually for Pavlov and Watson human behaviour is machine-like.
>
> (Roszak 1972: 180)

Some while ago, an article I had submitted to the editor of a technical journal was returned to me with the reports of three referees enclosed. One review was fair, the others recommended rejection because 'the paper was not based on research'. My impulse was to object to the editor. The paper summarized a substantial number of surveys and studies of the kind quite acceptable to the servants of normal management science. Unfortunately, it addressed a sensitive topic – the pathologies of 'professionalizing the work-force' and, in order to emphasize its relevance to us all, the language employed was in places emotive. Well, the passage of time has not moderated my indignation but has led to this more explicit outburst of private views I have long harboured.

I wish to explore three related themes here. The first starts with criticism of 'the scientific method'. The rejection of normal science and its methodologies already has advocates in plenty (e.g. Roszak 1972; Phillips 1977; and Feyerabend 1975); indeed it is fast becoming a popular sport, though few of its critics focus their criticism on the place of literacy in maintaining the institutions of science and the authority of the scientific estate. The second theme, which the title of the paper reflects, is an outline of personal research strategies and my own divergence from the critical posture. Far from denying dominant science and its rituals, my own predisposition has been to exploit them in getting into more fruitful games that are more personally satisfying. The third, concluding theme uses this post-paradigm mode of enquiry to explore the meaning and politics of literacy – the basis of the authority exercised by all our major institutions.

Old games gone wrong

I don't want to engage in detailed arguments against the scientific estate here. Others, including those cited above, have already done that with greater competence than I could muster. Besides, it's not politically astute to give undue attention to a cause from which you are diverging if you have your own trumpet to blow. The tenor of my objections are as follows. I see old, textbook science and its prescribed research methods as an essentially fraudulent, collusive and debilitating game. Any methodology which denies the anarchistic tradition in discovery, learning and advance is poor science. The rot sets in once the methods of science cease to reflect the limitless ways by which man subjects any phenomenon to observation, scrutiny and criticism. Through the process of institutionalization, science also ceases to be fun. Tedium and lethargy take over as the flight of the initiated from doing 'research' bears witness. This is particularly true of the so-called social sciences.

At this moment I fancy myself in a sort of spiritual exile from my colleagues in the occupations associated with psychology, sociology and management studies. This is a status freely chosen. I cannot deny my experiences nor the vast privileges gained from twenty-five years of association with the professional communities attached to these subjects. But if there is a limit to the extent to which we can collude with each other in the maintenance of a deception, then I have exceeded mine. For this deception is no trivial matter. Through the denial of feelings, imagination and the human spirit, concealed assumptions, rigid, sterile and inappropriate methods of enquiry, and the enlargement of trivia into problems of consequence, we, you and I, preserve our employment prospects to the detriment of our souls, our fellow men, and society.

My strongest objections are reserved for the positivists and those who hold to the 'value-free' claims for science. I am a child of this school and recognize the enormous authority it continues to exercise over social enquiry to this day. These assertions are not, however, influenced by conventional political allegiances. Indeed, my criticisms apply equally to those middle-class, educated, format Marxists who wait for history and working people to hand them power but for whom they show not the slightest sympathy in the language of their writings, their associations, and their styles of living. Nobody can put ideology before man and claim to be ennobling man.

Though there is nothing new in rejecting normal science, the tone of most objections has been muted for fear no doubt of being accused of subjectivity and irrationality – 'those instruments of tyranny'. The objectified/reductionist current runs so powerfully through social enquiry that when more adventurous souls seek to address themselves to meaningful issues they feel obliged to take recourse to zany language, joky aphorisms and gimmicks. Two such examples are Norman Mailer and Marshall McLuhan, both astute observers of our social order and much criticized by their establishments. Since we are given to demeaning ourselves, any departure from this tradition cannot be taken seriously.

More on personal prejudices

I do believe that the elevation of human dignity must be the overriding and continuing concern of any social enquiry. This disposition is different, I hope, from the 'caring, sharing, wanting to help others' phoney humanism that is currently riding high. Behind such apparently noble causes lie coercive games and the reducing effects of bureaucratized welfare and proceduralized democracy. An elevated view of man necessitates locating the authority for all social action within man's own frame. If this means that the quest for truth must take place then so be it. This does not mean that our cultural edifices and artefacts are neither relevant nor necessary. It does mean that our institutions and all that accompanies them are judged to be the consequence of human frailty, as a creation of and for our lesser selves rather than as the authoritative monuments we currently make of them. This notion of man as the measure of all things is nearly as old as the hills and goes back, in our philosophical tradition, to the Sophists and no doubt before.

Now an elevated image of man, his mysteries and actions recommends a simpler evaluation of his artefacts. The search for similarities in our cultural artefacts, an approach structuralists have been taking for some time, might follow. This is, of course, quite contrary to industrial man's predisposition for mystifying and complexifying the social fabric with which he surrounds himself. How convenient it would be if common cause for the overriding problems we now face could be found in the very mechanisms by which we transfer authority from ourselves to our social edifices.

Guidance in this direction originates from the aphorism which most aptly summarizes Marshall McLuhan's ideas – 'the medium is the message' and the further rider that industrial society is a visual/literary order (McLuhan 1964). In other words, we allow the mechanical sequence, advances in technology and an educational system based on 'the three Rs' to ensure that the critical information is transferred from the human brain to records, books, reports, cases, papers, computer tapes, legislation, procedures, microfilm and the rest. Each reinforces and is reinforced by the linear, sequential, rational view of the world. The primacy of literacy in communication gives us one-dimensional man and trivializes our other senses (Pym 1976). And what of the role of the scientific estate, the so-called protector of the open society? It adds weight to the tyranny by stressing the importance of precision, classification, objectivity, consistency, facts as visual/literary details and the quest for truth with prescribed method as the guarantor of that truth.

I am not disputing the qualitative outcomes of literacy – fine literature and mathematics and the capacity both afford to detail the intricacies of so many phenomena. I am against the authoritative role of literary media in our lives. For all its contributions to describing, defining and classifying the world, totalitarian literacy also imposes a highly fragmented time and space which imprisons and alienates. It makes, too, for scientific reductionism, bureaucratic excess and the insanities of spurious employment to mention just a few of its liabilities.

Like the fish in water, industrial literate man has no grasp of the meaning and politics of the medium in which he swims. Because this medium underlies the methodologies of normal science, the likelihood that conventional 'scientific' methods might be used to explore the dimensions and dynamics of literacy is not great. Different perspectives and approaches need to be found and these, according to Kuhn, can only emerge in a public sense when critical people within the industrial community find the norms and values of the old paradigm no longer useful in tackling the problems they identify. And more important, I would add, identifying pseudo problems to sustain their employment ceases to be a game worth playing.

A case for perversion

The quest for more appropriate methods of enquiry to fit with an elevated view of man can take place on many fronts. The enquirer might begin with his own private, preferred ways of exploring, examining and formulating the world as those we reckon to be 'the greats' have always done (see Feyerabend 1975). Descartes' visions, Poincares' subliminal self, Blake's religious romanticism, Rimbaud's drug-guided hallucinations, Bacon's distortions of the human anatomy, and McLuhan's probes are illustrations of the anarchistic enterprise. For the less adventurous and less creative mind (mine and probably yours) there is also scope to work away from the old paradigm with its associated theories and methods. Let me elaborate a little.

Unfortunately, advice on this approach is often unrealistic. Take, for example, March's suggestions with which many readers will be familiar. He begins by identifying the three most powerful prejudices within normal social science – the pre-existence of purpose, the necessity for consistency and the primacy of rationality. It is fundamental to this view of the world, he goes on,

> that thinking should precede action, that action should serve a purpose, that purpose should be defined in terms of a consistent set of pre-existent goals and that choice should be based on a consistent theory of the relation between action and its consequences.
>
> (March 1971: 3)

March then explores another approach which derives much from our observations of behaviour among children, i.e. before we are socialized into the dominant industrial culture. He wants us to emulate children. He asks us to consider when and where it may be more appropriate to act before we think and to re-examine our strictures against 'imitation, coercion and rationalisations' (p. 5). There is too, through the encouragement of play, the chance to 'suspend rational imperatives towards consistency' (p. 5). However, March's technology of foolishness seems to lack the practical steps which might get us going. He wants to treat goals as hypotheses, make intuition and hypocrisy real, treat memory as enemy and use experience as the basis for theory. These are all wise ideas and I for one have no argument with them – and if we were still children no doubt there would be no difficulty in implementing them. Unfortunately, you and I are no longer children and most of us are crippled by our adherence to the folklores of normal industrial social science – trained to incapacity, Veblen called it.

Let us start instead with our handicaps and predispositions. But, instead of perceiving that experience as the basis for theory let's call it prejudice. Our experiences in normal social science predispose us to approach our affairs in certain ways. If these ways are boring, unhelpful, and demeaning of ourselves and those we study, let us give them a dirty label. (Personally I can't recognize the difference between theory and prejudice but this is not the place for exploring my ignorance.)

When I go out to do research in the context of my employment I am always proceeding within the frame of some authority out there – business, education or government. The purposes of this enquiry and the methods acceptable to that authority fall neatly into the dominant paradigm. Publicly I am playing their game. It used to be my game too but it has not been so for over ten years. That is, I have been engaging in a collusive exercise. I acknowledge publicly the authority and power of my sponsors (they have little of either to act differently, i.e. outside the paradigm). They value me as a social scientist (objective, authoritative, etc., which is not so). We engage in a reciprocal game of maintaining our false selves.

The opportunity to diverge from the usual pattern of enquiry comes less from actual methods than what it is we attend to, *what constitutes information*. In reality the methods of normal science are not conducive to learning and discovering but to confirming and extending the status quo. If we divide 'enquiry' crudely between information gathering and decision taking, then any rule following associated with the scientific method gets us straight into a decision-taking posture. All the incidents which don't fit are ignored, questioned, kicked out, are given rough, unloving treatment. But conventional enquiry is so boring. All the fun is taken out of it if the rules are properly followed. What keeps me at this game called research is a little intellectual curiosity and a personal way of proceeding which I believe is most appropriate for post-paradigm enquiry.

In order to preserve the information-gathering phase of enquiry I found myself ignoring the confirmatory data and recording events which required my own personal interpretation and judgements. In short, I found myself determining significant information as that which seemed to me to be odd, peculiar, discrepant, contradictory, nonsensical, and the like. On reflection this strategy is close to the sophists' advice to make the weaker case the stronger and thereby to sustain the motion of the whole (Feyerabend 1975: 30). How, you may ask, does an event meet the description above? It does so by falling outside our predispositions and expectations, i.e. it is the very information that normal science recommends we discount, control or ignore. Facts in this situation *start* as events which *fail* to elaborate a framework. In the same way that we can use this method to transcend the restrictions of normal science, we can also use it to escape our own prejudices. But first we must acknowledge those prejudices even if we call them theories.

Here I had found for myself, if for nobody else, something useful to make of my own strong prejudices and, what is more, a technique which emphasizes those very existential characteristics of enquiry that others like March have been recommending to us – the authority of inconsistency and playfulness; the notion of memory as an enemy; a concern with impulse, intuition, and faith, etc.

I want now to outline how I have used this simple technique in an examination of the meaning and politics of literacy, but before I do a little more scene-setting.

On the meaning and politics of literacy

Over the past ten years I have not written a single paper which did not refer critically to the excesses of literacy in our lives today. It seems to be at the centre of everything I deem to be a problem. This is now a very strong prejudice of mine, an obsession which most recently has led me to examine the workings of the Other Economy (see Pym 1981) where, not surprisingly, written communications are practically non-existent. My public references to literary have depended very much on McLuhan's work. However, McLuhan carefully side-stepped the political implications of his interest in media (McLuhan 1964). No doubt he had his reasons for doing so. My own reticence had a lot to do with the problem of acceptable evidence. McLuhan's own methods of presentation and his lack of deference for the truth offended many visual/literary minds. But what McLuhan has to say is deadly serious. Man and his society have changed little in many fundamental ways through the centuries but the techniques which extend (or reduce) our senses and central nervous system have certainly evolved at a pace over the past few decades. In a different context, partly created by these changes, where the conventional means for proceeding are in dispute, it becomes timely to look more closely at that single feature which most distinguishes the institutions of industrial society from those of other societies – their dependence in transactions on written words and numbers.

Herewith five short, personal stories on the meaning and politics of literacy that are typical of the incidents which shaped my views.

Back in 1962 while at Birkbeck College I was involved in an intelligence and aptitude testing programme among children in several north London schools. The purpose of the exercise was to establish norms for vocationally guiding school leavers. In developing these instruments testers are keen on such things as their reliability and validity. Tests can't do the job expected of them unless they *discriminate between people*. Nearly all IQ tests are made up of verbal and numerical puzzles as well has having written instructions for their completion – that is, they measure visual/literary acuity. There are exceptions. One such test is the Ravens Matrices, a non-verbal measure requiring the testee to choose between a set of alternative symbols to create a larger picture. The explicit literary factor is removed but not the linear sequential or rational method of solving problems which underlies literacy. The Matrices is an old test millions of people throughout the world have taken. There are norms for the test that go back to the last war when it was used extensively in military recruitment and placement. That, essentially, is the orthodoxy of this situation; now for the discrepancy.

When marking the early batches of completed tests we found that our population of kids were scoring high on the Matrices. To put it personally, many in the bottom streams of the school were getting a higher score on the Matrices than I could obtain. However, the test was not serving the psychologist's purposes, so, after using it at a few more schools it was dropped from the battery. In the mean time, my curiosity had been roused. Many of the children were completing the exercise before the allotted time was up. They seemed to be guessing. Yet they were getting the puzzles right. They were *not* solving them by the literary (rational) fashion but by what appeared to be some kind of pattern recognition. (Faced with a visual overload we have no alternative but pattern recognition, see McLuhan 1969.) Here was a real opportunity to explore an aspect of mental functioning and we dismissed it because it made a nonsense of the psychologist's ideas on tests and his literary view of intelligence. By such mechanisms, those we judge to be dim are kept in cultural prisons.

In 1965 I was engaged in the evaluation of an organizational development programme at Esso's Fawley Refinery. Eight middle-managers, men mostly in their 30s and 40s, had been chosen from within the company to provide Coverdale training for the refinery staff and to assist them in implementing their training experiences through on-the-job coaching. They were attempting to change the culture of the refinery by way of an ambitious training programme.

From the start, the level of commitment on the venture was very high. Long hours were spent by the eight examining the refinery organization, evolving strategies for change and establishing the ground rules. However, one aspect of the team's behaviour struck me as inconsistent with their ages and roles. Morale fluctuated wildly. They behaved like kids. Sometimes they were going about their tasks with evangelical zeal, and on other occasions depression and lethargy dominated their conduct. I asked one of them to confirm my observation (which he did) and explain it. 'The trouble is', he told me, 'we do not have jobs'. While several of his colleagues agreed I disputed the explanation, pointing out that they did as much course training as I did teaching and that their on-the-job coaching and general planning work provided them with more than a job. 'It's just that we don't have any routines', he went on. Again I disagreed. 'You see', he said finally, 'we have no paper to push'. These men did not fit my image of the bureaucrat. Yet it is seems even among production managers, work, like education, gains its meaning from literacy.

Another event I recall in different time and space: a rain-threatened, damp winter's evening in Melbourne in 1969 and the company of anti-Vietnam war demonstrators. Six sociology students and myself were observing crowd behaviour. There were perhaps 1,000 souls drawn from a dull city's questioning few, rallied in a park in preparation for a march on the US consulate. We talked intermittently in anxious huddles. Every few minutes the group I had quietly joined was visited by an earnest caller who dealt out leaflets on his own particular club, society or organization. It was clear that most of those present were students. But it was now dark. Strange to be given written material to read in such circumstances. I withdrew from my group to get a better picture of the whole. As I watched the callers' ritual, I became aware of an intensified murmur and even more frenetic behaviour among the callers – the crowd's nervous energy had intensified, and then, behind me, I caught my first glimpse of blue uniforms still largely concealed by the darkness. The police had arrived in numbers and surrounded us. My mind leapt to wild connections. These papers in our hands comprised our only defence against the enemy out there – middle-class man's weapon against the reality of action, and I was struck by helplessness. There were a few speeches, poor stuff, and as the rain began to fall we lurched off on the march to the consulate leaving our damp weapons to the street-cleaners.

In 1971, I was asking school-leavers at Holland Park Comprehensive about their job-seeking activities. As I was about to talk to a few of the youngsters in my very first session, a concerned teacher took me aside. 'You aren't going to give them questionnaires?' she demanded. 'Why?' I asked. She told me how in the previous week a young researcher from the LSE had presented this same group with forms to complete, whereupon one of their number had punched him on the nose. (Do we need reminding, questionnaires are not value-free providers of information but instruments for imposing *our* values and frames on others? For the less literate their imposition may even represent an act of aggression.)

Now we move to a context in which my views on literacy and the institutions it props up are well established. In 1977 my wife and I were called by the headmaster of the local secondary school to discuss our second son's 'poor educational progress'. I had not met the man before and this meeting followed efforts on our part to get the school to acknowledge his particular problem and the remedial aid this required. The school is a mile away from our home and we went to the interview in our working clothes. Our dress and my son's disability no doubt gave the headmaster his defensive cue. After the usual pleasantries he addressed his remarks to me. 'Boys emulate their fathers' he commented. I nodded in agreement. 'Do you read?' he asked. The question amused me and as I hesitated to answer he took my slowness as a sign that his line of questioning might be above me. 'Do you read a newspaper?' he went on. Still silent I looked at my wife who showed signs of bursting into laughter. To save the situation I murmured that my son's brother and sister read a lot. After a few more trivial exchanges, the headmaster took us to look over that educational cure-all, the library! We left the school with the status quo unmolested and our peasant disguises still intact, knowing a little more about insanity. The boy –

well, he's doing fine on as little schooling as he is prepared to put up with.

From such incidents my fascination with literacy (and literary media) became an obsession: the limitations it imposes on human imagination; the phoney purchase it offers on immortality; its role in sustaining the authority of large enterprises in our lives and within them the major function of professionals in replacing the more traditional rituals of our social order with less authentic rites based on literacy.

My interest in the proliferation of unauthentic ritual in complex organizations developed from observing the ways in which professionals replace the more traditional rites shaped around task, process or product by their more 'rational' preoccupations with control, efficiency, growth, achievement and the like (Pym 1978). But planning, budgeting, accounting, staff appraisals, objective-setting exercises, agendized meetings and the rest are not rational exercises which we repeat. They are paper-based activities in which the connections between stated ends and means are difficult to make. They too possess the characteristics of ritual. However, our complaints about them derive from their meaninglessness; the time and energy they absorb; their use in exporting anxiety and tension to another party and the paucity of their aesthetic value. These, in essence, are bad rituals. To the extent that such rituals diminish the commitment of us all to the dominant industrial institutions, middle-class man is destroying his own power base through literary excess.

Today, I am interested in oddities, exceptions and nonsenses of a different kind, but literary man remains insensitive to the mess he makes of himself and the world around him. We are still too dependent on the instrument with which we make machines and mere roles of ourselves and deny our person.

In summary, in this chapter I have advocated a role for perversion in social enquiry. The old 'means and ends' are neither helpful in understanding our world nor in dealing with its pressing problems, nor are they much fun to pursue. But they are our ways so I am suggesting that we use them, while we need to, to gain access to the universe in which we are interested. However, once in that situation, we record as *relevant information* that which doesn't fit our presuppositions. Politically this is about exploiting our biases. Ignoring its deficiencies, the limitations to proceeding in this fashion are the enquirer's personal confidence and self-awareness. Wisdom, not knowledge, is the key.

Notes

Introduction

1 The editors would like to thank Peter Anthony (Cardiff), Peter Armstrong (East Anglia), Peter Clark (Aston), Andrew Friedman (Bristol), Michael Reed (Lancaster), David Silverman (Goldsmiths), and Barry Turner (Exeter) for their contributions to the *New Perspectives* programme.
2 For the originals of this debate consult David Silverman's *The Theory of Organizations* (1970). More recent work in this area can be found in Burrell and Morgan (1979), Clegg and Dunkerley (1975, 1980), Morgan (1983, 1986), Donaldson (1985), and Reed (1986).

2 Breaking up the mono-method monopolies in organizational analysis

1 This chapter has grown out of discussions with Joseph McGrath, Barry Straw, Richard Kulka, Eugene Webb, James G. March, John Van Maanen, and Richard Hackman. I am also grateful for the helpful comments of Meryl Louis, Gareth Morgan, and Richard Daft.
2 A colleague who reviewed an earlier draft of this chapter noted that it might be helpful to distinguish method and methodology, as follows. Method refers to the instruments or techniques used to gather and analyse data. For example, a survey is a method for gathering data and regression analysis is a method for interpreting that data. Ethnography is a method which implies certain procedures for collecting, analysing, and even displaying data. Methodology, on the other hand, denotes the study, discussion, or practice of particular methods.
3 Some qualitative research takes the position that the search for general laws of social behaviour is misguided because each social event is unique. Thus, qualitative methods can yield a deep understanding of a unique event, even though there is no possibility of extracting general laws. Others argue that both quantitative and qualitative techniques can uncover general laws concerning stable, reproducible phenomena (cf. Gergen 1976). The scope of this chapter does not include such ontological issues or epistemological rationales for preferring one method rather than another.
4 Some philosophers of science have observed that data that appears to be

objective inevitably has subjective elements (e.g. Popper 1959; Kuhn 1970; Feyerabend 1975; Bateson 1979). This position is consistent with the social construction of reality argument that social knowledge is a subjective rather than an objective phenomenon (cf. Berger and Luckmann 1966). Similarly, sociologists have demonstrated that a researcher's historical position, socio-economic status, and/or ideological commitments may influence the content of research findings (e.g. Ossowski 1963; Stark 1967; Horowitz 1968), possibly explaining the pro-management bias found in much organizational research (e.g. Frost 1980).

Ratcliffe offers an articulate variant of this point of view. He observes that numbers, like words, are symbols (Ratcliffe 1980). Thus, whether words or numbers are used to describe or re-present an experience, the process inevitably and always involves a translation from one logic system (experience) to another (symbolic). There is always an interpreter between an event and recorded data.

Even the act of studying a phenomenon can change it. For example, the traces left by atomic particles in a cloud chamber are not the particles themselves; 'The particle must be inferred by the researcher, and that inference is a qualitative process' (Ratcliffe 1980: 2). In experiments, animals are more likely to behave in accord with hypotheses if the person running the experiment is aware of the hypotheses and the experimental conditions to which the animals have been assigned – even when that person is unaware of having done anything to influence the animals' behaviour (Rosenthal and Rosnow 1969). Campbell's observation on this point is relevant to all types of quantitative research, although he refers specifically to experiments: '. . . .much of what we think of as experimental measures, recorded on the occasion of pretest and posttest for both experimental and control groups, are in fact quantifications of subjective judgments' (Campbell 1974: 17, quoted in Ratcliffe 1980: 3–4). Because of these considerations, this chapter does not associate the qualitative-quantitative distinction with judgements about degree of subjectivity and objectivity.

5 It is unclear whether, as McGrath argues, it is desirable to maximise all three of these criteria (see footnote 3 above). Agreement on this issue, however, is not a prerequisite for agreeing with the results of McGrath's analysis.

6 I am grateful to Richard Daft for this idea.

7 Burrell and Morgan have argued that method choices necessarily reflect epistemological preferences (Burrell and Morgan 1979). According to this point of view, because epistemologies conflict, it would be intellectually difficult, if not illogical, to endorse more than one type of method. Although a necessary association between epistemologies and method choices is debatable (for example, perhaps an integrated epistemology is possible), Burrell and Morgan's analysis does convincingly indicate that some researchers believe in a single epistemological approach and feel that the approach justifies a mono-method point of view.

One might expect a more catholic methodological tolerance from researchers who believe that knowledge is 'knowable' only from within the context in which it is embedded. Even researchers working within this epistemological paradigm (e.g. Spender 1983) are generally unwilling to admit that their own context has limitations no less significant than the limitations of other points of view (Burrell and Morgan 1979: 395).

8 Burrell and Morgan suggest a solution to the difficulties posed by conflicting epistemologies. They argue that advocates of a minority point of view should stop reacting to the dominant position and, instead, isolate themselves in order to develop the strengths of their chosen approach to its fullest potential. This solution might have some desirable effects. Isolation may give adherents to minority paradigms a short-term means of strengthening their chosen approaches. The development of mid-range theories might be facilitated. However, in the long term this strategy would hinder the transfer of knowledge across paradigm boundaries, thus impeding the development of organizational theory.

3 Beyond paradigmatic closure in organizational enquiry

1 The author would like to thank David Knights and Ivan Filby for their comments on an earlier draft of this chapter.

2 It is no exaggeration to say that the most stoical defenders of orthodox organization theory have defined their task *in opposition* to the wider analysis of social structure (Reed 1985). The technocratic orientation of so much organization analysis has been systematically exposed by Alvesson (1987). In the most articulate defence of orthodox analysis, Donaldson (p. 118) argues that,

> The study of society reveals larger structures and processes of stratification, socialization, conflict and international relations, all decidedly worthy of enquiry, but already central to the programme of general sociology .... To require that all sociological studies 'begin with a research problem relating to the structure of society rather than to the organization itself' (Silverman 1968: 224) is to prevent the build-up of the sort of knowledge which comes from study of 'the organization itself'. Questions about the consequences of variations in size on structure, technology on satisfaction, diversification on divisionalization, or complexity on innovation might never have been posed let alone answered if organization-level enquiries had not been pursued.

It is worth noting that Donaldson contrives to omit all reference to the Bravermanian tradition of labour process analysis when castigating (Marxian) sociology for its failure to theorize organizational phenomena (e.g. Braverman 1974; Littler 1982; Thompson 1983).

3 This is a very crude differentiation of forms of analysis. It is not intended to provide a comprehensive picture of the range of approaches, but to identify the most distinctive theoretical orientations. For a more discriminating account, see Pfeffer (1982).

4 Silverman's observations on the unreflexive use of common sense knowledge are no less relevant for neo-Marxist theorizing than for orthodox organization theory,

> the common sense knowledge employed by the observer (and the participants) for defining features, seeing relationships and recognizing regularities is specifically uninteresting. They are things to be glossed as 'what may be taken for granted', and the like, so that the 'real' business of the exercise (recording instances of relationships and regularities) may proceed . . . . The 'short-circuiting' of the issues of objectification which [Cicourel] describes ensures that the problematic nature of the process, whereby messages are relayed and received from the social world, never arises.
>
> (Silverman 1975: 273)

5 Of studies that have sought to link organization theory and class theory, Braverman's *Labor and Monopoly Capital* (1974) has probably been the most influential. As Littler and Salaman (1982: 251) have observed, 'by re-asserting the inherently class-based nature of work organization', the appearance of *Labor and Monopoly Capital* rejuvenated this theoretical approach. Braverman draws upon Marx's chapters on the capitalist labour process (Marx 1976) to argue that changes in the organization of work are expressive of the dynamics of the capitalist totality in which the dominance and pervasiveness of the market is an instrument of capital in which everything becomes a (commodified) object of the drive to accumulate. Increasing opportunities arise for an expansion of work that is primarily concerned with the planning, implementation and monitoring of the processes of production and distribution to ensure that a surplus is indeed generated. By substituting capital for traditional forms of manual and skilled labour, the proportion of the workforce engaged in these 'unproductive' tasks grows relative to those performing 'productive' tasks (e.g. managers) who are employed primarily to ensure that the mixing of capital and labour yields a surplus for investors. New skills are recognized to emerge with the development of new material and social technologies. But the organizing principle of capitalism, which systematically privileges the accumulation of capital over the emancipation of labour, continuously seeks the latter's routinization and degradation. Braverman's influence on the development of radical organization theory is somewhat paradoxical since, with the notable exception of Taylorism and a passing reference to Human Relations, Braverman omits reference to orthodox organization theory (e.g. Barnard 1938; March and Simon 1958). For critical assessments of labour process theory, see Littler 1982; Thompson 1983; Wood 1982; Knights and Willmott 1985, forthcoming).

6 For example, in *The Social Construction of Reality*, the 'subjective' and 'objective' elements are treated as separate moments in the process of social reproduction with minimal appreciation of how, in practice, they are fused (cf. Benson 1977; Pfeffer 1982; Astley and Van de Ven 1983). Approaching their task rather mechanistically, Berger and Luckmann first theorize modes and mechanisms of institutionalization before turning to consider the processes of socializing and re-socializing individuals in which objective realities are subjectively appropriated (i.e. internalized). But, equally, it is worth noting that the dismissal of all such attempts by locating

them firmly in one paradigm or another is an inevitable consequence of an unbending faith in paradigmatic closure.

7 As Giddens (1984: xxiii) puts it, by the recursive nature of everyday life, 'I mean that the structured properties of social activity . . . are constantly recreated out of the very resources that constitute them'.

8 Considering the attention given by Giddens to the work of other influential social theorists, his discussion of Berger and Luckmann's work is notable for its absence.

9 Of course, such generalizations are dangerous and potentially invidious. There can be little doubt that *The Social Construction of Reality* can open its reader's eyes to the humanly constituted nature of social reality, and thereby 'reawaken our wonder at this astonishing phenomenon' (Berger and Luckmann 1967: 211). In so far as it serves to dereify and relativize the reality of social institutions, it can serve to widen the horizons of human possibility. Similarly, the understanding of the social world provided by Giddens' theory of structuration may prompt a more critical attitude towards society that encompasses a change in one's relations with others. However, because neither book attends directly to the experience of oppression and suffering, it is more likely that their impact will be restricted to the level of what Giddens terms 'discursive consciousness', that is, what actors are able to give verbal expression to about social conditions, and its penetration of 'practical consciousness' – the tacit ways in which actors orientate themselves to the world which are not directly accessible to their consciousness.

9 Chronological codes and organizational analysis

1 I am heavily indebted to my colleagues in the ESRC's *Work Organization Research Centre* (1982–87) for their contributions towards a strategic vision of organization transitions. This chapter was consolidated whilst on sabbatical leave at the School of Business at Queens University, Canada. My host, Professor David Rutenberg, provided an energetic, constructive critique of the initial thoughts and made positive suggestions for examining corporate transitions within the perspective of the international business enterprise. Professor Norman McIntosh, Professor Steve Arnold and members of the Doctoral Programme emphasized the significance for organization processes of a macro-market dimension. I am also indebted to the seminar organized at the project for Time in Organization by Alan Bluedorme at the University of Columbia, Missouri, and Peter Monge at the Allenberg Centre, University of South Carolina.

10 Organization/disorganization

1 I am very grateful to Peter Manning of the Centre for Socio-Legal Studies, Wolfson College, Oxford, for extensive and constructive comments on a draft version of this chapter.

2 Even in General Systems Theory, a discipline reputed to have laid bare the

lineaments of a general theory of systems of any and every kind, one seeks in vain for a full and proper treatment of the boundary concept. In L von Bertalanffy's *General System Theory* (1971), widely recognized as an authoritative text on systems by a founding father of the subject, the concept of boundary is scantily dealt with and no definition is offered. The related idea of 'difference' is introduced in terms of its possible mathematization by means of differential equations – and then abruptly dropped. It therefore seems that the very concept which originates the system – namely, boundary or division – is the one which is most neglected.

3 This bias is equivalent to the 'imperative of selection' discussed earlier, i.e. the included/preferred vs excluded/nonpreferred structure of the frame analysed by Bateson.

4 We may suppose that it is for this reason that theorists of social systems such as Parsons and Blau treat key social concepts such as 'inter-action', 'differentiation', 'representation' as taken-for-granted terms which do not require analysis.

5 The works of the semiologist Roland Barthes are also variously caught up with the distinction between *free* play and fixed meaning: in *Writing Degree Zero* (1967), *The Pleasure of the Text* (1975), where the concept of zero degree is defined as that which is 'deprived of fixed meaning'; in essays such as 'From work to text' (where zero degree assumes the metaphor of the 'text that plays with itself') and 'The death of the author', both from Barthes (1977). In relation to Lévi-Strauss on myth, it is also instructive to read Barthes' (1972) essay on 'Myth today' which offers a different definition of myth – one based on signification of metalanguage – than the former's but which views the non-mythical stratum of communication (the object-language) in terms of zero degree.

6 Guy Oakes' careful introduction to Simmel's (1980) *Essays on Interpretation in Social Science* helps fill out the above overly brief sketch of Simmel as a theorist of the zero degree; see especially p. 84.

7 This essay pursues the thesis that aggression as a form of power is based on the 'purity' of the 'inside' against the 'impurity' of the 'outside'. For a similar argument, see Ryan (1982), especially Chapter 7, which uses the work of Derrida, Habermas and Lacan as general background for a critique of 'rationality' in capitalist society.

8 In an editorial introduction to this edition, Harold Beaver provides information on the factual background of *Billy Budd.*

9 Let us note, parenthetically, that 'formal' and 'pure' are conceptually related, with 'formal' usually meaning methodical, systematic, punctilious, etc. The study of 'formal organization' thus *predisposes* itself to the *exclusion* of the 'non-formal' or 'disorganized'.

10 In the study of social life, *prestige* and *status* are ways of talking about 'purity'. Everett Hughes' (1958) work in the sociology of occupations exemplifies this idea, especially in the hypothesis that occupational prestige is inversely related to 'dirty' work.

11 The conception of struggle as a cleansing process is used by Gaston Bachelard; see Canguilhem (1978).

12 For a similar argument, see Douglas and Isherwood (1979), especially Chapter 3.

11 Person, role and organization

1 One of Freud's major contributions – it is indeed the critical assumption on which psychoanalysis is based – was the contention that there was in all of us an unconscious sense of freedom and, hence, of responsibility and guilt. Freud called this sense of freedom 'the omnipotence of thoughts' and considered it to be the consequence of a distortion of reality, a distortion brought about by our instincts. By the thesis presented here this feeling of power – of freedom succeeding in its aims – need not be due to a distortion of reality – it could be due to our failure to grasp the existence of that reality in the first place. This, of course, implies that a grasping of outer reality leads to a loss of our sense of power and freedom.

2 It may be as well to discuss in a note a matter which nearly always complicates a discussion of Paiget's work – whether or not Paiget is right in asserting that nearly all (if not all) awarenesses of the unchanging must be learned. This criticism would appear to be at its most damaging when it concerns neonates – very young babies – who obviously have had no opportunity to learn. Thus it has been shown that a very young child indeed can be quite alert and need by no means be so unaware of the independents that surround him as Paiget has maintained.

To this objection, two points can be made. The first is that logic and fact should be kept rigidly separate and it is perfectly possible for Paiget to be factually wrong on every count – and for his logical position to remain unimpaired: even if children were born with perfect sight it would not deny the need to acquire such awareness – it would merely point to the possibility of inheriting such awareness. Not that Paiget's case is that disreputable (this is the second point that can be made on this issue). Paiget has indeed discovered a mass of intriguing findings about the development of the child's grasp of outer reality. And here Paiget can turn the tables on his empiricist critics. 'If empiricism is logically correct', he can ask, 'and we are passive before the inevitable outer fact, how can it *ever* be that such inevitable outer fact should be constantly redefined as we become more aware of it? And if it is constantly being redefined, then it must follow that outer fact, rather than being timeless criterion, is lawful consequence. And consequence cannot be criterion – not in the empiricist world which moves from the known to the yet unknown.'

3 Actually, the relational and the independent are not wholly symmetrical since it is possible to have independents in time (i.e. extended sequences – such as a tune or a 'law' in science – which can be recognized independently of different temporal contexts) so that any abiding continuity becomes, by that very token, independent. Thus awareness of the independent, assuming the universe is lawful (i.e. knowable), is to some extent asymptotic. (And if there were no change in context to allow us to recognize the independent as independent, then there would be no time and no thing – or sequence – to talk about.)

4 How the achieved becomes certain of itself and so assumes such dominance is something about which we can only speculate. Paiget tells us it is due to an 'equilibrium' of awareness (thus begging the question – is equilibrium itself assumed because awareness insists upon inevitability?); perhaps this phenomenon has something to do with memory: nothing can be more inflexible than memory. What is known cannot at times be unknown: memory is – or can be – just as independent, just as impervious to subsequent clause, as Plato's heaven. Perhaps it is our successful, reused memories that are the bases of that which become what cannot be otherwise – criteria.

Bibliography

Aberhams, R.D. (1987) 'Toward a sociological theory of folklore performing services', in R.H. Byington (ed.) *Working Americans: Contemporary Approaches to Occupational Folklore*, Washington D.C.: Smithsonian Folklore Studies: 19–42.
Abernathy, W.J. (1978) *The Productivity Dilemma: Roadblock to Innovation in the Automobile Industry*, Baltimore: Johns Hopkins.
Abernathy, W.J. *et al.* (1981) 'The new industrial competition', *Harvard Business Review*, October: 68–81.
Abernathy, W.J. *et al.* (1983) *Industrial Renaissance: Producing a Positive Future for America*, Boston: MIT Press.
Abrams, P. (1982) *Historical Sociology*, London: Open Books.
Aktouf, O. (1985) 'Business internal image: conflictual representation systems', *Dragon* 1 (1): 104–18.
Aldrich, H.E. (1979) *Organizations and Environments*, Englewood Cliffs, New Jersey: Prentice Hall.
Albrow, M. (1970) *Bureaucracy*, London: Macmillan.
Alvesson, M. (1986) 'Organizations, image and substance: some aspects of the cultural context of cultural management research', unpublished paper, University of Linkoping.
——(1987) *Organization Theory and Technocratic Consciousness*, Berlin: de Gruyter.
Anders, G. (1987) 'Die Antiquiertheit des Menschen. Vol. 1: Uber Die Seele im Zeitalter den zweiten Industriellen Revolution' Munchen: C.H. Beck.
Anthony, P.D. (1977) *The Ideology of Work*, London: Tavistock.
——(1985) 'The metamorphosis of management: from hero to villain', in Bengtove Gustavsson, *et al.*, *Work in the 1980s*, Aldershot: Gower.
Aredal, A. (1986) 'Procrustes: a modern management pattern found in a classical myth', *Journal of Management* 12: 403–14.
Astley, W.G. and Van de Ven, A. H. (1983), 'Central perspectives and debates in organizational theory', *Administrative Science Quarterly* 28: 245–73.
Baldamus, W. (1961) *Efficiency and Effort*, London: Tavistock.
Bandura, A. (1986) *Social Foundations of Thought and Action: A Social Cognitive Theory*, Englewood Cliffs, New Jersey: Prentice-Hall.
Barley, S. R. (1986) 'Technology as an occasion for structuring evidence from

observations of CT scanners and the social order of radiology departments', *Administrative Science Quarterly* 31: 78–108.
Barnard, C. (1938) *The Functions of the Executive*, Cambridge, Massachusetts: Harvard University Press.
Barthes, R. (1967) *Writing Degree Zero*, London: Cape.
——(1972) *Mythologies*, London: Cape.
——(1975) *The Pleasure of the Text*, New York: Hill & Wang.
——(1977) *Image-Music-Text*, London: Fontana/Collins.
Bateson, G. (1972) *Steps to an Ecology of Mind*, London: Intertext.
——(1972) 'A Theory of Play and Phantasy', in G. Batesons, *Steps to an Ecology of Mind*, New York: Chandler Publishing Company; 177–93.
——(1979) Mind and Nature, New York: E.P. Dutton.
Batstone, E. (1978) 'Management and industrial democracy' in *Industrial Democracy: International Views*, London: Social Science Research Council.
——(1984) *Working Order*, London: Basil Blackwell.
Baudrillard, J. (1985) 'The ecstasy of communication', in H. Fosters (ed.) *Post-Modern Culture*, London: Pluto Press.
Beck, B. (1987) 'Using ethnographic video in development work: the concept', *SCOS Note-Work* 6: 65–8.
Becker, E. (1974) *The Denial of Death*, New York: Free Press.
Benson, J.K. (1977) 'Organizations: a dialectical view', *Administrative Science Quarterly*, 22: 1–21.
——(1983) 'A dialectical method for the study of organizations', in G. Morgan (ed.) *Beyond Method*, Beverly Hills, California: Sage: 331–46.
Berg, P.O. and Asplund, C.J. (1981) 'Organizational sagas', unpublished paper presented to the EGOS Colloquium, Glasgow, Scotland.
Berg, P.O. (1984) 'Techno-culture', unpublished paper presented to the First International Conference on Organizational Symbolism and Corporate Culture, Lund, Sweden.
Berger, P.L. and Luckmann, T. (1966) *The Social Construction of Reality*, Garden City, New York: Doubleday.
Berger, P. and Pullberg, S (1966) 'Reification and the sociological critique of consciousness', *New Left Reveiew*, 35: 56–71.
Bertalanffy, L.von (1971) *General System Theory*, London: Allen Lane.
Beynon, H. (1973) *Working for Ford*, Harmondsworth: Penguin.
Bhakar, R. (1975) *A Realist Theory of Science*, Hassocks, Sussex: Harvester Press (second edition, 1978).
Bittner, E. (1965) 'On the Concept of Organization', *Social Research* 32: 239–55.
——(1973) 'The police on skid row', in G. Salaman and K. Thompson (eds) *People and Organizations*, London: Longman.
——(1974) 'The concept of organization', in R. Turner (ed.) *Ethnomethodology: selected readings*, Harmondsworth: Penguin.
Blau, P.M. (1965) 'The comparative study of organizations', *Industrial and Labour Relations Review* 28: 323–38.
——(1974) *On the Nature of Organizations*, New York: Wiley.
Bluedorne, A.C. (1987) 'Primary rhythms information processing and

planning: directions for a new temporal technology', working paper, *Project on Time and Organization*, University of Missouri, Columbia.
Blyton, P., Hassard, J., Hill, S., and Starkey, K. (1989) *Time, Work and Organization*, London: Routledge.
Borneman, E. (1985) 'Recht und Sexualitat im griechischen Mythos', in E. Lessing (ed.), *Die griechischen Sagen*, Munchen: Bertelsmann Verlag: 231–60.
Bordieu, R. (1977) *Outline of a Theory of Practice*, Cambridge: Cambridge University Press.
Bottomore, T. (1975) 'Competing pardigms in macrosociology', in A. Inkeles *et al.* (eds) *Annual Review of Sociology*, New York: Annual Reviews.
Braudel, F. (1984) *The Perspective of the World*, London: Collins.
Braverman, H. (1974) *Labor and Monopoly Capital*, New York: Monthly Review Press.
Broms, H. and Gahmberg, H. (1982) *Mythology in Management Culture*, Helsinki: Helsinki School of Economics, D–58.
——(1983) 'Communication to self in organizations and cultures', *Administrative Science Quarterly*, 28: 482–95.
Brown, N.D. (1968) *Life Against Death: The Psychoanalytical Meaning of History*, London: Sphere.
Brown, W. *et al.* (1981) *The Changing Contours of British Industrial Relations*, London: Basil Blackwell.
Buckley, W. (1967) *Sociology and Modern Systems Theory*, Englewood Cliffs, New Jersey: Prentice Hall.
Burawoy, M. (1985) *The Politics of Production*, New York: Verso.
Burges, R.G. (ed.) (1982) *Field Research*, London: Allen & Unwin.
——(1984) *In the Field*, London: Allen & Unwin.
Burns, T. (1977) *The BBC: Public Institution and Private World*, London: Macmillan.
——(1982) 'A comparative study of administrative structure and organizational process in selected areas of the national health service', Social Science Research Council.
Burns, T. and Stalker G.M. (1961) *The Management of Innovation*, London: Tavistock.
Burrell, G. (1981) 'Towards a radical organization theory', paper presented at the Annual Meeting of the Academy of Management, San Diego, California.
Burrell, G. and Morgan, G. (1979) *Sociological Pardigms and Organizational Analysis*, London: Heinemann.
Campbell, D.T. (1974) 'Qualitative knowing in action research', paper presented at the meeting of the American Psychological Association, New Orleans, Los Angeles.
Campbell, D.T. and Cook, T.D (1979) *Quasi-Experimentation: Design and Analysis for Field Settings*, Chicago, Illoinos: Rand McNally & Company.
Campbell, D.T. and Stanley, J.C. (1963) *Experimental and Quasi-Experiemental Designs for Research*, Chicago, Illinois: Rand McNally & Company.
Campbell, J. (1973) *Myths to Live By*, New York: Bentham Books.

Camus, A. (1948) *The Plague*, New York: Modern Library.
Canguilhem, G. (1978) *On the Normal and the Pathological*, Dordrecht: Reidel.
Carpenter, E. (1975) *Oh What a Blow that Phantom Gave Me!*, London: Paladin.
Carse, J.P. (1987) *Finite and Infinite Games*, Harmondsworth: Penguin.
Chandler, A.D. (1977) *The Visible Hand: The Managerial Revolution in America*, Cambridge: Belknap.
Chandler, A.D., and Daems, H. (1980) *Managerial Hierarchies: Comparative Perspectives on the Rise of the Modern Industrial Enterprise*, Boston: Harvard University Press.
Child, J. (1972) 'Organizational structure, environment and performance: the role of strategic choice', *Sociology* 6: 1–22.
——(1985) 'Managerial strategies, new technology and the labour process', in D. Knights *et al. Job Redesign: Critical Perspectives on the Labour Process*, Aldershot: Gower.
Christensen, S. and Kreiner, K. (1984) 'Corporate culture and culture-in-work', unpublished paper presented to the First International Conference on Organizational Symbolism and Corporate Culture, Lund, Sweden, June 1984.
Cicourel, A.V. (1972) *Cognitive Sociology*, Harmondsworth: Penguin.
Clark, B. (1970) *The Distinctive College: Antioch, Reed and Swarthmore*, Chicago, Illinois: Aldine Publishing Company.
Clark, P.A. (1985a) 'A review of theories of time and structure for organizational sociology', in S.B. Bachrach and S.M. Mitchel (eds) *Research in the Sociology of Organizations* 4, Greenwich, Conneticut: JAI Press.
——(1986a) 'The economy of time and the managerial division of labour in the British construction industry, 1965–1985', *Proceedings of the 7th Bartlett International Summer School*, London: University College, London University.
——(1986b) 'Le capitalisme et la reglemantation du temps de travail: une critique de la thèse d'E.P. Thompson', *Temps Libre*, March 2732.
——(1987) *Anglo American Innovation*, Berlin: de Guyter.
Clark, P.A. and Starkey, K. (1988) *Organization Transitions and Innovation-design*, London: Pinter.
Clark, P.A. and Windebank, J. (1985) 'Innvation and Renault: 1900–1982. Product, Process and Work Organization', ESRC Work Organization Research Centre, Working Paper Series Number 13, Aston University.
Clawson, D. (1980) *Bureaucracy and the Labour Process*, New York: Monthly Review Press.
Clegg, S. (1976) 'Power, Theorizing and Nihilism', *Theory and Society* 1,3: 65–87.
Clegg, S. and Dunkerley, D. (1980) *Organization, Class, and Control* London: Routledge & Kegan Paul.
Cohen, A. (1987) *The Symbolic Construction of Community*, London: Tavistock.
Cohen, D., March, J.G., and Olsen, J.P. (1972) 'A garbage can model of

organizational choice', *Administrative Science Quarterly*, 17: 1–25.
Connerton, P. (1980) *The Tragedy of Enlightenment: An Essay on the Frankfurt School*, Cambridge: Cambridge University Press.
Crafts, N.F.R. (1984) *British Economic Growth During the Industrial Revolution*, Oxford: Clarendon Press.
Crozier, M. (1964) *The Bureaucratic Phenomenon*, London: Tavistock.
——(1973) *The Stalled Society*, New York: Viking Press.
——(1984) *The Trouble with America*, Berkeley: University of California Press.
Cusumano, M.A. (1985) *The Japanese Automobile Industry: Technology and Management at Nissan and Toyota*, Boston: Harvard University Press.
Daft, R.L. (1980) 'The evolution of organization analysis in ASQ, 1959–1979', *Administrative Science Quarterly* 25: 632–6.
Dandridge, T. (1986) 'Ceremony as an integration of work and play', *Organization Studies* 7: 159–68.
Daniel, W., and Millward N. (1983) *Workplace Industrial Relations in Britain*, London: Heinemann.
Dawe, A. (1979) 'Theories of social action', in T. Bottomore and R. Nisbet (eds) *A History of Sociological Analysis*, London: Heinemann.
Deal, T.E., and Kennedy, A.A. (1982) *Corporate Cultures*, Reading, Massachusetts: Addison-Wesley.
Deam, R., and Salaman G. (eds) (1986) *Work, Culture and Society*, Milton Keynes: Open University Press.
Derrida, J. (1978) *Writing and Difference*, London: Routledge & Kegan Paul.
——(1981) *Dissemination*, London: Athlone Press.
——(1982) *Margins of Philosophy*, Hassocks, Sussex: Harvester.
Dill, W.R. (1962) 'The impact of environment on organizational development', in S. Maillick and E.H. Van Ness (eds) *Concepts and Issues in Administrative Behaviour*, New York: Prentice Hall.
DiMaggio, B., and Powell, W.W. (1983) 'The iron cage revisited: institutional isomorphism and collective rationality in organizational fields', *American Sociological Review* 82: 147–60.
Disco, C. (1976) 'Ludwig Wittgenstein and the end of wild conjectures', *Theory and Society* 3: 265–87.
Ditton, J. (1979) 'Baking time', *Sociological Review* 21, 1: 157–68.
Donaldson, L. (1985) *In Defence of Organization Theory: A Reply to the Critics*, London: Cambridge University Press.
Douglas, J. (ed.) (1971) *Understanding Everyday Life*, London: Routledge & Kegan Paul.
Douglas, M., and Isherwood, B. (1979) *The World of Goods*, London: Allen Lane.
Downey, H.K., and Ireland, R.D. (1979) 'Quantitative versus qualitative: the case of environment assessment in organizational studies', *Administrative Science Quarterly* 24: 630–8.
Dubinskas, F.A. (1987) *Making Time: Ethnographies of Culture, Time and Organization in High Technology*, Philadelphia: Temple Press.
Dunne, J.S. (1965) *The City of Gods: A Study in Myth and Morality*, New York: Macmillan.

——(1975) *Time and Myth: A Meditation on Storytelling as an Exploration of Life and Death*, Notre Dame: University of Notre Dame Press.

Ebers, M. (1985) 'Understanding organizations: the poetic mode', *Journal of Management* 11: 51–62.

Eckburg, D.L., and Hill, L. jun. (1979) 'The paradigm concept and sociology: a critical review', *American Sociological Review* 44: 925–37.

Eckman, B. (1986) 'Moon colonisation and the imagination: a psychological interpretation of Robert A. Heinlein's "Requiem"', in C.H. Holbrow, A.M. Russell, and G.F. Sutton (eds) *Space Colonisation: Technology and the Liberal Arts*, American Institute of Physics Conference Proceedings 148, New York: AIP.

Edgren, L., and Carson, P. (1987) 'Totems in a computer service company?', unpublished paper presented to the Third International Conference on Organization Symbolism and Corporate Culture, Milano, Italy, June.

Edwards P.K. (1986) *Conflict at Work: A Materialist Analysis of Workplace Relations*, London: Basil Blackwell.

——(1987) *Managing the Factory*, London: Basil Blackwell.

Edwards, R. (1979) *Contested Terrain: The Transformation of the Workplace in the Twentieth Century*, London: Heinemann.

Elias, N. (1985) *The Loneliness of the Dying*, Oxford: Basil Blackwell.

Ellsworth, P.C. (1977) 'From abstract ideas to concrete instances: some guidance for choosing natural research settings', *American Psychologist* 32: 604–15.

Evans-Pritchard, E.E. (1940) *The Nuer*, Oxford: Oxford University Press.

Evered, R., and Louis, M.R. (1981) 'Inquiry from the inside' and 'Inquiry from the outside', *Academy of Management Review* 6: 385–96.

Fairhurst, E. (1981) 'A sociological study of the rehabilitation of elderly patients in an urban hospital', PhD Thesis, University of Leeds.

——(1983) 'Organizational rules and the accomplishment of nursing work on geriatric wards', *Journal of Management Studies* 210: 315–32.

Feyerabend, P.K. (1975) *Against Method*, London: New Left Books.

Fine, G. (1984) 'Negotiated orders and organizational cultures', *Annual Review of Sociology* 10: 239–62.

Fiske, D. W., and Campbell, D.T. (1959) 'Convergent and discriminant validation by the multitrait–multimethod matric', *Psychological Bulletin* 56: 81–105.

Follet, M.P. (1941) *Dynamic Administration*, New York: Management Publications.

Forrester, J. (1983) 'Critical theory and organizational analysis', in G. Morgan (ed.) *Beyond Method*, Beverly Hills, California: Sage: 234–46.

Fox, A. (1985) *History and Heritage: The Social Origins of the British Industrial Relations Systems*, London: Allen & Unwin.

Fox, F.V., and Staw, B.M. (1979) 'The trapped administrator: effects of job insecurity and policy resistance on commitment to a course of action', *Adminstrative Science Quarterly* 24: 449–72.

Frankfort, H., and Frankfort, H.A. (1949) 'Myth and reality', in H. Frankfort, H.A. Frankfort, J.A. Wilson and T. Jacobsen *Before Philosophy: The Intellectual Adventure of Ancient Man*, Baltimore: Penguin.

Friedheim, E.A. (1979) 'An empirical comparison of Ritzer's paradigms and similar metatheories', *Social Forces* 58: 59–66.
Friedman, A. (1977) *Industry and Labour: Class Struggle at Work and Monopoly Capitalism*, London: Macmillan.
Friedrichs, R. (1970) *A Sociology of Sociology*, New York: Free Press.
Friere, P. (1972) *Pedagogy of the Oppressed*, Harmondsworth: Penguin.
Frost, P.J. (1980) 'Toward a radical framework for practising organization science', *Academy of Management Review*, 5: 501–7.
Gadamer, H.-G. (1975) *Truth and Method*, translated by G. Barden and J. Cumming, New York: Seabury Press.
Garfinkel, H. (1967) *Studies in Ethnomethodology*, Englewood Cliffs, New Jersey: Prentice Hall.
——(1974) 'The origins of the term "ethnomethodology"', in R.Turner (ed.) *Ethnomethodology: Selected Readings*, Harmondsworth: Penguin.
——(in press) *A Manual for the Study of Naturally Organized Ordinary Activites*, London: Routledge.
Garfinkel, H.L. and Sacks, H. (1970) 'On formal structures of practical actions', in J.C. McKinney and E.A. Tiryakian (eds) *Theoretical Sociology* New York: Appleton Century.
Geertz, C. (1973) *The Interpretation of Cultures*, New York: Basic Books.
Gephart, R. (1978) 'Status degradation and the organizational succession problem', *Administrative Science Quarterly*, 22: 553–81.
Gergen, K.J. (1976) 'Social psychology, science, and history', *Personality and Social Psychology Bulletin* 2: 373–83.
Geuss, R. (1981) *The Idea of A Critical Theory: Habermas and the Frankfurt School*, Cambridge: Cambridge University Press.
Gherardi, S., Turner, B.A., and Strati, A. (in press) 'Industrial democracy and organizational symbolism', in C. Lammers and G. Szell (eds) *Organizational Democracy: Taking Stock*, Oxford: Oxford University Press.
Giddens, A. (1973) *The Class Structure of the Advanced Societies*, London: Hutchinson.
——(1976) *New Rules of Sociological Method*, London: Hutchinson.
——(1979) *Central Problems in Social Theory*, London: Cambridge.
——(1982) 'Power, the dialectic of control and class structuration', in A. Giddens and G. Mackenzie (eds) *Social Class and the Division of Labour*, Cambridge: Cambridge University Press.
——(1984) *The Constitution of Society*, Cambridge: Polity Press.
Goff, J. Le (1980) *Time, Work and Culture in the Middle Ages*, Chicago: Chicago University Press.
Goffman, E. (1975) *Frame Analyses: An Essay on the Organization of Experience*, Harmondsworth: Penguin.
Gordon, D., Edwards, R., and Reich, F. (1982) *Segmented Work, Divided Workers*, Cambridge: Cambridge University Press.
Gospel, H (1983a) 'The development of management organization in industrial relations: a historical perspective', in K. Thurley, and S. Wood (eds) *Industrial Relations and Management Strategy*, Cambridge: Cambridge University Press.

——(1983b) 'Managerial structures and strategies: an introduction', in H. Gospel and C. Littler, *Managerial Strategies and Industrial Relations*, London: Heinemann.
Gouldner, A. (1954a) *Patterns of Industrial Bureauracy*, New York: Collier Macmillan.
——(1954b) *Wildcat Strike*, New York: Antioch Press.
——(1959) 'Organizational analysis', in R.K. Merton, L. Broom and L.S. Cottrell (eds) *Sociology Today*, New York: Basic Books.
——(1971) *The Coming Crisis in Western Sociology*, London: Heinemann.
——(1973) *For Sociology*, London: Allen Lane.
Grafton-Small, R., and Linstead, S. (1986) 'The everday professional: skill in the management of occupational kinship', in A. Strati (ed.) *The Symbolics of Skill*, Trento: Dipartimento di Politica Socialie.
Gregory, K.L. (1983) 'Native-view paradigms: multiple cultures and culture conflicts in organizations', *Administrative Science Quarterly*, 28: 359–76.
Gross, N. *et al.* (1971) *Implementing Organizational Innovation, A Sociological Analysis of Planned Educational Change*, New York: Basic Books.
Gurvitch, G. (1964) *The Spectrum of Social Time*, Dordrecht: Reidel.
Habermas, J. (1970) *Towards a Rational Society*, London: Heinemann.
—(1972) *Knowledge and Human Interests*, London: Heinemann.
——(1979) *Communication and the Evolution of Society*, London, Heinemann.
— (1981) *Theorie des kommunikativen Handelns*, Frankfurt: Suhrkamp.
——(1984) 'Questions and counterquestions', *Praxis International* 4, 3: 229–9.
Habermas, J. and Luhmann, N. (1973) *Theorie der gesellschaft oder Sozialtechnologie Was leistet die Systemforschung?* Frankfurt: Suhrkamp.
Hackman, R. (series ed.) (1982) *Studying Organizations: Innovations in Methodology*, Beverly Hills, California: Sage.
Halberstram, D. (1986) *The Reckoning*, New York: Avon.
Hammersley, M., and Atkinson, P. (1983) *Ethnography: Principles in Practice*, London: Tavistock.
Hampshire, S. (1959) *Thought and Action*, London: Chatto and Windus.
Hanson, N.R. (1958) *Patterns of Discovery*, Cambridge: Cambridge University Press.
Hantrais, L.P., Clark, P., and Samuel S. (1984) 'Time space dimensions of work, family and leisure in France and Great Britain', *Leisure Studies* 3: 301–8.
Harris, C. (1982) *Fundamental Concepts and the Sociological Enterprise*, London: Croom Helm.
Hartt, J.N. (1963) *The Lost Image of Man*, Baton Rouge, LA: Louisiana State University Press.
Hassard, J. (1988) 'Overcoming hermeticism in organization theory', *Human Relations* 41: 247–59.
——(1989a) 'Time and industrial sociology', in P. Blyton, J.Hassard, S. Hill, and K. Starkey, *Time, Work and Organization*, London: Routledge.
——(1989b) 'Time and organization', in P. Blyton, J. Hassard, S. Hill, and K.

Starkey, *Time, Work and Organization*, London: Routledge.
——(1989c) 'Toward a qualitative paradigm for working time', *International Social Science Journal.*
——(ed.) (1990) *The Sociology of Time*, London: Macmillan.
——(forthcoming) *Analysing Organizations, Cambridge: Cambridge University Press.*
Held, D. (1976) *Introduction to Critical Theory: Horkheimer to Habermas*, London: Hutchison.
Heller, E. (1958) *The Ironic German*, Cambridge: Cambridge University Press.
Heyderbrand, W.V. (1983) 'Organization and praxis', in G.Morgan (ed.) *Beyond Method*, Beverly Hills, California: Sage.
Hickson, D., Butler, R., Cray, D., Mallory, G., and Wilson, D. (1985) 'Playing the game of strategic decision-making', in J.M. Pennings (ed.) *Organizational Strategy and Chance*, San Francisco: Jossey-Bass.
Hillman, J. (1980, 1981) 'Silver and the white earth', *Spring: an Annual of Archetypal Psychology and Jungian Thought*, Part I: 21–48: Part II: 21–66.
Hofstede, G. (1980) *Culture's Consequences*, London: Sage.
Horkheimer, M. and Adorno T. (1972) *The Dialectic of Englightenment*, New York: Seabury Press.
Horowitz, I.V. (1968) *Professing Sociology: Studies in the Life Cycle of Social Science*, Chicago, Illinois: Aldine Publishing Company.
Hounshell, D. (1984) *From the American System of Mass Production, 1800–1932: The Development of Manufacturing Technology in the United States*, Baltimore: Johns Hopkins University.
Hughes, E. (1958) *Men and Their Work*, Glencoe, Illinois: Free Press.
Huizinga, J. (1970) *Homo Ludens*, London: Paladin.
Hyman, R. (1987) 'Strategy or structure: capital, labour and control', *Work, Employment and Society* 1: 25–6.
Jackson, N., and Willmott, H.C. (1987) 'Beyond Epistemology and Reflective Conversion: Towards Human Relations', *Human Relations* 40: 361–80.
Jaques, E. (1970) 'Death and the mid-life crisis', in E. Jaques, *Work, Creativity, and Social Justice*, New York: International University Press.
Jay, M. (1973) *The Dialectical Imagination: A History of the Frankfurt School and the Institute of Social Research 1923–1950*, London: Heinemann.
——(1984) 'Habermas and Modernism', *Praxis International* 4: 1–14.
Jelineck, M., Smircich, L., and Hirsche, P. (eds) (1983) 'Special issue on organizational culture', *Administrative Science Quarterly* 20: 331–8.
Jermier, J.M. (1981) 'Infusion of critical theory into organizational analysis: implications for studies of work adjustment', in D. Dunkerley and G. Salaman (eds) *International Yearbook of Organizational Studies*, London: Routledge.
Jick, T.D. (1979) 'Mixing qualitative and quantitative methods: triangulation in action', *Administrative Science Quarterly* 24: 620–1.
Johnson, B. (1980) *The Critical Difference*, Baltimore: The Johns Hopkins University Press.
Johnson, H.T., and Kaplan, H.S. (1987) *Relevance Lost: The Rise and Fall of*

Management Accounting, Boston: Harvard Business School Press.
Jones, B. (1982) 'Destruction or redistribution of engineering skills: the case of numerical control', in S. Wood (ed.) *The Degradation of Work?* London: Hutchinson.
Kanter, R.M. (1984) *The Change Masters, Corporate Entrepreneurs at Work*, London: Allen & Unwin.
Klein, M. (1959) 'Our adult world and its roots in infancy', *Human Relations* 12: 291–303.
Kenny, A.J.P. (1973) *Wittgenstein*, London: Allen Lane.
Knights, D., and Willmott, H.C. (1985) 'Power and identity in theory and practice', *Sociological Review* 33: 22–46.
Knights, D., and Willmott, H.C., (forthcoming) (eds) *Labour Process Theory*, London: Macmillan.
Knorr, K.D. (1979) 'Tinkering toward success: prelude to a theory of scientific practice', *Theory and Society* 8: 22–43.
Konecki, K. (1987) 'Interactional aspects of the culture of an organization', unpublished paper presented to the Third International Conference on Organizational Symbolism and Corporate Culture, Milano, Italy, June.
Krupp, S (1961) *Patterns in Organizational Analysis*, Philadelphia: Chiltern.
Kuhn, T.S. (1962) *The Structure of Scientific Revolutions*, Chicago: University of Chicago Press.
——(1970) *The Structure of Scientific Revolutions*, Chicago: University of Chicago Press, second edition (enlarged).
——(1970a) 'Reflections on my critics', in I. Lakatos and A. Musgrave (eds) *Criticism and the Growth of Knowledge*, Cambridge: Cambridge University Press.
——(1974) 'Second thoughts on paradigms', in F. Suppe (ed.) *The Structure of Scientific Theories*, Chicago: University of Illinois Press.
Lakatos, I. (1970) 'Falsification and the methodology of scientific research programmes', in I. Lakatos and A. Musgrave (eds) *Criticism and the Growth of Knowledge*, Cambridge: Cambridge University Press.
Lakatos, I., and Musgrave, A. (eds) (1970) *Criticism and the Growth of Knowledge*, Cambridge: Cambridge University Press.
Lammers, C.J., 'Mono- and poly-paradigmatic developments in natural and social sciences', in R. Whitley (ed.) *Social Processes of Scientific Development*, London: Routledge & Kegan Paul.
Landes, D.J. (1983) *Revolution in Time*, Boston: Belknap.
Lang, C.L. (1981) 'Good cases, bad cases: client selection and professional prerogative in a community mental health centre', *Urban Life* 10: 289–309.
Lawrence, P.R., and Dyer, R. (1983) *Renewing American Industry*, New York: Free Press.
Lawrence, W.G. (1979) 'A concept for today: the management of oneself in role', in W.G. Lawrence (ed.) *Exploring Individual*, Chichester: John Wiley & Sons.
——(1982) 'Some psychic and political dimensions of work experiences', London: The Tavistock Insitute of Human Relations, Occasional Paper No. 2.
——(1985) 'Beyond the frames', in M. Pines (ed.) *Bion and Group*

Psychotherapy, London: Routledge & Kegan Paul.
——(1987) 'Stress, death and life itself', in N.N. & H. Meyer (eds) *Stress, Opinions, Theories and Results*, Berlin: Springer Verlag.
Leach, E. (1966) 'Ritualisation in man in relation to conceptual and social development', *Philosophical Transactions of The Royal Society of London*, Series B, ccli, 772: 403–8.
Levinson, D.J. *et al.* (1979) *The Seasons of a Man's Life*, New York: Knopf.
Levi-Strauss, C. (1950) 'Introduction', in M. Mauss, *Sociologie et Anthropologie*, Paris: Presses Universitaires de France.
——(1966) *The Savage Mind*, London: Weidenfeld and Nicholson.
——(1979) *The Raw and the Cooked*, London: Routledge & Kegan Paul.
Light, D., jun. (1979) 'Surface data and deep structure: observing the organization of professional training', *Administrative Science Quarterly* 24: 551–60.
Lincoln, Y. (ed.) (1985) *Organization Theory and Inquiry: The Paradigm Revolution*, Beverly Hills, California: Sage.
Linstead, S., and Grafton-Small, R. (1987) 'Artefact as theory: all roses lead to Milano', unpublished paper presented to the Third International Conference on Organizational Symbolism and Corporate Culture, Milano, Italy, June.
Littler, C.R. (1982) *The Development of the Labour Process in Capitalist Societies* London: Heinemann.
Littler, C. R., and Salaman, G. (1982) 'Bravermania and beyond: recent theories on the labour process', *Sociology* 16: 251–69.
Lofland, J. (1971) *Analyzing Social Settings*, New York: Wadsworth.
Louis, M. R. (1985) 'An investigator's guide to workplace culture', in P.J. Frost, M.R. Louis, C.C. Lundberg, and J. Martin (eds) *Organization Culture*, Beverly Hills, California: Sage.
Luhmann, N. (1969) 'Die praxis der theorie', *Soziale Welt* 20: 129–144.
Lynch, M, (1979) 'Art and artefacts in laboratory science: a study of shopwork and shoptalk in a research laboratory', PhD. Thesis, University of California at Irvine.
Lynxwiler, J., Shaver, W., and Clelland, D. A. (1987) 'The organisation and impact of inspector discretion in a regulatory bureaurcracy', *Social Problems* 30: 425–36.
Lyotard, J-F. (1984) *The Postmodern Condition: A Report on Knowledge*, Manchester: Manchester University Press.
McCarthy, T. (1985) *The Critical Theory of Jurgen Habermas*, Cambridge, Massachusetts; MIT Press.
McClintock, C.C., Brannon, D, and Maynard-Moody, S. (1979) 'Applying the logic of sample surveys to qualitative case studies: the case cluster method', *Administrative Science Quarterly* 24: 612–30.
McGrath, J.E. (1982) 'Dilemmatics: the study of choices and dilemmas in the research process', in J.E. McGrath, J. Martin, and R.K. Kulka (eds) *Judgement Calls in Research*, Beverly Hills, California: Sage.
McGrath, J.E., Martin, J., and Kulka, R.A. (eds) (1982) *Judgement Calls in Research*, Beverly Hills, California: Sage.
McHugh, P. (1968) *Defining the Situation*, New York: Bobbs Merrill.

McIntyre, A. (1981) *After Virtue: A Study in Moral Theory*, New York: Duckworth.
Mackenzie, G. (1982) 'Class boundaries and the labour process', in A. Giddens and G. Mackenzie (eds) *Social Class and the Division of Labour*, Cambridge: Cambridge University Press.
McLuhan, M. (1964) *Understanding Media*, London: Routledge & Kegan Paul.
——(1965) *Counterblast*, London: Rapp & Whiting.
McMillan, C.J. (1985) *The Japanese Industrial System*, Berlin: de Gruyter.
McNeil, K. (1978) 'Understanding organizational power: building on the Weberian legacy', Administrative Science Quarterly, 23:1, 65–90.
Manning P. (1977) *Police Work*, Cambridge, Massachusetts: MIT Press.
March, J.G. (1971) 'A technology of foolishness', *Civilokonomen*, Copenhagen, 18: 1–21.
——(1987) 'Overview of Papers', Address to Conference of Political and Organizational Culture, Tromso, September.
March, J.G. and Simon, H.G. (1958) *Organizations*, New York: Wiley.
Marcuse, H. (1964) *One-Dimensional Man*, London: Routledge & Kegan Paul.
——(1968) *Negotiations*, London: Allen Lane.
Martin, J. (1981) 'Stories and scripts in organizational settings', in A. Hastroft and A. Isen (eds) *Cognitive Social Psychology*, New York: Elsevier-North Holland, Incorporated.
——(1982) 'The garbage can model of the process of making research decisions', in J.E. McGrath, J. Martin, and R.A. Kulka (eds) *Judgement Calls in Research*, Beverly Hills, California: Sage.
Muruyama, M. (1974) 'Paradigms and Communication', *Technological Forecasting* 6: 3–32.
Marx, K. (1976) *Capital*, Volume 1, Harmondsworth: Penguin.
Melville, H. (1970) *Billy Budd, Sailor and Other Stories*, Harmondsworth: Penguin.
Miles, R.H. (1980) *Macro Organizational Behaviour*, Santa Monica: Goodyear.
Miller, A. (1981) *The Drama of the Gifted Child*, New York: Basic Books.
Miller, D., and Friesen, P.H. (1984) *Organizations, A Quantum View*, Englewood Cliffs, New Jersey: Prentice Hall.
Mintzberg, H. (1983) *Structure in Fives: Designing Effective Organizations*, Englewood Cliffs: Prentice Hall.
Mitroff, I. and Mason, R. (1982) 'Business policy and metaphysics', *Academy of Management Review* 7: 361–70.
Moore, W.E. (1963) *Man, Time and Society*, New York: Wiley.
Morgan, G. (1980) 'Paradigms, metaphors and puzzle-solving in organization theory', *Administrative Science Quarterly* 25: 605–22.
——(1986) *Images of Organization*, Beverly Hills, California: Sage.
——(ed.) (1983) *Beyond Method*, Beverly Hills, California: Sage.
Morgan, G., and Smircich, L. (1980) 'The Case for Qualitative Research', *The Academy of Management Review* 5: 491–500.
Mosteller, F., and Tukey, J.W. (1968) 'Data Analysis Including Statistics' in G. Lindzey and E. Aronson (eds) *The Handbook of Social Psychology*

volume 2, Menlo Park, California: Addison-Wesley Publishing Company.
Mushashi, M. (1974) *A Book of Five Rings*, translated by V. Harris, London: Allison & Busby.
Novak, M. (1970) *The Experience of Nothingness*, New York: Harper & Row.
Odiorne, G.S. (1984) 'Strategic Management of Human Resources: A Portfolio Approach, London: Jossey-Bass.
Ohmae, K. (1982) *The Mind of the Strategist*, Harmondsworth: Penguin.
Ossowski, W. (1963) *Class Structure in the Social Consciousness*, New York: Free Press.
Ott, K.K. (1984) 'Two problems that threaten organizational culture research', unpublished paper presented to the First International Conference on Organizational Symbolism and Corporate Culture, Lund, Sweden, June.
Ouchi, W.G. (1981) *Theory Z: How American Business Can Meet the Japanese Challenge*, Menlo Park, California: Addison-Wesley Publishing Company.
Pahl, R.E., and Winkler, J. (1974) 'The economic elite: theory and practice', in P. Stanworth and A. Giddens (eds) *Elites and Power in British Society*, Cambridge: Cambridge University Press.
Parkes, M.S. (1976) 'A generalized model for automating judgemental decisions', *Management Science*, 16: 841–51.
Parsons, T. (1951) *The Social System*, London: Routledge & Kegan Paul.
Pascale, R.J., and Athos, A. (1981) *The Art of Japanese Management: Applications for American Executives*, New York: Simon & Schuster.
Perrow, C. (1972) *Complex Organizations: A Critical Essay*, Illinois: Scott Foresman.
Peters, T. J., and Waterman, R.H. (1982) *In Search of Excellence: Lessons from America's Best Run Companies*, New York: Harper & Row.
Pettigrew, A. (1985) *The Awakening Giant: Continuity and Change in ICI*, London: Basil Blackwell.
Pfeffer, J. (1982) *Organizations and Organization Theory*, Boston: Pitman.
Phillips, D. (1973) *Abandoning Method*, London: Jossey-Bass.
——(1977) *Wittgenstein and Scientific Knowledge*, London: Macmillan.
Phillipson, M. (1972) 'Phenomenological philosophy and sociology', in P. Filmer *et al.* (eds) *New Directions in Sociological Theory*, London: Collier-Macmillan.
Piore, M.J., and Sabel, C.A. (1984) *The Second Industrial Divide: Possibilities for Prosperity*, New York: Basic Books.
Polanyi, K. (1969) *Primitive, Archaic and Modern Economies*, London: Hutchinson.
Pollner, M. (1974) 'Mundane reasoning', *Philosophy of the Social Sciences* 4: 35–54.
Pondy, L.R., Frost, P. J., Morgan, G., and Dandridge, T.C. (eds) (1983) *Organizational Symbolism*, Greenwich, Conneticut: JAI Press.
Popper, K.R. (1968) *The Logic of Scientific Discovery* (Logik der Forschung), London: Hutchinson.
——(1970) 'Normal science and its dangers', in I. Lakatos and A. Musgrave (eds) *Criticism and the Growth of Knowledge*, Cambridge: Cambridge University Press.

Priestley, J.B. (1934) *English Journey*, London: Heinemann.
Purcell, J. (1983) 'The management of industrial relations in the modern corporation: agenda for research', *British Journal of Industrial Relations*: 100–15.
Purcell, J., and Sisson, K. (1983) 'Strategies and practice in the management of industrual relations', in G. Bain (ed.) *Industrial Relations in Britain*, London: Basil Blackwell.
Pym, D. (1976) 'The demise of management and the ritual of employment', *Human Relations* 28: 675–98.
——(1978) 'Employment as bad ritual', *The London Business School Journal* 3: 1.
——(1981) 'Emancipation and organization', in T. Wall (ed.) *Essays on the Theory and Practice of Organizational Psychology*, London: Academic Press.
——(1986) *The Employment Question and Other Essays*, London: Freedom Press.
Quinn, R.E. (1977) 'Coping with Cupid', *Administrative Science Quarterly* 22: 30–45.
Ranson, S., Hinings, B., and Greenwood, R. (1980) 'The structuring of organizational structures', *Administrative Science Quarterly* 25: 1–17.
Raspa, R. (1984) 'The refocusing of folkloric expression under stress in the automobile industry', unpublished paper presented to the First International Conference on Organizational Symbolism and Corporate Culture, Lund, Sweden, June.
Ratcliffe, J.W. (1980) 'Notions of validity in qualitative research methodology', paper presented at Grounded Theory and Qualitative Methods Group, University of Exeter.
Reed, M. (1984) 'Management as a social practice', *Journal of Management Studies* 21:3.
——(1985) *Redirections in Organizational Analysis*, London: Tavistock.
——(1989) *The Sociology of Management*, London: Wheatsheaf.
Reynaud, E.M. (1983) 'Change in collective identities', in C. Crouch and F. Heller (eds) *Organizational Democracy and Political Processes*, New York: Wiley.
Riley, P. (1983) 'A structurationist account of political culture', *Administrative Science Quarterly*, 28: 414–37.
Ritzer, G. (1975) *Sociology: A Multiple Paradigm Science*, New York: Allyn & Bacon.
Roberts, K.H., Hunlin, C.L., and Rousseau, D.M. (1978) *Developing An Interdisciplinary Science of Organizations*, San Fransisco: Jossey-Bass.
Rorty, R. (1984) 'Habermas and Lyotard on post-modernity', *Praxis International* 4: 32–44.
Rose, M., and Jones, B. (1985) 'Managerial strategy and trades union response in work re-organization schemes at establishment level', in D. Knights, H.C. Willmott, and D. Collinson *Job Redesign: Critical Perspectives on the Labour Process*, Aldershot: Gower.
Rosen, M. (1985) 'Breakfast at Spiro's: dramaturgy and dominance', *Journal of Management* 11: 31–48.

Rosenberg, N. (1982) *Inside the Black Box: Technology and Economics*, New York: Cambridge University Press.
Rosenthal, R., and Rosnow, R.K. (1969) *Artefact in Behavioural Research*, New York: Academic Press.
Roszak, T. (1972) *Where the Wasteland Ends*, London: Faber & Faber.
Roth, J.A. (1963) *Timetables: Structuring the Passage of Time in Hospital Treatment and Other Careers*, New York: Bobbs Merrill.
Roy, D. (1960) 'Banana time: job satisfaction and informal interaction', *Human Organization* 18: 156–68.
Runkel, P.J., and McGrath, J.E. (1972) *Research on Human Behaviour: A Systematic Guide to Method*, New York: Holt, Rinehart & Winston.
Ryan, M. (1982) *Marxism and Deconstruction*, Baltimore: The Johns Hopkins University Press.
Sacks, H., Schegloff, E.A., and Jefferson, G. (1974) 'A Simplist Systematics for the Organization of Turn-Taking for Conversation', *Language* 50: 696–735.
Salaman, G., and Thompson, K. (eds) (1973) *People and Organizations*, London: Longman.
Salaman, G. (1982) 'Managing the frontier of control', in A. Giddens and G. Mackenzie (eds) *Social Class and the Division of Labour*, Cambridge: Cambridge University Press.
——(1986a) 'Factory work', in R. Deam and G. Salaman (eds) *Work, Culture and Society*, Milton Keynes: Open University Press.
——(1986b) *Working*, London: Tavistock.
Salancik, J.R. (1978) 'Uncertainty, secrecy, and the choice of similar others', *Social Psychology* 41: 246–55.
Saussure, F. de (1974) *Course in General Linguistics*, London: Fontana/Collins.
Schegloff, E.A., and Sacks, H. (1973) 'Opening-up closings', *Semiotica* 7: 298–327.
Schneider, S., and Dunbar R.L.N. (1987) 'Takeover attempts: what does the language tell us?', unpublished paper presented to the Third International Conference on Organizational Symbolism and Corporate Culture, Milano, Italy, June.
Schutz, A., and Luckmann, T. (1974) *The Structures of the Life World*, London: Heinemann.
Schwartz, H. (1987) 'The symbol of the space shuttle and the deconstruction of the American dream', unpublished paper presented to the Third International Conference on Organizational Symbolism and Corporate Culture, Milano, Italy, June.
Scott, J. (1985) *Corporations, Classes and Capitalism*, London: Hutchinson.
Standing Conference on Organizational Symbolism (SCOS) (1984). Call for papers for the First International Conference on Corporate Culture and Organizational Symbolism, Lund, and also editorial material repeated in each issue of the journal *Dragon*.
Segal, H. (1964) *Introduction to the Work of Melanie Klein*, London: The Hogarth Press.
Selznick, P. (1949) *T.V.A. and the Grass Roots*, Berkeley: University of

California Press.
——(1957) *Leadership and Administration*, Evanston, Illinois: Row, Peterson.
Shapere, D. (1971) 'The paradigm concept', *Science* 17: 706–9.
Siehl, C., and Martin, J. (1984) 'The role of symbolic management: How can managers successfully transmit organizational culture?', in J.G. Hunt, D. Hosking, C. Schriesheim and R. Stewart (eds) *Leaders and Managers: International Perspectives on Managerial Behaviour and Leadership*, Elmsford, New York: Pergamon Press.
Sievers, B. (1984) 'Motivation as a surrogate for meaning', Arbeitspapiere des Fachbereichs Wirtschaftswissenschaft der Bergischen Universitäte – Gesamthochschule Wuppertal, 81.
——(1986a) 'Beyond the surrogate of motivation', *Organization Studies* 7: 335–51.
——(1986b) 'Participation as a collusive quarrel over immortality', *Dragon* 1: 72–82.
——(1987) 'Some thoughts on the symbolism of work, death and life itself in the socio-technological systems framework', *Dragon* 2: 41–56.
——(1987a) 'Leadership as a perpetuation of immaturity', in B. Sievers, *Work, Death and Life Itself*, Arbeitspapiere des Fachbereichs Wirtschaftswissenschaft der Bergischen Universität – Gesamthochschule Wuppertal, 98: 23–35.
—— (1987b) *Motivation als Sinnersatz*, Gruppendynamic 18, 2+3.
Silverman, D. (1968) 'Formal organizations or industrial sociology: towards a social action analysis of organizations', *Sociology* 2: 221–38.
——(1970) 'Accounts of organizations: organizational structure and the accounting process', in J.B. McKinley (ed.) *Processing People: Cases in Organizational Behaviour*, New York: Holt, Rinehart & Winston.
——(1979) *The Theory of Organization*, London: Heinemann.
Silverman D., and Jones, J. (1973) 'Getting-in', in J. Child (ed.) *Man and Organization*, London: George Allen & Unwin.
——(1976) *Organizational Work*, London: Collier-Macmillan.
Simmel G. (1950) *The Sociology of Georg Simmel*, New York: Free Press.
——(1968) *The Conflict in Modern Culture and Other Essays*, New York: Teachers' College Press.
——(1980) *Essays on Interpretation in Social Science*, Manchester: Manchester University Press.
Smircich, L. (1983) 'Organizations as shared meanings', in L.R. Pondy *et al.* (eds) *Organizational Symbolism*, Greenwich: Jai-Press: 55–65.
——(1983) 'Studying organizations as cultures', in G. Morgan (ed.) *Beyond Methods*, Beverly Hills, Calilfornia: Sage.
Smircich, L., and Calas, M.B. (1987) 'Organizational culture: a critical assessment', in F. Jablin, L. Putnam and L. Porter (eds) *Handbook of Organizational Communication*, Beverly Hills, California: Sage.
Smircich, L., and Morgan, G. (1982) 'Leadership: the management of meaning', *Journal of Applied Behavioural Science* 18: 257–73.
Smith, L.M., Prunty, J.P., Dwyer, D.C., and Klein, P.F. (1987) *The Fate of an Innovative School: Book 2*, London: Falmer Press.
Smith, C.W. (1983) 'A case-study of structuration: the pure-bred beef

business', *Journal for the Theory of Social Behaviour* 13: 3–18.
Smith, T.C. (1986) 'Peasant time and factory time in Japan', *Past and Present* 113: 165–97.
Sorokin, P.A., and Merton, R.K. (1937) 'Social time: a methodological and functional analysis', *American Journal of Sociology* 42: 615–29.
Spencer-Brown, G. (1969) *Laws of Form*, London: Allen & Unwin.
Spender, J.C. (1983) 'Executive myth-making: industry-level responses to uncertainty', unpublished manuscript, University of California at Los Angeles.
Stark, W. (1967) *The Sociology of Knowledge*, London: Routledge & Kegan Paul.
Starkey, K.P. (1985) 'Time and professional work in public sector organization: an examination of four occupational groups in education and medicine', Ph.D. Thesis, Aston University, Birmingham.
Staw, B., and Ross, J. (1980) 'Commitment in an experienting society: an experiment on the attribution of leadership from administrative scenarios', *Journal of Applied Psychology* 65: 249–60.
Storey, J. (1983) *Managerial Prerogative and the Question of Control*, London: Routledge & Kegan Paul.
——(1983) 'The means of management control', *Sociology* 19: 212.
——(in press) 'The phoney war? New office technology: organization and control', in D. Knights, and H. Willmott, *Management and the Labour Process*, London: Macmillan.
Strati, A. (ed.) (1986) *The Symbolics of Skill*, Trento: Dipartimento di Politica Sociale.
Sudnow, D. (1973) 'Normal crimes', in G. Salaman and K. Thompson (eds) *People and Organizations*, London: Longmans.
Sullivan, H.S. (1950) 'The illusion of personal individuality', *Psychiatry* 13: 317–32.
Tatham, P. (1982) 'Organisational symbols and myths', paper presented to Exeter Workshop on Organizational Symbolism, June.
Thompson, J.D. (1967) *Organisations in Action*, Englewood Cliffs, New Jersey: Prentice Hall.
Thompson, P. (1983) *The Nature of Work*, London: Macmillan.
Thompson, P., and Bannon, E. (1985) *Working the System: The Shop Floor and New Technology*, London: Pluto Press.
Thurley, K. and Wood, S. (1983) *Industrial Relations and Management Strategy*, Cambridge: Cambridge University Press.
Tiryakian, E.A. (1970) 'Structural sociology', in J.C. McKinney and E.A. Tiryakian (eds) *Theoretical Sociology: Perspectives and Development*, New York: Appleton.
Tomlinson, J. (1982) *Unequal Struggle: British Socialism and the Capitalist Enterprise*, London: Methuen.
Trompenaars, F. (1985) *The Organization of Meaning and the Meaning of Organization*, Pennsylvania: Wharton School of the University of Pennsylvania.
Turner, B.A. (1971) *Exploring the Industrial Subculture*, London: Macmillan.
Turner, R. (ed.) (1974) *Ethnomethodology: Selected Readings*,

Harmondsworth: Penguin.
Turner, V.W. (1969) *The Ritual Process*, London: Routledge & Kegan Paul.
Van Maanen, J. (1979) 'The fact of fiction in organizational ethnography', *Administrative Science Quarterly* 24: 539–51.
——(1981) Some thoughts (and afterthoughts) on context, interpretation and organization theory', paper presented at the Annual Meeting of the Academy of Management, San Diego, California.
Van Maanen, J., Dabbs, J.M., and Faulkner, R.R. (1982) *Varieties of Qualitative Research*, Beverly Hills, California: Sage.
Vaught, C., and Smith, D. (1980) 'Incorporation and mechanical solidarity in an underground coal mine', *Sociology of Work and Occupations* 7: 159–87.
Watkins, J. (1970) 'Against 'Normal Science'', in J. Lakatos and A. Musgrave (eds) *Criticism and the Growth of Knowledge*, Cambridge: Cambridge University Press.
Watson, T. (1983) 'Towards a general theory of personnel and industrial relations management', Trent Business School, Occasional Paper Series, 2.
Webb, E.J., Campbell, D.T., Schwartz, R.D., and Sechrest, L. (1972) *Unobtrusive Measures: Non Reactive Research in the Social Sciences*, Chicago, Illinois: Rand McNally & Company.
Webb, E.J., and Ellsworth, P.C. (1975) 'On nature and knowing', in H.W. Sinaiko and L.A. Broedling (eds) *Perspectives on Attitude Measurement: Surveys and Their Alternatives*, Washington: Smithsonian Institution.
Weber, M. (1968) *Economy and Society: An Outline of Interpretative Sociology*, New York: Bedminster.
Weick, K.E. (1969) *The Social Psychology of Organizing*, Reading, Massachusetts: Addison-Wesley (second edition 1979).
Weider, L. (1974) 'Telling the code', in R. Turner (ed.) *Ethnomethodology: Selected Readings*, Harmondsworth: Penguin.
Wellmer A. (1985) 'On the dialectic of modernism and postmodernism', *Praxis International* 4: 337–62.
Whipp, R., and Clark P.A. (1986) *Innovation and the Auto Industry: Product, Process and Work Organization*, London: Frances Pinter.
White, O.F. (1983) 'Improving the prospects for heterodoxy in organization theory', *Administration and Society* 15: 257–72.
White, O.F., and McSwain, C. (1983) 'Transformational theory and organizational analysis', in G. Morgan (ed.) *Beyond Method*, Beverly Hills, California: Sage.
Whitley, R. (1987) 'Taking firms seriously as economic actors: towards a sociology of firm behaviour', *Organizational Studies* 8: 125–47.
Wilden, A. (1982) 'Semiotics as praxis: strategy and tactics', *Recherches Semiotique: Semiotic Inquiry* 1: 1–34.
Wilkins, A. (1979) 'Organizational stories as an expression of management philosophy: implications for social control in organizations', unpublished doctoral dissertation, Stanford University.
Williams, B.A.O. (1983) 'Auto-de-fe', *New York Review of Books* 30:7.
Willmott, H.C. (1981) 'The structuring of organizational structure: a note', *Administrative Science Quarterly* 26: 470–4.
——(1984) 'Images and ideals of managerial work: a critical examination of

conceptual and empirical accounts', *Journal of Management Studies* 21: 369–84.
——(1986) 'Unconscious sources of motivation in the theory of the subject: an exploration and critique of Giddens' dualistic models of action and personality', *Journal for the Theory of Social Behaviour* 16: 105–21.
——(1987) 'Studying managerial work: a critique and a proposal', Journal of Management Studies 24: 249–70.
Winch, P. (1958) *The Idea of a Social Science*, London: Routledge & Kegan Paul.
Witkin, R.W. (1987) 'The aesthetic imperative of a rational-technical machinery: a study in organizational control through the design of artefacts', unpublished paper presented to the Third International Conference on Organizational Symbolism and Corporate Culture, Milano, Italy, June.
Witkin, R.W., and Poupart R. (1986) 'Running a commentary on imaginatively relived events: a method for obtaining qualitatively rich data', in A. Strati (ed.) *The Symbolics of Skill*, Trento: Dipartimento di Politica Sociale: 79–86.
Winkler, J. (1974) 'The Ghost at the bargaining table', *British Journal of Industrial Relations* 12: 191–212.
Winnicott, D.W. (1950) 'Some thoughts on the meaning of the word democracy', *Human Relations* 3: 175–86.
Wittfogel, K.A. (1957) *Oriental Despotism: A Comparative Study of Total Power*, Massachusetts: Yale University Press.
Wittgenstein, L. (1953) *Philosophical Investigations*, London: Basil Blackwell.
—— (1958) *The Blue and Brown Books*, London: Basil Blackwell.
Wood, S. (ed.) (1982) *The Degradation of Work?*, London: Hutchinson.
——(1986) 'Work organization', in R. Deam and G. Salaman (eds) *Works, Culture and Society*, Milton Keynes: Open University Press.
Zerubavel, E. (1978) 'Timetables and scheduling: on the social organization of time', *Sociological Inquiry* 46: 87–94.
Ziegler, J. (1982) *Die Lebenden und der Tod*, Frankfurt: Ullstein.
Zimbalist, A. (ed.) (1979) *Case Studies on the Labour Process*, New York: Monthly Review Press.
Zimmerman, D. (1971) 'Record-keeping and the intake process in a public welfare bureaucracy', in S. Wheeler (ed.) *On Record*, New York: Russell Sage.
——(1973) 'The practicalities of rule use', in G. Salaman and K. Thompson (eds) *People and Organizations*, London: Longman.
Zimmerman, D. and Pollner, M. (1971) 'The everyday world as a phenomenon', in J. Douglas (ed.) *Understanding Everyday Life*, London: Routledge & Kegan Paul.
Zucker, L. (1979) 'The role of institutionalization in cultural persistence', *American Sociological Review* 42: 726–43.

Index

UNIVERSITY OF GLAMORGAN
PRIFYSGOL MORGANNWG
Learning Resources
Centre